Betty Crocker®

Diabetes COOKBOOK

Great-Tasting, Easy Recipes for Every Day

BETTY CROCKER®

Diabetes
COOKBOOK

Great-Tasting, Easy Recipes for Every Day

International Diabetes Center, Park Nicollet Health Services, Minneapolis
Richard M. Bergenstal, M.D., and Diane Reader, R.D. C.D.E.

WILEY
John Wiley & Sons, Inc.

GENERAL MILLS

Editorial Director: Jeff Nowak

Assistant Manager, Marketing Services:
Christine Gray

Editors: Cheri Olerud, Grace Wells

Editorial Assistant: Kelly Gross

Food Editors: Andrea Bidwell,
Catherine Swanson

Nutritionist: Elyse Cohen, M.S., L.N.

Recipe Development and Testing:
Betty Crocker Kitchens

Photography: General Mills
Photography Studios and Image Library

Photographers: Chuck Nields, Rich Wong

Food Stylists: Nancy Johnson, Sue Brue

JOHN WILEY & SONS, INC.

Publisher: Natalie Chapman

Associate Publisher: Jessica Goodman

Executive Editor: Anne Ficklen

Senior Editor: Linda Ingroia

Production Editor: Abby Saul

Cover and Interior Book Design:
Tai Blanche

Layout: Indianapolis Composition Services

Manufacturing Manager: Tom Hyland

The Betty Crocker Kitchens seal guarantees
success in your kitchen. Every recipe has
been tested in America's Most Trusted
Kitchens™ to meet our high standards of
reliability, easy preparation and great taste.

Find more great ideas at
BettyCrocker.com
and EatBetterAmerica.com

Cover images: General Mills Photography Studios and Image Library

Cover design: Tai Blanche

This book is printed on acid-free paper. ∞

For general information on our other products and services or for technical support, please contact our Customer Care Department within the United States at (877) 762-2974, outside the United States at (317) 572-3993 or fax (317) 572-4002.

Wiley publishes in a variety of print and electronic formats and by print-on-demand. Some material included with standard print versions of this book may not be included in e-books or in print-on-demand. If this book refers to media such as a CD or DVD that is not included in the version you purchased, you may download this material at http://booksupport.wiley.com. For more information about Wiley products, visit www.wiley.com

Library of Congress Cataloging-in-Publication Data is available upon request.

ISBN 978-1-118-18087-7 (pbk.), 978-1-118-28781-1 (ebk.), 978-1-118-28782-8 (ebk.), 978-1-118-28848-1 (ebk.)

Manufactured in the United States of America

10 9 8 7 6 5 4 3 2 1

Cover photos: Triple-Berry and Jicama Spinach Salad (page 196), Veggie-Stuffed Omelet (page 46), Dark Chocolate–Cherry Multigrain Cookies (page 246), Baked Berry Cups with Crispy Cinnamon Wedges (page 230), Buffalo Chicken Pizza (page 88), Slow Cooker Chipotle Beef Stew (page 110), Pork Mole Quesadillas (page 122), and African Squash and Chickpea Stew (page 162)

Dear Readers,

Have you recently been diagnosed with diabetes? Or do you know someone who has diabetes? Whatever your particular situation, this book will be a great addition to your cookbook library for a variety of reasons. You will be able to learn about how to cook and eat deliciously even though you are dealing with a complex disease. With the direct, accurate medical information, easy-to-follow menus, fun-to-read tips from the diabetes team and fabulous recipes, you'll be able to follow simple guidelines to provide meals that everyone will enjoy.

In this second edition of *Betty Crocker's Diabetes Cookbook,* Betty has again teamed up with the International Diabetes Center to create a complete reference guide to cooking for diabetes. Because sound nutrition and good eating habits are at the heart of diabetes care, we've made it a priority to include recipes that are both delicious and good for you.

This updated edition includes 40 new great recipes and all-new photographs. Because we know that some recipes are asked for often, we've kept some of those in the book. Variety is the key to enjoying food, so a great range of recipes is included—from main dishes, salads and breakfast ideas to desserts and breads for everyday eating. We also know that many who have diabetes also are gluten-intolerant, so there is even a gluten-free chapter of recipes for you to choose from. Plus, every recipe gives you clear information on exchanges and carbohydrate choices so it's easy to put meals together.

So go ahead and browse the book—then start planning your next meal. Diabetes does change your life, but with this cookbook at your fingertips, you're on the road to living well and enjoying some delicious eating!

Richard M. Bergenstal, M.D.
Diane Reader, R.D., C.D.E.

CONTENTS

Living Well with Diabetes   8

1 Day-Starter Breakfasts   36

2 Smart Snacks and Breads   62

3 Pleasing Poultry, Fish and Meat   86

4 Stand-Out Meatless Meals   126

5 Great Grains, Legumes and Pasta   154

6 Vital Vegetables and Salads   182

7 Best Gluten-Free Recipes   208

8 Delightful Desserts   228

Index   258

Metric Conversion Guide   264

Living Well with Diabetes

With the comprehensive information included in this chapter, you'll see that the goal is to help you feel in control of your diabetes. The easy-to-follow health information includes all of the resources that you need to live well with diabetes.

What Is Diabetes?

To understand diabetes, it's important to understand how your body uses glucose and insulin. Glucose, a form of sugar, is the main fuel the body needs and uses for energy. It is made when the food you eat is broken down during digestion. Glucose travels through the bloodstream and enters the cells in the body with the help of insulin. Insulin, a hormone made in the pancreas, is the "key" that "opens" cells so glucose can get inside to provide the body with energy.

Diabetes develops when insulin is either completely absent, in short supply or poorly used by the body. Without insulin, too much glucose stays in the bloodstream rather than entering the cells to be used for energy. If diabetes is not diagnosed and treated, blood glucose levels continue to rise, and over time this can lead to serious health problems—the "complications" of diabetes, such as blindness, heart and blood vessel disease, stroke, kidney failure, nerve damage and limb amputation. Taking care of your diabetes by eating the right foods, exercising regularly and taking your medication, if prescribed, helps you feel great and provides the best defense against complications.

THE TYPES OF DIABETES

There are three main types of diabetes:

TYPE 1

This type occurs most often in children and young adults under the age of thirty. This is an autoimmune disease in which the body's own immune system destroys the beta cells in the pancreas that produce insulin. The diagnosis of type 1 diabetes is usually signaled by common symptoms such as extreme thirst, significant weight loss and frequent urination. People with type 1 diabetes need to take daily insulin injections to stay alive.

TYPE 2

About 90 percent of people with diabetes have type 2 diabetes. It usually develops in adults over age forty, but a growing number of cases in younger people, including teens and children, are diagnosed each year. With type 2 diabetes, the cells in the body "resist" the action of insulin, and glucose doesn't get into the cells very well. This is called insulin resistance. Over time, the insulin-producing cells in the pancreas wear out, in part because they're working too hard trying to overcome the body's insulin resistance.

GESTATIONAL

Gestational diabetes occurs when the hormonal changes of pregnancy demand more insulin than the body can make or use well, and 3 to 5 percent of pregnant women develop it, usually during the second or third trimester (24 to 28 weeks). Though gestational diabetes usually disappears after the baby is born, its occurrence significantly increases the risk for developing type 2 diabetes later in life.

Diabetes in the United States

More than 25 million Americans have diabetes. That's more than 8.3 percent of the U.S. population. One-third of Americans who have diabetes aren't even aware that they have it, and another third of Americans have "prediabetes." This is a condition in which blood glucose is higher than normal but not yet high enough to be diabetes. In most cases, prediabetes will eventually progress into diabetes unless some action is taken. For those who are overweight, the most effective action appears to be losing weight and exercising regularly. There are also certain medications that may help to prevent the development of diabetes. Your health-care provider can discuss your options with you.

Diabetes is indeed epidemic. Why? In large part, rates of diabetes have increased because diets high in fat and calories and lack of exercise have led to obesity, a major risk factor for diabetes. A similar trend is occurring globally as well. As people in other countries become more affluent, consume more food and are less active, the rate of diabetes is increasing rapidly. It's estimated that there will be 300 million people with diabetes worldwide by the year 2025.

Vietnamese Meatball Lollipops with Dipping Sauce, page 82

Greek Chicken Burgers with Tzatziki Sauce, page 92

Eating Well for Good Health

Most people agree that eating is one of the greatest joys in life, and that does not need to change just because you have diabetes. Food plays a key role in many family celebrations and social situations. Viewing diabetes as an opportunity to prepare and eat the best possible foods to maintain your body will help you deal with the daily challenge of diabetes.

At first, it may be a struggle when others are planning a "normal" holiday dinner, for example; but with experience, you'll be able to modify recipes or situations to fit your needs. And it's likely that eventually you'll like your new way of eating much better than the old way. An added benefit is you will feel better, both physically and emotionally.

The Role of Carbohydrate Foods

Food contains three main nutrients: carbohydrates, protein and fat. It's the carbohydrate foods that raise your blood glucose level, so you need to pay attention to how much you eat.

Carbohydrate foods are necessary for good nutrition. They provide important nutrients, fiber, vitamins and minerals, and they give your body the energy it needs. Without carbohydrates, your body cannot function properly, although, as with any foods, it's wise to eat carbohydrates in moderation to avoid excess calories and weight gain.

Carbohydrate foods include grains and grain-based foods such as bread, cereal and pasta, and starchy vegetables such as corn, squash and potatoes. Milk and yogurt, fruits and fruit juices and sweets are also carbohydrate foods. All carbohydrates provide four calories per gram. Eating consistent amounts of carbohydrate according to your diabetes food plan will help control your blood glucose levels.

What Is Carbohydrate Counting?

"Counting" carbohydrates with Carbohydrate Choices helps you track the amount of carbohydrate in a meal and balance that with your medication and activity (see also Carbohydrate Choices, page 13). Counting carbohydrates and testing your glucose level after you eat give you the information to keep your diabetes in good control. And that means you don't have to give up foods you like or that taste great. Can you ever have a piece of cake again? Yes! Once you know how to count carbohydrates, you'll be able to fit a wide variety of foods into your food plan, including sweets.

If you have diabetes, you've come to the right place—this cookbook offers the latest and easiest way to count Carbohydrate Choices. These guidelines are easier than the exchange system because you only need to keep track of one thing: the amount of carbohydrate that you eat for each meal and snack. If you're used to keeping track of food exchanges, that information is included for you, too.

To create this cookbook, we enlisted the experienced help of an endocrinologist (a diabetes specialist doctor) and diabetes dietitian who have many years of experience working with people with diabetes. Teamed with the trusted recipes of the Betty Crocker Kitchens, the result is a cookbook you're sure to refer to again and again.

The recipes in this cookbook were developed for healthy eating with diabetes, and each recipe lists the Carbohydrate Choices per serving, removing the guesswork for you. Keeping overall health and all-family appeal in mind, we kept the fat, sugar and calories down, added whole grains, boosted the fiber and used a variety of spices and herbs to limit sodium without sacrificing the delicious satisfying flavor of the food. Be sure to check out the Special-Occasion Menus on page 23—plus there are also sample meals on page 22 to show you how to put a meal together with the ideal number of Carb Choices.

A diagnosis of diabetes may make you feel like your life is spinning out of control. One positive way to approach this news is to think of having diabetes as an opportunity to take charge of your health and find great pleasure in the foods you select and eat. Along with having great food options, it's important to know as much as you can about diabetes, how to take good care of yourself and how your diabetes care team can help you. With all of this in mind, the cookbook is packed with information that will guide you in taking the best possible care of your diabetes and provide fabulous recipes to enjoy. All the information you need is here at your fingertips.

Diabetes Nutrition 101

The primary goal in diabetes care is to control blood glucose, followed closely by the need to control blood fats and blood pressure and to lose weight or minimize weight gain, all of which play a significant role in diabetes health.

At the foundation of achieving all of these goals is good nutrition. A nutritious, well-balanced diet provides the building blocks for healthy body functioning, physical energy, satisfaction in eating and just feeling good!

Carbohydrate Choices

Carbohydrate is measured in grams. A gram is a small unit of weight in the metric system. The trick to carbohydrate counting is to know how many carbohydrate grams you are eating at any given time. (See also What is Carbohydrate Counting?, page 11.) Carbohydrate counting provides you with a tool to help with blood glucose control and enables you to select the amount of carbohydrate recommended by your healthcare provider for a well-balanced diet.

Bllueberry-Almond Brown Bread, page 68

Thai Broccoli Slaw, page 200

Dark Chocolate Cupcakes, page 240

Pork Chops with Raspberry-Chipotle Sauce and Herbed Rice, page 118

CHOOSING MYPLATE

The USDA recently unveiled a food symbol called MyPlate to help you build a healthy plate at meal times—and to make healthier food choices. The MyPlate symbol shows the five food groups (fruit, vegetable, grain, protein and dairy) within a place setting—and includes awareness of portion sizes. The symbol indicates that half the plate should be made up of fruits and vegetables—with a lesser emphasis on protein and dairy than grains. See www.ChooseMyPlate.gov to learn more.

MyPlate replaces the MyPyramid image as the primary food group symbol to help you meet the *2010 Dietary Guidelines for Americans*. MyPlate and the Dietary Guidelines suggest these practices:

- Enjoy your food, but eat less.
- Avoid oversized portions.
- Make half your plate fruits and vegetables.
- Switch to fat-free or low-fat (1%) milk.
- Make at least half your grains whole grains.
- Compare sodium in foods—and choose foods with lower numbers.
- Drink water to keep calories down.

Your body needs foods from all of the food groups shown in MyPlate.

Your dietitian will help you develop a personal food plan that tells the specific number of servings from each group that you need to eat each day for good nutrition. Eating consistent amounts of food at consistent times is a key factor in your blood glucose control. Counting Carbohydrate Choices makes it easier to eat consistently from day to day.

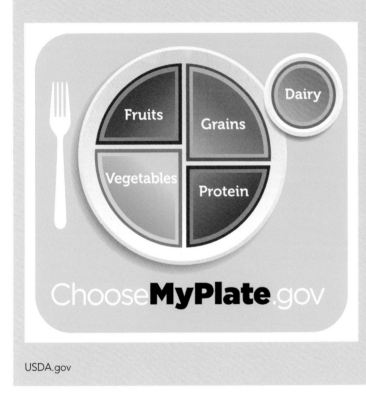

USDA.gov

A Carbohydrate Choice is a serving of food that contains 15 grams of carbohydrate. This is the approximate amount of carbohydrate in one serving of:

- Potato (½ cup)
- Rice (⅓ cup)
- Bread (1 slice)
- Cereal (½ to ¾ cup)
- Milk (1 cup)
- Apple (1 small)

If you eat two small apples, it counts as 2 Carbohydrate Choices. If you consume 1 slice of bread plus 1 cup of milk, that also counts as 2 Carbohydrate Choices. Your customized food plan will include the right number of Carbohydrate Choices for you. (See page 20 for Carbohydrate Choices of Common Foods.)

A typical diabetes food plan includes 3 to 5 Carbohydrate Choices (or 45 to 75 grams of carbohydrate) for meals, depending upon your gender, activity level, weight change goal and food planning goals. Snacks are usually 1 to 2 Carbohydrate Choices, if they are included in your plan. You and your dietitian will determine how much carbohydrate you should eat each day. Then together you will find the best way to space carbohydrate foods throughout the day

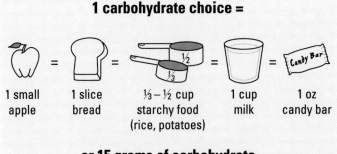

1 carbohydrate choice =

1 small apple = 1 slice bread = ⅓–½ cup starchy food (rice, potatoes) = 1 cup milk = 1 oz candy bar

or 15 grams of carbohydrate

Used with permission from International Diabetes Center, Minneapolis, MN

HOW MANY CARBOHYDRATE CHOICES?

Use this conversion guide to convert the number of carbohydrate grams to Carbohydrate Choices. If a food has 5 or more grams of fiber, subtract half of the grams of fiber from the total carbohydrate before determining the Carbohydrate Choices. (See Fabulous Fiber, page 203, for more information.)

Carb Grams		Carb Choices
0–5	=	0 choices
6–10	=	½ choice
11–20	=	1 choice
21–25	=	1½ choices
26–35	=	2 choices
36–40	=	2½ choices
41–50	=	3 choices
51–55	=	3½ choices
56–65	=	4 choices
66–70	=	4½ choices
71–80	=	5 choices

Used with permission from International Diabetes Center, Minneapolis, MN

so that you get the energy you need without overwhelming your body's insulin supply. Or, if you take insulin, your diabetes care provider will help determine the right doses to match the amount of carbohydrate foods you eat. Every meal and snack needs to include carbohydrate foods, because they provide the energy your body "runs" on.

It's best to follow your food plan. "Saving" Carbohydrate Choices from one meal or snack to have at another time can lead to low or high blood glucose levels. If you want to eat more than your food plan calls for, you'll need to make up for it with extra exercise or additional insulin.

Your dietitian can tell you more about eating "outside" your food plan. But be careful—eating more of any food adds calories and may lead to weight gain, whether you have diabetes or not.

Carbohydrate on Food Labels

While there are many "standard" 1 Carbohydrate Choice foods, such as milk, fruit and bread, you may also want to eat carbohydrate-containing foods such as pizza, frozen dinners or frozen yogurt. How do these foods translate into Carbohydrate Choices? Look to the nutrition label on the food package. See the Fiber One® cereal label, at right, as an example.

Nutrition Facts

Serving Size ½ cup (30g)
Servings Per Container about 15

Amount Per Serving	Fiber One	with ½ cup skim milk
Calories	60	100
Calories from Fat	10	10

	% Daily Value**	
Total Fat 1g*	1%	1%
Saturated Fat 0g	0%	0%
Trans Fat 0g		
Polyunsaturated Fat 0.5g		
Monounsaturated Fat 0g		
Cholesterol 0mg	0%	1%
Sodium 105mg	4%	7%
Potassium 100mg	3%	9%
Total Carbohydrate 25g	8%	10%
Dietary Fiber 14g	57%	57%
Soluble Fiber 1g		
Sugars 0g		
Other Carbohydrate 11g		
Protein 2g		

Vitamin A	0%	4%
Vitamin C	10%	10%
Calcium	10%	25%
Iron	25%	25%
Vitamin D	0%	10%
Thiamin	25%	30%
Riboflavin	25%	35%
Niacin	25%	25%
Vitamin B₆	25%	25%
Folic Acid	25%	25%
Vitamin B₁₂	25%	35%
Phosphorus	6%	15%
Magnesium	4%	8%
Zinc	25%	30%

* Amount in cereal. A serving of cereal plus skim milk provides 1g total fat, less than 5mg cholesterol, 170mg sodium, 300mg potassium, 31g total carbohydrate (6g sugars), and 6g protein.

** Percent Daily Values are based on a 2,000 calorie diet. Your daily values may be higher or lower depending on your calorie needs:

	Calories	2,000	2,500
Total Fat	Less than	65g	80g
Sat Fat	Less than	20g	25g
Cholesterol	Less than	300mg	300mg
Sodium	Less than	2,400mg	2,400mg
Potassium		3,500mg	3,500mg
Total Carbohydrate		300g	375g
Dietary Fiber		25g	30g

Ingredients: Whole Grain Wheat, Corn Bran, Modified Wheat Starch, Guar Gum, Color Added, Cellulose Gum, Salt, Baking Soda, Aspartame*. **Vitamins and Minerals:** Calcium Carbonate, Zinc and Iron (mineral nutrients), **Vitamin C** (sodium ascorbate), **A B Vitamin** (niacinamide), **Vitamin B₆** (pyridoxine hydrochloride), **Vitamin B₂** (riboflavin), **Vitamin B₁** (thiamin mononitrate), **A B Vitamin** (folic acid), **Vitamin B₁₂**.

***PHENYLKETONURICS: CONTAINS PHENYLALANINE**

CONTAINS WHEAT INGREDIENTS.

DISTRIBUTED BY GENERAL MILLS SALES, INC., MINNEAPOLIS, MN 55440 USA
SSG 3229892109 F 3220904109

CARBOHYDRATE COUNTING TIPS

- A good start is to remember that 15 grams of carbohydrate is 1 Carbohydrate Choice.

- One starch, fruit or milk exchange is equal to 1 Carbohydrate Choice. All the foods in these three groups raise blood glucose about the same amount.

- Meats and fats aren't counted because they do not contain carbohydrate and therefore do not directly raise blood glucose.

- Non-starchy vegetables (any vegetable except corn, peas, squash and potatoes) are not counted unless eaten in large (3 cups raw or 1½ cups cooked) quantities.

- If a food has 5 or more grams of fiber, subtract half of the grams of fiber from the total grams of carbohydrate before determining the Carbohydrate Choices. This is only necessary if you are counting carbs to determine your mealtime insulin dose.

HELPING HANDS

½ cup is about the size and thickness of your palm without the fingers (examples: peas, corn)

1 cup is about the size of your first (examples: milk, soup, squash)

1 snack choice is a moderate handful (examples: chips, pretzels)

1 bread choice is about the size of your open palm and half your fingers (examples: bread slice, tortilla, pancake, waffle)

1 tablespoon is about the size of your thumb (examples: jelly, syrup, honey)

Used with permission from International Diabetes Center, Minneapolis, MN

Nutrition labels on packaged foods provide the carbohydrate content of that specific product. Finding the carbohydrate on a Nutrition Facts panel of a food package is easy. Begin by looking at the serving size of the food. Looking down the panel, locate the carbohydrate grams for that serving. "Total Carbohydrate" includes all starches, sugars and dietary fiber.

You can use the guide entitled How Many Carbohydrate Choices? (page 15) to convert the number of carbohydrate grams on any label to the number of Carbohydrate Choices.

What About Sugar?

Sugar is a carbohydrate. It affects your blood glucose in the same way that other carbohydrates do. Contrary to what many believe, people with diabetes can eat some sweets and foods with added sugar as long as the carbohydrates are counted.

Desserts and tempting sweets can pack a big carbohydrate wallop—even in small portions. If you decide to eat a food with added sugar, you need to plan by substituting it for other carbohydrates in your food plan. For example, a 2-inch-square piece of cake with frosting has the same amount of carbohydrate as 1 ear of corn or 2 slices of bread, but it also contains more fat and calories than the corn or the bread.

Often, foods high in added sugar have little or no nutritional value other than calories. And often where there is sugar, there is also fat, so it makes good sense to monitor the sweets you eat.

About Exchange Lists

If you've had diabetes for a while, you may have learned to use the Exchange Lists and already know a lot about food groups and counting. What's the advantage of Carbohydrate Choices over diet or Food Exchanges? In exchange lists, foods are listed with their serving sizes, which are usually measured after cooking. When you begin, measuring the size of each serving will help you learn to "eyeball" correct serving sizes. Carbohydrate counting is an easier way to manage the food you eat and offers more flexibility in food selection, making meal planning easier.

To use exchanges, the following chart shows the amount of nutrients in one serving from each list.

FOOD EXCHANGES

Groups/Lists	Carbohydrate (grams)	Protein (grams)	Fat (grams)	Calories
Carbohydrate Group				
Starch	15	3	0–1	80
Fruit	15	—	—	60
Milk				
Fat-free, low-fat	12	8	0–3	90
Reduced-fat	12	8	5	120
Whole	12	8	8	150
Other carbohydrates	15	varies	varies	varies
Nonstarchy vegetables	5	2	—	25
Meat and Meat Substitutes Group				
Very Lean	—	7	0–1	35
Lean	—	7	3	55
Medium-fat	—	7	5	75
High-fat	—	7	8	100
Fat Group	—	—	5	45

Essential Nutrients for Good Health

In addition to carbohydrates, there are several nutrients needed every day to maintain optimal health. It's important to balance your intake of protein and fat as well as carbohydrates as part of a healthy diet. Just as eating too much carbohydrate may lead to excess calories and weight gain, a diet that's too high in protein and fat but low in carbohydrate won't provide your body with the energy and balanced nutrition it needs for proper functioning. The bottom line is moderation. Low-fat meat and dairy products (with an emphasis on increasing monounsaturated fats) along with a moderate amount of nutritious carbohydrate foods that fit your food plan are the keys to healthy, satisfying eating.

Protein is found in meats, poultry, fish, milk and other dairy products, eggs, dried peas and beans and nuts. Starch and vegetables also have small amounts of protein. Your body uses protein for growth and maintenance. Protein provides 4 calories per gram. Most Americans eat more protein than their bodies need. Your dietitian will help you determine how much protein is right for your body. Eating 5 to 7 ounces of protein foods per day is recommended. Choosing low-fat meats and dairy products also offers heart-healthy benefits to people with diabetes.

Fat is found in butter, margarine, oil, salad dressing, nuts, seeds, cheese, meat, fish, poultry, snack foods, ice cream, cookies and many desserts. Your body needs some fat for good nutrition, just as it needs protein and carbohydrate. But certain types of fat are better for you than others. There are three different types of fat: monounsaturated, polyunsaturated and saturated. Unsaturated fats are sometimes hydrogenated (hydrogen is added to them) to help make them solid at room temperature.

This hydrogenation process creates trans fatty acids. Health professionals recommend eating less saturated and trans fats. These are found in meats, dairy products, coconut, palm and palm kernel oils as well as partially hydrogenated oils and fats that are hard at room temperature such as butter, shortening and margarine. Saturated fats and trans fats have been shown to contribute to heart disease. The best choice is monounsaturated fat, which has been shown to improve the cardiovascular system. Monounsaturated fat is found in canola oil, olive oil, nuts and avocados. Polyunsaturated fat, found in corn oil, soybean oil and sunflower oil, is also a better choice than saturated fat.

Fat provides 9 calories per gram. This is more than twice the calories found in carbohydrate or protein. Excess calories from fat are very easily stored in the body as fat and can

MAKE WISE FOOD CHOICES A HABIT

These tips are based on sound nutrition principles and are good for everyone—with or without diabetes.

- **Don't Skip Meals.** For many reasons, you may be tempted to skip meals. This isn't a good idea, particularly if you have diabetes. When you skip meals, maintaining stable blood glucose levels becomes difficult. To make matters worse, people usually end up overeating at the next meal. So stick to your food plan, and for times when it's not possible, talk to your dietitian to find appropriate snack choices to hold you over until your next meal.

- **Plan Meals and Snacks.** Planning what to eat for meals and snacks may seem overwhelming at first, but in time you'll become an expert on what foods work best for you. If you don't plan, you may find yourself eating whatever is available, which may not be the best choice. Before shopping, decide on healthy meals and snacks to eat at home or take to work or school for the upcoming week.

- **Eat a Variety of Foods.** Grains, fruits and vegetables are packed with vitamins, minerals and fiber. Foods differ in nutrient content, so eat a variety of colors and kinds, and be sure to include protein in your daily diet. Variety helps to ensure your body gets the nutrients it needs for good health. Variety also helps to avoid boredom and enhances the pleasure of eating.

- **Choose Low-Fat Foods Often.** Whenever you have the choice, drink fat-free (skim) milk; eat low-fat cheeses, yogurt and puddings; and use low-fat ingredients for cooking and baking, such as yogurt and light sour cream. Also, choose lean meats, and remove the skin from chicken. When buying processed foods, look for those that contain 3 grams of fat or less per 100 calories.

Fiber is necessary to maintain a healthy digestive tract and to help lower blood cholesterol levels. Experts recommend at least 25 grams of fiber daily. To get enough fiber each day, include:

- Bran cereals or whole-grain breads, cereals, rice, pasta and other whole-grain products.

- Vegetables and fruits, especially those with edible skins, seeds and hulls.

- Legumes (dried beans and peas) and nuts.

lead to weight gain. It's not healthy to completely cut fats from your diet, especially monounsaturated fats. But most people can afford to reduce the amount of calories they get from fat. Two of the best steps you can take are to reduce your fat intake and switch to a more beneficial type of fat.

Fiber rich foods are a good choice. If a food has 5 or more grams of fiber, you can subtract half of the grams of fiber from the total grams of carbohydrate before determining the number of Carbohydrate Choices. For an example, look at the Fiber One® cereal label (page 15).

The total number of fiber grams in one serving is 14. Since that is more than 5 grams, you can subtract half of it from the total carbohydrate grams in one serving. That leaves you with 18 grams of carbohydrate per serving or 1 Carbohydrate Choice. It's that simple! Most foods do not contain more than 5 grams of fiber, so check the food label carefully. Your best bet for finding high-fiber packaged foods are cereals, foods with bran and dried beans and peas (legumes). For more about fiber, see page 203.

Water is essential for good health. Experts generally recommend eight to ten glasses of water daily for healthy individuals who do not have trouble with eliminating fluids from the body. Drink even more when it's hot, you're exercising or you don't feel well.

Vitamins help release energy from the fuel sources of carbohydrate, protein and fat. Your vision, hair, skin and the strength of your bones all depend on the vitamins that come from the foods you eat. The more variety you have in your diet, the more likely you are to get all the vitamins your body needs.

Minerals help your body with many functions. Iron, for example, carries much-needed oxygen to your body cells. Calcium is key to strong bones and teeth, and potassium is important for proper nerve and muscle function. Magnesium is also very important for muscle function, and it helps the body produce energy from carbohydrates, protein and fats and is often deficient in people with diabetes. The best way to get enough of the minerals you need is through a varied diet, although people with certain health conditions, including people with diabetes, sometimes need a supplement. It's a good idea to check with your health-care provider about your individual needs.

Nutrition in the Recipes

In addition to the number of Carbohydrate Choices, each recipe in this cookbook lists the calories, calories from fat, total fat, saturated fat, cholesterol, sodium, carbohydrate, dietary fiber and protein per serving. Food exchanges are also listed on each recipe. Based on criteria set by the American Dietetic Association and the American Diabetes Association, exchanges are listed as whole or half. To calculate the nutrition content of recipes, these guidelines were followed:

- The first ingredient is used whenever a choice is listed (such as ⅓ cup plain yogurt or sour cream—the analysis would use yogurt).

- The first ingredient amount is used whenever a range is given (such as 2 to 3 teaspoons—the analysis would use 2 teaspoons).

- The first serving number is used whenever a range is given (such as 4 to 6 servings—the analysis would use 4 servings).

- "If desired" ingredients are not included in the nutrition calculations, whether mentioned in the ingredient list (such as "parsley, if desired") or in the recipe directions as a suggestion (such as "top with sour cream if desired").

- Only the amount of a marinade or frying oil that is absorbed during preparation is calculated.

Celery and Apple Salad
with Cider Vinaigrette, page 204

Carbohydrate Choices of Common Foods

A Carbohydrate Choice is the amount of a food that has about 15 grams of carbohydrate. (To read more about Carbohydrate Choices, see page 12.) Here are some common foods and the number of Carbohydrate Choices they contain:

Food	Carbohydrate Choices
Grains, Beans, Starchy Vegetables	
Bagel, large (most bagel shops), 4 to 5-inch	4 to 5
Beans, baked, ⅓ cup	1
Beans (black, garbanzo, pinto, red), canned or cooked, ½ cup	1
Bread, wheat or white, 1 slice (1 oz)	1
Bun, hamburger or hot dog, 1 bun	1½ to 2
Cereal, cooked, unsweetened, ½ cup	1
Cereal, unsweetened (Cheerios®, Wheaties®), ¾ cup	1
Corn, ½ cup or 5 to 6-inch cob	1
Dinner roll, 1 roll (1 oz)	1
English muffin, 1 muffin (2 oz)	2
French fries, regular cut, frozen, 10 to 15 fries	1
Muffin, small, 2½-inch	2
Pancake, 4-inch	1
Pasta (macaroni, noodles, spaghetti), cooked, ⅓ cup	1
Peas, green, ½ cup	1
Potato, sweet or white, baked or broiled, medium, 4-inch (6 oz)	2 to 2½
Potato, sweet or white, mashed, ½ cup	1
Rice, brown or white, cooked, ⅓ cup	1
Squash, acorn or butternut, cooked, 1 cup	1
Tortilla, flour, 8-inch	1½
Waffle, frozen, 4-inch	1

Tropical Fruit 'n Ginger Oatmeal, page 56

Food	Carbohydrate Choices
Fruits, Fruit Juices	
Berries (blueberries, raspberries, strawberries), 1 cup	1
Cherries, 12 (1 cup)	1
Fruit, canned, in light syrup or juice, ½ cup	1
Fruit (apple, banana, pear), whole, large	2
Fruit (kiwi, orange, peach, tangerine), whole, medium	1
Fruit (clementine, plum), whole, small, 2	1
Grapefruit, ½ large	1
Grapes, small, 17 (½ cup)	1
Juice (apple, grapefruit, orange, pineapple), ½ cup	1
Juice (cranberry, grape, prune), ⅓ cup	1
Melon, (cantaloupe, honeydew, watermelon), 1 cup	1

Food	Carbohydrate Choices
Raisins, dried cranberries, other dried fruit, ¼ cup	2
Milk, Yogurt, Milk Substitutes	
Milk, skim or 1%, 1 cup (8 oz)	1
Milk, 2% or whole, 1 cup (8 oz)	1
Rice beverage, 1 cup (8 oz)	1 to 1½
Soymilk, plain or flavored, 1 cup (8 oz)	1 to 2
Yogurt, low-fat, artificially sweetened or plain, ¾ to 1 cup (6 to 8 oz)	1
Yogurt, low-fat, sweetened, ¾ to 1 cup (6 to 8 oz)	2 to 2½
Snacks, Sweets	
Brownie or cake, frosted, 2-inch square	2
Candy, hard, round, 3 pieces (½ oz)	1
Candy bar, chocolate, snack-size, about 2-inch (1 oz)	1
Chips, potato or tortilla, regular, 10 to 15 chips	1
Cookie, 3-inch	1
Crackers, snack, 5 to 6 crackers	1
Doughnut, 3-inch cake or 4-inch raised	1½ to 2½
Frozen yogurt, nonfat or low-fat, ½ cup	1 to 2
Gelatin, regular, ½ cup	1
Granola bar, 1 bar (1 oz)	1
Honey or table sugar, 1 tablespoon	1
Ice cream, light or regular, ½ cup	1
Jam or jelly, regular, 1 tablespoon	1
Popcorn, microwave, popped, light or regular, 3 cups	1
Pretzel twists, mini, 15 pretzels (¾ oz)	1
Syrup, light, 2 tablespoons	1
Syrup, regular, 1 tablespoon	1

Food	Carbohydrate Choices
Combination Foods	
Asian entree (meat and vegetables), no rice, 1 cup	1
Burrito, bean, flour tortilla, frozen, 7-inch long	3
Burrito, meat, flour tortilla, frozen, 7-inch long	2
Casserole or hot dish, 1 cup	2
Chili, with meat and beans, 1 cup	1½ to 2
Frozen dinner, fewer than 350 calories, 8 to 11 oz	2 to 3
Hamburger, with bun, regular	2
Lasagna, frozen, 3-inch x 4-inch	2
Mixed vegetables with corn, pasta, or peas, 1 cup	1
Pasta or potato salad, ½ cup	1 to 1½
Pizza, frozen, thick-crust, medium, ⅛ pizza	2
Pizza, frozen, thin-crust, medium, ⅛ pizza	1
Sauce, tomato or marinara, canned, ½ cup	1
Soup (bean, noodle, rice, vegetable), 1 cup	1 to 2
Soup (cream), 1 cup	1 to 2
Sub sandwich, 6-inch	3
Taco, corn shell, 5-inch across	½

Buffalo Chicken Pizza, page 88

Everyday Meal Menus (3 to 5 Carb Choices Each)

We realize that planning meals can be a challenge for anyone who is living with diabetes. To help you, we have created a variety of meals that will give you a starting point to do your own planning.

The general guideline for diabetes food plans is to have 3 to 5 Carb Choices or 45 to 75 grams of carb at each meal. All of our meals follow this guideline.

It will be important for you to have a personalized food plan that best fits how you like to eat and fits your diabetes. Ask your doctor to refer you to a registered dietitian who will help you to create your own food plan and learn more about carb counting. Page 11 has some information you can read now about carb counting.

Easy-Does-It Chicken Dinner for 4
- **Baked Chicken Dijon,** page 91 (2 carbs)
- **Asparagus-Pepper Stir-Fry,** page 187 (½ carb)
- **Fresh Blueberries and Strawberries,** 1 cup per serving (1 carb)

Burger Special for 6
- **Broiled Dijon Burgers,** page 112 (1½ carbs)
- **BLT Potato Salad,** page 202 (1 carb)
- **Sliced Tomatoes and Cucumbers,** 1 cup per serving (1 carb)

Soup and Salad for 4
- **Roasted Red Pepper Soup with Mozzarella,** page 138 (2 carbs)
- **Chopped Vegetable Salad with Italian Dressing,** 1 cup per serving (0 carb)
- **Onion–Poppy Seed Scones,** page 64 (1 carb)

Pizza Night for 6
- **Buffalo Chicken Pizza,** page 88 (2 carbs) **OR Veggie-Tofu Pizza,** page 150 (2 carbs)
- **Tossed Green Salad with Vinaigrette Dressing,** 1 cup per serving (0 carb)
- **Melon Chunks,** 1 cup per serving (1 carb)

Take-Out Thai for 6
- **Thai Beef Noodle Bowls,** page 160 (½ carb)
- **Thai Broccoli Slaw,** page 200 (½ carb)
- **Small Dinner Rolls,** 1 per serving (1 carb)

- **Orange Sections,** ½ cup per serving (1 carb)
- **Double-Ginger Cookies,** page 248 (½ carb)

Southwestern Restaurant Dinner for 4
- **Spicy Shrimp Fajitas,** page 109 (2 carbs)
- **Cucumber-Mango Salad,** page 198 (1 carb)
- **Pomegranate–Tequila Sunrise Jelly Shots,** page 236 (½ carb)

Everyday Breakfast for 4
- **Tropical Fruit 'n Ginger Oatmeal,** page 56 (2 carbs)
- **Grapefruit,** ½ large per serving (1 carb)
- **Scrambled Egg,** 1 per serving (0 carb)

Gluten-Free Dinner for 6
- **Glazed Meat Loaf,** page 220 (½ carb)
- **Mashed Potatoes,** ½ cup per serving (1 carb)
- **Steamed Baby Carrots,** ½ cup per serving (0 carb)
- **Pumpkin–Chocolate Chip Cookies,** page 218 (1 carb)

Chunky Garden Noodles, page 178

Special-Occasion Menus (3 to 5 Carb Choices Each)

Don't let celebrations be a challenge—instead embrace the choices that you make to eat well. Use the following menus as a starting point for whatever occasion on your calendar, and then customize for your own eating plan. Each one of the menus provides up to 5 Carbohydrate Choices per serving. Refer to Carbohydrate Choices on pages 12 and 20 and other recipes in the cookbook for a variety of foods you could substitute to suit your taste.

And remember, if you do go off your meal plan a bit during the holidays, don't worry. Just get back on your plan the next day.

Christmas Dinner for 6

- **Standing Rib Beef Roast,** 4 oz per serving (0 carb)
- **Steamed New Potatoes,** ½ cup per serving (1 carb)
- **Triple-Berry and Jicama Spinach Salad,** page 196 (1 carb)
- **Mini Chocolate Cheesecakes,** page 244 (1½ carbs)
- **Sparkling Water with Sugar Free Cranberry Juice** (0 carb)

Thanksgiving Celebration for 6

- **Roast Turkey,** 4 oz per serving (0 carb)
- **Bread Stuffing** ½ cup (1 carb)
- **Mashed Russet or Sweet Potatoes,** ½ cup per serving (1 carb)
- **Herb-Roasted Root Vegetables,** page 190 (1 carb)
- **Broccoli and Squash Medley,** page 186 (½ carb)
- **Coffee or Tea** (0 carb)

Spring Brunch for 6

- **Corn, Egg and Potato Bake,** page 43 (1 carb)
- **Chocolate Chip-Cherry Scones** (1½ carbs)
- **Mixed Fresh Berries,** ½ cup per serving (1 carb)
- **Flavored Sparkling Water** (0 carb)

Summer Grilling Gathering for 4

- **Sirloin Steaks with Cilantro Chimichurri,** page 116 (0 carb)
- **Strawberry-Blueberry-Orange Salad,** page 195 (1 carb)
- **Small Dinner Rolls,** 1 per serving (1 carb)
- **BLT Potato Salad,** page 202 (1 carb)
- **Iced Tea** (0 carb)

Cobia with Lemon-Caper Sauce, page 106

Fireside Dinner for 4

- **Cobia with Lemon-Caper Sauce,** page 106 (½ carb)
- **Celery and Apple Salad with Cider Vinaigrette,** page 204 (1 carb)
- **Sweet Potato Oven Fries with Spicy Sour Cream,** page 72 (1 carb)
- **White Wine,** 4 oz per serving (0 carb)

New Year's Celebration for 8

- **Greek Salad Kabobs,** page 74 (0 carb) **OR Vegetable Kabobs with Mustard Dip,** page 78 (½ carb)
- **Roasted Carrot and Herb Spread,** page 75 (1 carb)
- **Vietnamese Meatball Lollipops with Dipping Sauce,** page 82 (½ carb)
- **Deviled Eggs,** ½ egg per serving (0 carb)
- **Mixed Melon Bowl,** ½ cup per serving (1 carb)
- **Mini Rosemary Scones,** page 67 (1 carb)
- **Flavored Sparkling Water or Champagne,** 4 oz per serving (0 carb)

Ask the Dietitian

Diane Reader, a registered dietitian with over 20 years of experience in nutrition counseling, answers some of the most frequently asked questions from people with diabetes.

Q Do I have to give up foods made with sugar?

A No. People who have diabetes can eat foods that contain sugar. Sugar is a carbohydrate that raises your blood glucose. But it doesn't raise it higher than other types of carbohydrates. To control your blood glucose you need to watch your total intake of carbohydrates, not just sugar. Carbohydrates are contained in starchy foods like potatoes, beans, squash, corn, rice, bread and pasta. They're also found in fruits, fruit juices, dairy products, sweets and sugar.

Foods that contain little or no carbohydrate include meats, poultry, fish, eggs, non-starchy vegetables and fats. It is important to recognize which foods contain carbohydrates and which do not. Then, try to consume a consistent, moderate amount of carbohydrate at meals. That will help you keep your blood glucose levels steadier and in your target range. If you want to choose a sweet food, you can substitute it for another carbohydrate.

Q If all carbohydrates raise blood glucose, should I avoid all carbohydrates?

A No. Carbohydrates are an essential source of energy, fiber and micronutrients. The brain and central nervous system have an absolute requirement for glucose from carbohydrates as an energy source. Restricting your total carbohydrate intake to less than 130 grams per day is not recommended.

Different kinds of carbohydrates offer different benefits. Grains give your body fiber and B vitamins. Fruits provide fiber and vitamin C. Milk and dairy products are a source of calcium and vitamin D. Vegetables contain needed fiber, vitamins and minerals.

For people with diabetes, it's all about counting carbohydrates. Because carbohydrates raise blood glucose after meals, counting them is the key to controlling your glucose levels. Each 15 gram serving of a carbohydrate equals 1 Carbohydrate Choice. Check the "Total Carbohydrate" section of food labels to find the grams per serving, then count 1 Carbohydrate Choice for every 15 grams (ignore the sugar grams). Examples of 1 Carbohydrate Choice include: 1 small apple, 1 cup of milk, 1 slice of bread, or 1 "fun size" candy bar.

Q So how many carbohydrates can I have each day?

A It depends on your personal goals and body weight. A reasonable place to begin is having 3 to 4 Carbohydrate (Carb) Choices per meal. Each Carb Choice is 15 grams, so you can have 45 to 60 grams of carbohydrate per meal. If your goal is to lose weight, reduce your Carb Choices to 2 to 3 per meal. For men or very active women, 4 to 5 Carb Choices per meal may be needed to maintain weight. Snacks are usually not necessary but may be added if you get hungry. Keep snack portions limited to 15 to 30 grams of carbohydrate (1 to 2 Carb Choices). That gives you a total of 9 to 16 Carb Choices per day.

Q Should I use low-carb products?

A If you like low-carb products, feel free to use them—but there is no need to. There are three ways that food manufacturers reduce carbohydrate in a product. The first is to substitute artificial sweeteners like aspartame in place of sugar, such as in diet soda. The second is to use less starch and substitute with more fiber, such as in low-carb, high-fiber breads. The third way is to substitute sugar alcohols for sugar. An example is a "sugar-free" candy bar that contains sorbitol instead of sugar. Using sugar alcohols can be misleading because many low-carb products claim to have no sugar carbohydrates, when they actually contain sugar alcohols. In general, half of the sugar alcohol amount should be considered carbohydrate. Sugar alcohols are not completely absorbed from the small intestine into the blood. Unabsorbed sugar alcohols are fermented in the large intestine and may produce some abdominal gas and discomfort.

Compared to regular foods, low-carb products often contain similar amounts of calories. If you like a low-carb product, it's okay to use it. But low-carb products are frequently more expensive and higher in fat, and may not taste as good. The key point is that people who have diabetes don't need special foods. They just need to monitor or count their intake of carbohydrates in regular foods.

Q I've heard about the glycemic index. What is it?

A The glycemic index is a rating system that predicts how high blood glucose levels will rise after you eat a specific food containing carbohydrates. It uses a scale of numbers to show which foods cause the lowest to the highest rises in blood glucose. Choosing carbohydrates that cause a lower rise in blood glucose may help control the surge in blood glucose that occurs after eating. Legumes, nuts, fruit, dairy and non-starchy vegetables are low-glycemic foods. To discover this for yourself, test your blood glucose before eating and two hours after. You will notice that some foods raise your blood glucose higher, even though they have the same amount of carbohydrate.

Not everyone agrees that using the glycemic index is the best way to plan your carbohydrate intake. Most carbohydrate foods aren't eaten alone. Once foods are mixed, the glycemic response in your body may change. Also, the glycemic index doesn't take the nutritional values of foods into account. If you would like more information about the potential benefit of the glycemic index, discuss it with your diabetes care team.

Q Can I still have a beer or glass of wine?

A Yes. Studies have found that drinking alcohol can lower blood glucose. A relationship has been shown between drinking a small amount of alcohol and an improvement in insulin resistance, a decrease in the development of diabetes and a reduced risk of coronary artery disease. Keep in mind, though, that you shouldn't consume more than a maximum of 1 to 2 drinks per day (defined as a 12-ounce beer, a 5-ounce glass of wine, or a 1½-ounce shot of liquor). If you are drinking beer, choose light beer, as it contains fewer carbohydrates. Twelve ounces of regular beer has about 13 grams of carbohydrate, compared to 5 to 11 grams in light beer (depending on the brand). A 5-ounce glass of wine or a shot of liquor has only trace amounts of carbohydrate. Because alcohol lowers glucose, there is a potential for hypoglycemia for people who are taking medication to lower blood glucose. To prevent low blood glucose, alcohol should be consumed with carbohydrate food.

Diabetes Care: You're in Charge

To live well with diabetes, you need to take charge of your care. Your diabetes knowledge, self-care skills and emotional health are in the palm of your hand. Your diabetes care team provides the medical care you need to achieve your treatment goals, keeping good health at your fingertips. It's all in your hands.

Used with permission from International Diabetes Center, Minneapolis, MN

Take Charge of Your Care

It takes a team to manage diabetes, and you are the central person on your team. Your diabetes care team may include your primary care provider, a nurse educator, a dietitian, an endocrinologist (diabetes specialist) and a mental health professional. Their expertise and guidance are invaluable, so seek them out whenever necessary.

Just remember, it's your body, and you know it better than anyone else. Listen to your body, and talk with your team about what you "hear." They can help you interpret and understand the signals you receive. Diabetes self-care means knowing what to do to take care of your diabetes and how to do it. Ongoing diabetes care and education will help ensure that you keep on track and stay healthy.

A. Diabetes Knowledge

Knowing about diabetes empowers you to take control of it, instead of allowing diabetes to take control of you. Understanding what is happening in your body and why it's happening can help you appreciate how you can make real differences in your health.

If you have not met with a diabetes educator or have not attended a diabetes education class, ask your health-care provider about these opportunities. If it's been a while since you've had diabetes education, check with your provider to see if there is a refresher or an advanced class you can take. New information and approaches to diabetes treatment are emerging as scientists continue to study the disease. Ongoing diabetes education will ensure that you are informed of new advances as they evolve.

B. Self-Care Skills

In diabetes education, you also learn the skills and lifestyle behaviors that contribute to controlling blood glucose levels day to day. These include testing your blood glucose, following a food plan and incorporating physical activity. Many people bring a family member, friend, spouse or significant other to education visits, which is a great way to include them and to get support for your diabetes self-care. Having someone in your life who understands diabetes can be very helpful and comforting.

Diabetes Treatment Goals

The overall goals of diabetes treatment are to:

- Achieve and maintain blood glucose control.
- Achieve and maintain optimal blood lipid (fat) levels.
- Achieve and maintain healthy blood pressure levels.
- Prevent or effectively treat diabetes complications.
- Improve overall health.

Blood Glucose Testing

Regularly testing your blood glucose with a blood glucose meter and keeping a record of your test results helps you and your health-care team assess how well your treatment plan is working. Testing also helps you:

- Evaluate your blood glucose control.
- Decide what treatment or lifestyle changes to make to improve your control.
- See how treatment or lifestyle changes affect your blood glucose levels.

Your health-care provider can help you select a blood glucose meter that fits your needs. Diabetes technology is constantly advancing; several meters are available with a variety of features and capabilities. Some even allow you to test just a small pinpoint of blood on your arm instead of your finger, and some give a reading in just seconds. There are also new devices that allow you to get a blood sample with very little discomfort.

Blood glucose targets for people with diabetes are a little higher than the normal range. Although we have excellent treatments for diabetes, they are not yet perfect, and many things in daily life affect blood glucose levels. So your blood glucose test results may sometimes be outside your target range—that's okay. Your blood glucose levels don't have to be perfect. The goal is to have at least half of your test results within the target range.

Many meters can use a computer for downloading blood glucose readings. You can download at home, or your diabetes care team can do it for you. If your blood glucose readings are frequently too high (hyperglycemia) or too low (hypoglycemia), your team can help you get back on track.

Food Planning

Of all the care skills, food planning is of primary importance to any diabetes treatment plan, because what, when and how much you eat directly affects your blood glucose levels. A diabetes food plan usually includes three meals per day, and it may or may not include snacks, depending on personal preferences and your medications. You don't have to eat special foods, and there is no special diabetes diet. Just take a look at the recipes in this book, and you'll see that meal planning when you have diabetes can be both delicious and easy!

If you've met with a registered dietitian, the two of you probably developed an individualized food plan. Important considerations include your food likes and dislikes, your daily schedule, what kind of job you have and other lifestyle factors that affect eating and physical activity.

The key to success with your food plan is learning to count carbohydrates. Carbohydrate foods are an important part of a nutritious diet, and they provide the glucose your body needs for energy. Carbohydrate foods also make your blood glucose levels go up, so you need to balance your intake with activity and your medications in order to ensure that glucose gets into your body's cells. Carbohydrate counting helps you do this. For more information about carbohydrate counting, see page 12, or make an appointment to see a dietitian. (If you count food exchanges, see page 17.)

Physical Activity

One of the most beneficial things you can do for yourself is to find the physical activity that's right for you—and commit to it. Exercise helps lower high blood pressure, improves blood cholesterol levels and helps with weight management. For people with diabetes, there is an added benefit: Regular physical activity helps lower blood glucose levels by making the body's cells more sensitive to insulin. And for people at risk for diabetes, exercise can even help prevent the disease from developing.

Physical activity is always an important part of diabetes treatment. In type 2 diabetes, exercise can greatly enhance blood glucose control, with or without the help of diabetes medications. In type 1 diabetes, it's necessary to plan and sometimes make adjustments for physical activity because it can actually cause blood glucose levels to go too low when significant insulin is circulating. But that's no reason not to exercise! There are many ways to incorporate exercise safely.

C. Emotional Health

It's sometimes easy to forget that your emotional health is just as important to your overall well-being as your physical health. When you feel good about yourself emotionally, you tend to feel better physically. When you take care of your body, you often feel better emotionally.

Responding emotionally to having diabetes is normal, just as it would be with any disease. Feelings such as denial ("If I stop thinking about it, maybe it will go away"), fear ("What will happen to me?") and anger ("It's not fair that I have diabetes") are common. Guilt ("If I had eaten better, then I wouldn't have gotten diabetes"), sadness ("I feel so bad about this") and frustration ("Now what do I have to do? This is so hard!") also are normal.

Fortunately, bolstered by a little insight and knowledge, you also can feel relief ("It could be worse"), hopefulness ("I can care for my body and my diabetes"), adaptation ("I don't like it, but I'll deal with it") and, finally, acceptance ("I have diabetes, but I'm still going to enjoy my life").

Instead of thinking about diabetes as the worst thing that could happen to you, view diabetes as a wake-up call that can lead to healthier living and a longer life. Even small changes, practiced over a long time, can be a big help on the road to better health.

If you take care of your emotional self, you can accept diabetes as one part—and not all—of your life. This doesn't happen overnight. So give yourself the time and patience needed to work through any feelings you experience. Look to family, friends and mental health professionals if you feel you need help, and ask for it. It will be better for you and for the people who love you.

Take time to congratulate yourself on maintaining good blood glucose levels and other accomplishments. It's easy to focus too much on areas that still need work and forget to notice all the successes. Perhaps you've worked up to exercising four times a week, and you feel great. Or all of a sudden, you find that your craving for sweets has gone away! Maybe your latest achievement is much smaller—you've made it through a whole week without being so tired. Even small accomplishments deserve to be celebrated.

Certified Diabetes Educator

Nurses and dietitians who specialize in diabetes care are often certified as experts in the field (often designated by "CDE," or Certified Diabetes Educator). They help people with diabetes and their families to understand the following:

- What diabetes is.
- How glucose and insulin work together to provide energy.
- How food and activity affect blood glucose levels.
- Different diabetes medications and how they work.
- The purpose, importance and how-to's of daily self-care.

Diabetes Treatment

Diabetes knowledge, self-care skills and emotional support provide the foundation for your treatment plan and help support appropriate medical therapies. Food planning and physical activity are important components of care. For certain people, medications are sometimes needed as well.

BLOOD GLUCOSE TARGET LEVELS

Best Time	Diabetes Target (mg/dL)	My Target	No Diabetes/ Prediabetes (mg/dL)
Before a meal	70–120		Less than 100
2 hours after the start of a meal	Less than 160		Less than 140

* Random glucose test cannot be used to diagnose pre-diabetes.

Used with permission from International Diabetes Center, Minneapolis, MN, *Type 2 Diabetes BASICS, 3rd edition*, 2010

1. Blood Glucose Control

The number one goal of diabetes care is to keep your blood glucose levels as close to normal as possible. Every member of your care team has a role in helping you to achieve this goal. A big part of your role is to test your blood glucose as recommended by your health-care provider. Be sure you receive and understand your self-tested blood glucose targets. You need to have a target for before meals and a target for two hours after the start of meals (post-meal blood glucose). Common times and targets for blood glucose tests are shown on the opposite page. Self-testing your blood glucose is critical for monitoring and managing daily control.

Hemoglobin A1C Test

There is a laboratory test today that indicates your average blood glucose over the past two to three months. Commonly called a Hemoglobin A1C test, or just A1C, it is available through any medical office and is the standard measure for evaluating overall blood glucose control. It's the best indicator of your risk for developing diabetes complications. If you have not had an A1C measurement, be sure to talk with your health-care provider about it. It's recommended that people with diabetes have an A1C test every three to four months. As for blood glucose self-tests, the goal is to keep your A1C target as close to normal as possible. See the Diabetes Care Schedule on page 34 for A1C and other diabetes care targets.

The Best Plan for You

Your treatment plan is based on what your body needs. Anyone with type 1 diabetes needs to take insulin injections coordinated with a personalized food plan, activity and lifestyle needs. Individuals with type 2 diabetes may or may not need medication; sometimes a personalized food plan along with increased physical activity is enough to control blood glucose levels. But over time, or even right at diagnosis if warranted, your health-care professional may recommend adding a diabetes medication. You may need oral medication, insulin or both to keep your blood glucose level in target. It's important to note that diabetes medications alone cannot replace the benefits of following your food plan and staying physically active. Healthy eating and exercising dramatically improve the effectiveness of medications.

Diabetes Medications

There are three types of diabetes medication:

- Oral medications.
- Insulin injections.
- Non-insulin injectables—the newest category.

BLOOD TESTS:
Doctor's Tool to Diagnose

If you have two or more risk factors, you should be tested for diabetes as part of your regular checkup. Four different blood tests may be used to diagnose diabetes:

❶ HEMOGLOBIN A1C TEST

Done at any time of day, this test measures your average glucose level over the last two to three months.

❷ FASTING BLOOD GLUCOSE TEST

Blood is drawn after at least 8 hours of not eating or drinking anything (usually first thing in the morning).

❸ RANDOM GLUCOSE TEST

Blood may be drawn at any time.

❹ GLUCOSE TOLERANCE TEST

Blood for this test is drawn two hours after drinking a special glucose solution. The chart below shows blood glucose ranges for prediabetes and diabetes.

BLOOD TEST TABLE

Diagnosis	A1C	Fasting Glucose	Random Glucose*	2-hour OCGTT
Diabetes	6.5% or higher	126 mg/dL or higher	200mg/dL or higher with symptoms	200mg/dL or higher
Prediabetes	5.7–6.4%	100–125mg/dL		140–199mg/dL

* Random glucose test cannot be used to diagnose prediabetes.

Used with permission from International Diabetes Center, Minneapolis, MN, *Type 2 Diabetes BASICS, 3rd edition,* copyright 2010.

DIABETES TREATMENT OPTIONS

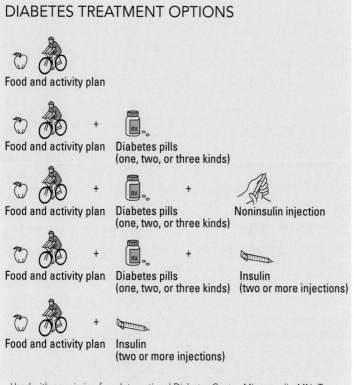

Food and activity plan

Food and activity plan + Diabetes pills (one, two, or three kinds)

Food and activity plan + Diabetes pills (one, two, or three kinds) + Noninsulin injection

Food and activity plan + Diabetes pills (one, two, or three kinds) + Insulin (two or more injections)

Food and activity plan + Insulin (two or more injections)

Used with permission from International Diabetes Center, Minneapolis, MN, *Type 2 Diabetes BASICS, 3rd edition, 2010*

Oral medications may also be called glucose-lowering pills, diabetes pills or oral agents. There are three main types of oral agents:

* Those that stimulate or push the pancreas to make more insulin.

* Those that help the body use insulin more efficiently.

* Those that help the pancreas cells work better.

Insulin-stimulating agents include those that are long-acting and taken once a day and those that are short-acting and taken before each meal. Insulin-sensitizing agents help the body use insulin more efficiently by reducing insulin resistance.

Non-insulin injectables are medications that help the body make more insulin. These medications work like a hormone that is made by the body. They prevent blood glucose from going too high after meals and can make you feel less hungry and lose weight. Sometimes they cause nausea.

Oral agents may be used alone or in combination with each other. If oral agents and non-insulin injectables are not effective in keeping blood glucose levels in your target range, insulin injections may be prescribed. Many people with type 2 diabetes now take both oral agents and insulin. Oral agents are generally not used for people with type 1 diabetes.

Insulin is taken by injection, usually several times per day depending on blood glucose patterns and goals for treatment. There are two classes of insulin: short- or rapid-acting mealtime insulin and intermediate- or long-acting background insulin. Short- or rapid-acting insulin provides a burst of insulin to cover a meal that is ready to be eaten. Mealtime insulin is also called bolus insulin. The more carbohydrate you have in the meal, the more insulin you need to help the body use it. This prevents blood glucose from going too high after eating. Background insulin provides a continuous supply of insulin to keep blood glucose in control overnight and between meals during the day. Background insulin is also called basal insulin. The newest type of background insulin, taken once a day, often in the evening, can be effective in type 2 diabetes when combined with oral agents taken during the day. It is also very effective when used with rapid-acting insulin before meals for both type 1 and type 2 diabetes.

People may not want to take insulin for various reasons, most commonly because it must be taken by injection. Fortunately, the needles on syringes are now very short and thin, so that they are barely felt. Also, many people now use insulin pens, which allow the appropriate insulin dose to be quickly injected without drawing insulin from a bottle. Pens with premixed bolus insulin and background insulin in one device are another option that can make insulin delivery easy.

Insulin injections are the most effective method of lowering blood glucose levels offered today. Studies show that most people with type 2 diabetes will eventually need insulin to control blood glucose levels. This is a natural result of having diabetes for a long time. It does not mean that the person has somehow failed or that their diabetes is getting worse. It is simply that the pancreas is making less insulin over time and the treatment must change to match the body's needs.

2. Blood Lipids (Fats) Control

Diabetes increases your risk for heart and blood vessel disease. High blood lipids (fats) and high blood pressure add to the risk. As with blood glucose control, food planning, exercise and medications play a crucial role in helping control these heart disease risks.

Blood lipids consist of cholesterol and triglycerides. These are both made in the body and are found in food. Most of the cholesterol in the bloodstream is actually made in the body. Triglycerides come mostly from food, particularly from added fat, such as butter and salad dressing, and from sweets. Cholesterol and triglycerides are carried through the bloodstream in small packages called lipoproteins. There are two main lipoproteins:

- HDLs (high-density lipoproteins), or "good" cholesterol, which carries "bad" cholesterol and triglycerides out of the blood.
- LDLs (low-density lipoproteins), or "bad" cholesterol, which deposits cholesterol in blood vessel walls, narrowing the vessel opening and irritating the lining of the vessel.

To keep track of your heart health, you need to know how much HDL, LDL and triglycerides are in your blood. The only way to know this is to have your doctor order a complete cholesterol profile for you every year. Blood for this test needs to be drawn first thing in the morning, before you eat. It's good to have high HDL levels and low LDL levels in your blood.

Increasing physical activity is the best way to improve HDL. Eating a healthy diet that is low in saturated fat and rich in omega-3 fatty acids and monounsaturated fats, nuts and legumes is the best way to lower LDLs and triglycerides.

Target goals for cholesterol and triglycerides are on the Diabetes Care Schedule (page 34).

3. Blood Pressure Control

High blood pressure puts extra strain on your heart and in the large blood vessels in the brain and legs. It can also damage small blood vessels in the eyes and kidneys. It adds to the risk for heart disease, stroke, visual impairment, kidney disease and other diabetes complications.

Blood pressure is recorded as two numbers. The upper number is the systolic blood pressure, the pressure when your heart is contracting. The lower number is the diastolic pressure, the pressure when your heart is relaxed. If either number is high, your risk for heart disease is increased. Make sure your blood pressure is checked at every health-care visit, and ask to see the results. Target goals for blood pressure are on the Diabetes Care Schedule (page 34).

Making food choices that are lower in sodium has been shown to help reduce blood pressure. The recommendation for daily sodium intake is 1,500 to 2,300 milligrams per day.

4. Prevent and Manage Complications

Long-term complications are caused by extended periods of high blood glucose levels, which damage small and large blood vessels. Damage to small blood vessels causes problems with the nerves (neuropathy), eyes (retinopathy) and kidneys (nephropathy). This is called microvascular disease. The walls of large blood vessels can be damaged by lipid buildup, high blood pressure and inflammation, which can lead to problems in the heart, brain and feet. This is called macrovascular disease.

Keeping blood glucose levels within the target range at least 50 percent of the time, as well as achieving an A1c result of less than 7 percent, greatly reduces the risk of long-term complications. Research confirms this, including data from the 10-year Diabetes Control and Complications Trial (DCCT), concluded in 1993, and the United Kingdom

Prospective Diabetes Study, concluded in 1999. The DCCT showed that blood glucose control can:

- Reduce eye disease by 76 percent.
- Reduce kidney disease by 56 percent.
- Reduce nerve damage by 60 percent.

While blood glucose control reduces heart disease in type 1 diabetes, its precise role in reducing heart disease in type 2 diabetes is still being studied.

Your diabetes care team members must do their parts in monitoring diabetes complications by checking your feet, eyes and kidney function regularly for signs of damage. It is very important to follow the recommendations in the Diabetes Care Schedule (page 34) for tests and exams; do not allow them to be overlooked. Despite your best efforts, some complications may develop. Your best defense is to learn about any problems early so that you and your team can take action.

5. Other Care Essentials

Diabetes affects every aspect of your health and your health care. Therefore, your provider may recommend other treatments contributing to your overall well-being, including the taking of:

- A daily aspirin dose to reduce the risk of heart attack, if you are over 50 years for men and over 60 years for women, particularly if you have a history of heart disease.
- Daily blood pressure medication (consider an ACE-inhibitor) for high blood pressure or to counteract the effects of kidney damage. (Some providers also prescribe these medications to prevent blood vessel damage.)
- Daily cholesterol-lowering medication (a statin is recommended) to treat high LDL cholesterol and to protect against heart damage. Consider taking after discussing with your doctor.

The Diabetes Care Schedule summarizes the laboratory tests, medical examinations and lifestyle behaviors that contribute to achieving and maintaining your diabetes and health goals. Work with your diabetes care team to ensure that you receive the regular care that you need. Your health depends on it!

Tap into Resources

The members of your diabetes care team are your first resource. Additional resources are also available.

- The International Diabetes Center (IDC) offers a wealth of information on diabetes and diabetes self-care, including food planning, exercise, planning for pregnancy, gestational diabetes, diabetes prevention, depression and diabetes, and much more. Visit their Web site and online store at http://www.internationaldiabetescenter.com or call 1-888-825-6315.
- The International Diabetes Center (IDC) publications used as resources for this book include:
  - Carbohydrate Counting for People with Diabetes
  - Insulin BASICS
  - My Food Plan
  - Blood Glucose Pattern Control
  - Staged Diabetes Management
  - Type 2 Diabetes BASICS
  - Top 10 Nutrition Questions
- The Academy of Nutrition and Dietitics can provide customized answers to your questions about nutrition. Call them at 1-800-877-1600 to obtain a referral to a registered dietitian in your area. You can also listen to recorded messages about food and nutrition. Check out The Academy's Web site at www.eatright.org.
- The American Diabetes Association (ADA) Web site at www.diabetes.org provides general information about diabetes. You can also call 1-800-DIABETES (1-800-342-2383) to request a free information packet. The American Diabetes Association also offers several books and pamphlets about diabetes.
- The American Association of Diabetes Educators (AADE) can help you locate a diabetes educator in your area. Check their Web site at www.diabeteseducator.org or call 1-800-338-3633.
- The Juvenile Diabetes Research Foundation (JDRF) is a leader in the type 1 diabetes community with a focus on unifying global efforts to cure, treat and prevent type 1 diabetes. To learn more about JDRF or to locate a chapter near you, visit their Web site at www.jdrf.org. Or call 1-800-533-CURE (1-800-533-2873).

CLINICAL RESEARCH

Individuals with diabetes may want to consider participating in a diabetes clinical research study. Clinical trials are an important part of determining which new drugs, medical devices or lifestyle choices can best help people with diabetes manage their disease and one day possibly lead to a cure. Participating in a clinical trial may benefit an individual by allowing them to test the latest new therapies and medical technology or by receiving special education or support to manage their diabetes. In addition, the research one participates in may benefit future generations of people with diabetes. One should always discuss the pros and cons of participating in clinical research with his or her medical team since it is always important to weigh the benefits and risks of being involved in clinical research. If one wants to find out more about what is involved in participating in clinical research here are some web sites with good explanations:

JDRF - https://trials.jdrf.org/patient

ADA - http://www.diabetes.org/news-research/research/clinical-trials

- dLife, a tv show dedicated to people with diabetes, was established to address the consumer need for real, practical solutions to the 24/7 challenge of managing diabetes. Check local tv schedules for show times.

- Don't forget support groups. You can find one through hospitals, workplaces or your community center. Or talk to your doctor, diabetes educator or dietitian about joining a group, and ask when and where it meets. Supportive people in similar situations are often able to learn from and help each other. Over time, you may find that sharing your experiences will help someone else who is just beginning to learn about dealing with diabetes.

Thai Beef Noodle Bowls, page 160

Southwestern Quinoa Salad, page 168

Diabetes Care Schedule

The Diabetes Care Schedule summarizes the laboratory tests, medical examinations and lifestyle behaviors that contribute to achieving and maintaining your diabetes and health goals. Work with your diabetes care team to ensure that you receive the regular care that you need. Your health depends on it!

LAB TEST/EXAM	TARGET	FREQUENCY
Hemoglobin A1C	Less than 7% for most Less than 8% for nearly everyone	Every 3 to 6 months
Total cholesterol	Less than 200 mg/dL	Yearly
LDL cholesterol ("bad")	Less than 100 mg/dL	Yearly
HDL cholesterol ("good")	Greater than 40 mg/dL	Yearly
Triglycerides	Less than 150 mg/dL	Yearly
Kidney Function —microalbumin test ratio —eGFR	Less than 30 mg/g CR Greater than 60 ml/min/1.73m^2	Yearly
TSH (thyroid function)	0.2 to 5.5 mIU/mL (normal range varies by lab)	As recommended
ECG (electro-cardiogram)	Normal or stable from last EKG	As recommended
Blood pressure	Less than 130/80 for most Less than 140/90 for nearly everyone	Every visit
Retinal eye exam	No signs of changes due to diabetes or stable from last visit	Yearly
Foot exam, comprehensive	Check for sores, blood flow, nerve damage	At least yearly
Dental exam	Regular check-up of teeth and gums	Every 6 months

VACCINES	RECOMMENDATION	FREQUENCY
Flu vaccine	All people with diabetes, 6 months or older if not allergic	Yearly
Pneumonia vaccine (PPV)	All people with diabetes, 2 years or older	Repeat as directed by doctor
Hepatitis B vaccine	All people with diabetes, ages 19 to 59 years	Once (age 60 and over, as directed by doctor)

LIFESTYLE AND DIABETES SELF-MANAGEMENT	RECOMMENDATION
Diabetes education	At diagnosis and yearly by nurse and diabetes care team
Blood glucose self-tests	Before meals: 70 to 120 mg/dL 2 hours after start of meals: less than 160 mg/dL Individualized blood glucose targets may be determined by health care professional
Food plan	3 meals per day; 2 to 4 carb choices (30 to 60 g)/meal Snacks not usually needed; < 30 grams carb/snack
Activity	30 minutes of activity most days of the week. A combination of fitness and strength training is ideal.
Overweight or obese	Lose 5 to 7 percent of total body weight to improve blood glucose control; for example, 10 to 14 pounds if you weigh 200 pounds
Foot exam, visual	Check for sores and redness
Smoke or tobacco use	Stop smoking—consider smoking cessation classes or prescription medications from your doctor

MEDICATION USE	RECOMMENDATION
Aspirin (thins blood and reduces inflammation of blood vessels)	Adults take an aspirin (usually low-dose 81 mg) if history of heart disease, or discuss with your doctor
ACE-inhibitor (blood pressure-lowering medication)	Take by prescription for hypertension, if urine protein is greater than 30 mg/g CR, or if recommended for heart and circulation protection
Statin (cholesterol-lowering medication)	Take by prescription for high LDL ("bad") cholesterol or if recommended for heart protection
Review treatment plan	Every visit

Adapted with permission from International Diabetes Center, Minneapolis, MN

CHAPTER 1

Day-Starter Breakfasts

2
Carbohydrate Choices

Berry–French Toast Stratas

PREP TIME: 15 min • **START TO FINISH:** 50 min • 6 servings (2 stratas with ½ cup fruit each)

1 SERVING: Calories 190 (Calories from Fat 15); Total Fat 1.5g (Saturated Fat 0g; Trans Fat 0g); Cholesterol 0mg; Sodium 280mg; Total Carbohydrate 31g (Dietary Fiber 5g; Sugars 18g); Protein 11g

% DAILY VALUE: Vitamin A 15%; Vitamin C 20%; Calcium 10%; Iron 10%

EXCHANGES: 1 Starch, ½ Fruit, ½ Other Carbohydrate, 1 Very Lean Meat

3	cups assorted fresh berries, such as blueberries, raspberries or cut-up strawberries
1	tablespoon granulated sugar
4	cups cubes (¾ inch) whole wheat bread (about 5 slices)
1½	cups fat-free egg product or 6 eggs
½	cup fat-free (skim) milk
½	cup fat-free half-and-half
2	tablespoons honey
1½	teaspoons vanilla
1	teaspoon ground cinnamon
¼	teaspoon ground nutmeg
½	teaspoon powdered sugar, if desired

1 In medium bowl, mix fruit and granulated sugar; set aside.

2 Heat oven to 350°F. Spray 12 regular-size muffin cups generously with cooking spray. Divide bread cubes evenly among muffin cups.

3 In large bowl, beat remaining ingredients, except powdered sugar, with fork or whisk until well mixed. Pour egg mixture over bread cubes, pushing down lightly with spoon to soak bread cubes. (If all egg mixture doesn't fit into cups, let cups stand up to 10 minutes, gradually adding remaining egg mixture as bread cubes soak it up.)

4 Bake 20 to 25 minutes or until centers are set. Cool 5 minutes. Remove from muffin cups, placing 2 stratas on each of 6 plates. Divide fruit mixture evenly over stratas; sprinkle with powdered sugar.

Betty's Success Tip

It's easy to sprinkle powdered sugar lightly and evenly over berries. Just use a wire-mesh strainer, tapping the side with a spoon.

2½
Carbohydrate Choices

Chocolate Pancakes with Strawberries

PREP TIME: 25 min • **START TO FINISH:** 25 min • 4 servings (2 pancakes and ¼ cup strawberries each)

1 SERVING: Calories 210 (Calories from Fat 45); Total Fat 4.5g (Saturated Fat 0g; Trans Fat 0g); Cholesterol 0mg; Sodium 260mg; Total Carbohydrate 36g (Dietary Fiber 3g; Sugars 11g); Protein 6g

% DAILY VALUE:
Vitamin A 6%; Vitamin C 20%; Calcium 15%; Iron 15%

EXCHANGES:
1½ Starch, 1 Other Carbohydrate, ½ Fat

¾	cup light chocolate soymilk
¼	cup fat-free egg product
1	tablespoon canola oil
¾	cup all-purpose flour
2	tablespoons sugar
2	tablespoons unsweetened baking cocoa
1	teaspoon baking powder
⅛	teaspoon salt
1	cup sliced fresh strawberries
	Sliced banana, if desired
	French vanilla fat-free yogurt, if desired

1 In medium bowl, beat soymilk, egg product and oil with whisk until smooth. Stir in remaining ingredients except strawberries, banana and yogurt.

2 Spray griddle or 10-inch skillet with cooking spray; heat griddle to 375°F or heat skillet over medium heat. For each pancake, pour slightly less than ¼ cup batter onto hot griddle.

3 Cook pancakes until puffed and dry around edges. Turn and cook other sides until golden brown. Serve with strawberries, banana and yogurt.

Betty's Success Tip

The key to making great pancakes lies in bringing the griddle or skillet to the right temperature. Heat the griddle or skillet over medium heat (375°F) before cooking.

Whole-Grain Strawberry Pancakes

PREP TIME: 30 min • **START TO FINISH:** 30 min • 7 servings

2 Carbohydrate Choices

1½ cups whole wheat flour

3 tablespoons sugar

1 teaspoon baking powder

½ teaspoon baking soda

½ teaspoon salt

3 eggs or ¾ cup fat-free egg product

1 container (6 oz) vanilla low-fat yogurt

¾ cup water

3 tablespoons canola oil

1¾ cups sliced fresh strawberries

1 container (6 oz) strawberry low-fat yogurt

1 Heat griddle to 375°F or heat 12-inch skillet over medium heat. Grease with canola oil if necessary (or spray with cooking spray before heating).

2 In large bowl, mix flour, sugar, baking powder, baking soda and salt; set aside. In medium bowl, beat eggs, vanilla yogurt, water and oil with egg beater or whisk until well blended. Pour egg mixture all at once into flour mixture; stir until moistened.

3 For each pancake, pour slightly less than ¼ cup batter onto hot griddle. Cook pancakes 1 to 2 minutes or until bubbly on top, puffed and dry around edges. Turn; cook other sides 1 to 2 minutes or until golden brown.

4 Top each serving with ¼ cup sliced strawberries and 1 to 2 tablespoons strawberry yogurt.

1 SERVING: Calories 260 (Calories from Fat 90); Total Fat 9g (Saturated Fat 1.5g; Trans Fat 0g); Cholesterol 95mg; Sodium 380mg; Total Carbohydrate 34g (Dietary Fiber 4g; Sugars 13g); Protein 8g

% DAILY VALUE: Vitamin A 4%; Vitamin C 20%; Calcium 15%; Iron 8%

EXCHANGES: 1½ Starch, ½ Other Carbohydrate, ½ Very Lean Meat, 1½ Fat

Diabetes Team Tip
Look for sugar-free syrup at the grocery store. The carbohydrate content is lower than regular syrup. If it's 20 calories or less per serving, it's a free food for you. —Diane Reader, Dietitian

Betty's Success Tip
We really like the strawberry yogurt topping on these pancakes, but you could use lemon or orange yogurt instead. If you like raspberries, why not add a few to the strawberries for a sweet surprise.

3½
Carbohydrate Choices

Whole Wheat Waffles with Honey–Peanut Butter Drizzle

PREP TIME: 35 min • **START TO FINISH:** 40 min • 8 servings (2 waffle squares, 1½ tablespoons syrup and 1 tablespoon granola each)

1 SERVING: Calories 360 (Calories from Fat 110); Total Fat 12g (Saturated Fat 2.5g; Trans Fat 0g); Cholesterol 60mg; Sodium 320mg; Total Carbohydrate 52g (Dietary Fiber 3g; Sugars 25g); Protein 10g

% DAILY VALUE: Vitamin A 4%; Vitamin C 0%; Calcium 20%; Iron 10%

EXCHANGES: 2 Starch, 1½ Other Carbohydrate, ½ Medium-Fat Meat, 1½ Fat

WAFFLES

- 2   eggs or 4 egg whites
- 1   cup whole wheat flour
- 1   cup all-purpose flour
- 2   cups buttermilk
- 1   tablespoon sugar
- 3   tablespoons canola oil
- 2   teaspoons baking powder
- ¼   teaspoon salt
- ½   cup low-fat granola

DRIZZLE

- ½   cup honey
- ¼   cup creamy peanut butter

1 Heat waffle iron; brush with canola oil if necessary (or spray with cooking spray before heating). In medium bowl, beat eggs with fork or whisk until foamy. Beat in remaining waffle ingredients except granola just until smooth.

2 Pour about 1 cup batter onto center of hot waffle iron. (Check manufacturer's directions for recommended amount of batter.) Close lid of waffle iron.

3 Bake about 5 minutes or until steaming stops. Carefully remove waffle. Repeat with remaining batter.

4 Meanwhile, in small microwavable bowl, mix honey and peanut butter. Microwave uncovered on High 40 to 60 seconds or until warm; stir until smooth. Drizzle over waffles. Sprinkle with granola.

Betty's Success Tip

Besides being low in fat because it's made with skim milk, buttermilk is a powerful ingredient to use in baking because it adds a terrific dairy flavor and makes a moist baked good. You'll love these easy waffles!

Corn, Egg and Potato Bake

PREP TIME: 20 min • **START TO FINISH:** 1 hr 30 min • 8 servings

1
Carbohydrate
Choice

4   cups frozen diced hash brown potatoes (from 2-lb bag), thawed

½   cup frozen whole-kernel corn (from 1-lb bag), thawed

¼   cup chopped roasted red bell peppers (from 7-oz jar)

1½   cups shredded reduced-fat Colby–Monterey Jack cheese (6 oz)

10   eggs or 2½ cups fat-free egg product

½   cup fat-free small-curd cottage cheese

½   teaspoon dried oregano leaves

¼   teaspoon garlic powder

4   medium green onions, chopped (¼ cup)

1   Heat oven to 350°F. Spray 11×7-inch (2-quart) glass baking dish with cooking spray. In baking dish, layer potatoes, corn, bell peppers and 1 cup of the shredded cheese.

2   In medium bowl, beat eggs, cottage cheese, oregano and garlic powder with whisk until well blended. Slowly pour over potato mixture. Sprinkle with onions and remaining ½ cup shredded cheese.

3   Cover and bake 30 minutes. Uncover and bake about 30 minutes longer or until knife inserted in center comes out clean. Let stand 5 to 10 minutes before cutting.

1 SERVING: Calories 240 (Calories from Fat 100); Total Fat 11g (Saturated Fat 5g; Trans Fat 0g); Cholesterol 280mg; Sodium 440mg; Total Carbohydrate 18g (Dietary Fiber 2g; Sugars 2g); Protein 16g

% DAILY VALUE: Vitamin A 10%; Vitamin C 4%; Calcium 20%; Iron 6%

EXCHANGES: 1 Starch, 2 Lean Meat, 1 Fat

Diabetes Team Tip
As your steps (or other physical activity) add up, so do the health benefits. Research shows that walking helps control blood pressure and cholesterol, while reducing the risk of diabetes, stroke and certain types of cancer.—Diane Reader, Dietitian

Betty's Success Tip
An easy way to cut calories is to use low-fat or fat-free dairy products, which contain fewer calories than regular-fat dairy products. You could use reduced-fat Cheddar cheese instead of the Colby–Monterey Jack cheese.

1
Carbohydrate
Choice

Chorizo Mexican Breakfast Pizzas

PREP TIME: 15 min • START TO FINISH: 25 min • 4 servings

1 SERVING: Calories 330 (Calories from Fat 170); Total Fat 19g (Saturated Fat 7g; Trans Fat 0g); Cholesterol 40mg; Sodium 1030mg; Total Carbohydrate 19g (Dietary Fiber 6g; Sugars 2g); Protein 20g

% DAILY VALUE: Vitamin A 10%; Vitamin C 4%; Calcium 8%; Iron 15%

EXCHANGES: 1 Starch, ½ Vegetable, ½ Lean Meat, 2 Medium-Fat Meat, 1½ Fat

6   oz chorizo sausage, casing removed, crumbled, or 6 oz bulk chorizo sausage

2   (10-inch) whole-grain lower-carb lavash flatbreads or tortillas

¼   cup chunky-style salsa

½   cup black beans with cumin and chili spices (from 15-oz can)

½   cup chopped tomatoes

½   cup frozen whole-kernel corn, thawed

¼   cup reduced-fat shredded Cheddar cheese (1 oz)

1   tablespoon chopped fresh cilantro

2   teaspoons crumbed cotija (white Mexican) cheese

1   Heat oven to 425°F. In 8-inch skillet, cook sausage over medium heat 4 to 5 minutes or until brown; drain.

2   On 1 large or 2 small cookie sheets, place flatbreads. Spread each with 2 tablespoons salsa. Top each with half the chorizo, beans, tomatoes, corn and Cheddar cheese.

3   Bake about 8 minutes or until cheese is melted. Sprinkle each with half the cilantro and cotija cheese; cut into wedges. Serve immediately.

Betty's Success Tip

Cotija cheese is a tasty type of crumbly Mexican cheese, and just a little bit adds great flavor. If cotija isn't available, substitute crumbled feta cheese.

0
Carbohydrate
Choices

Veggie-Stuffed Omelet

PREP TIME: 15 min • **START TO FINISH:** 15 min • 1 serving

1 SERVING: Calories 140 (Calories from Fat 50); Total Fat 5g (Saturated Fat 1g; Trans Fat 0g); Cholesterol 0mg; Sodium 470mg; Total Carbohydrate 6g (Dietary Fiber 2g; Sugars 3g); Protein 16g

% DAILY VALUE: Vitamin A 100%; Vitamin C 30%; Calcium 15%; Iron 20%

EXCHANGES: 1 Vegetable, 2 Very Lean Meat, 1 Fat

1   teaspoon olive or canola oil

2   tablespoons chopped red bell pepper

1   tablespoon chopped onion

¼   cup sliced fresh mushrooms

1   cup loosely packed fresh baby spinach leaves, rinsed

½   cup fat-free egg product or 2 eggs, beaten

1   tablespoon water
    Pinch salt
    Pinch pepper

1   tablespoon shredded reduced-fat Cheddar cheese

1 In 8-inch nonstick skillet, heat oil over medium-high heat. Add bell pepper, onion and mushrooms to oil. Cook 2 minutes, stirring frequently, until onion is tender. Stir in spinach; continue cooking and stirring just until spinach wilts. Transfer vegetables from pan to small bowl.

2 In medium bowl, beat egg product, water, salt and pepper with fork or whisk until well mixed. Reheat same skillet over medium-high heat. Quickly pour egg mixture into pan. While sliding pan back and forth rapidly over heat, quickly stir with spatula to spread eggs continuously over bottom of pan as they thicken. Let stand over heat a few seconds to lightly brown bottom of omelet. Do not overcook; omelet will continue to cook after folding.

3 Place cooked vegetable mixture over half of omelet; top with cheese. With spatula, fold other half of omelet over vegetables. Gently slide out of pan onto plate. Serve immediately.

Betty's Success Tip

To make two omelets, double all of the ingredients, cooking the egg mixture in two batches. Keep the first omelet warm by placing it on a warm plate. Topping each omelet with about 1 tablespoon salsa or hot sauce adds an extra burst of flavor.

2
Carbohydrate
Choices

Potato, Egg and Sausage Frittata

PREP TIME: 30 min • **START TO FINISH:** 30 min • 4 servings

1 SERVING: Calories 280 (Calories from Fat 110); Total Fat 12g (Saturated Fat 4.5g, Trans Fat 0g); Cholesterol 220mg; Sodium 590mg; Total Carbohydrate 26g (Dietary Fiber 3g, Sugars 5g); Protein 17g

% DAILY VALUE: Vitamin A 20%; Vitamin C 15%; Calcium 20%; Iron 10%

EXCHANGES: 1½ Starch, 2 Medium-Fat Meat

4   frozen soy-protein breakfast sausage links (from 8-oz box), thawed

1   teaspoon olive oil

2   cups frozen country-style shredded hash brown potatoes (from 30-oz bag)

4   eggs or 8 egg whites

¼   cup fat-free (skim) milk

¼   teaspoon salt

⅛   teaspoon dried basil leaves

⅛   teaspoon dried oregano leaves

1½ cups chopped plum (Roma) tomatoes

½   cup shredded mozzarella and Asiago cheese blend with garlic (2 oz)

    Pepper, if desired

    Chopped green onion, if desired

1 Cut each sausage link into 8 pieces. Coat 10-inch nonstick skillet with oil; heat over medium heat. Add sausage and potatoes; cook 6 to 8 minutes, stirring occasionally, until potatoes are golden brown.

2 In small bowl, beat eggs and milk with fork or whisk until well blended. Pour egg mixture over potato mixture. Cook uncovered over medium-low heat about 5 minutes; as mixture begins to set on bottom and side, gently lift cooked portions with spatula so that thin, uncooked portion can flow to bottom. Cook until eggs are thickened throughout but still moist; avoid constant stirring.

3 Sprinkle salt, basil, oregano, tomatoes and cheese over eggs. Reduce heat to low; cover and cook about 5 minutes or until center is set and cheese is melted. Sprinkle with pepper and green onion.

Betty's Success Tip

If you haven't tried the newest soy products lately, you're in for a pleasant surprise. Soy sausage is a tasty alternative to higher-fat regular sausage and an easy addition to this fresh-tasting frittata.

Stopping the Epidemic

As diabetes continues to increase worldwide, medical experts have been tackling an important question: Can diabetes be prevented? For type 1 diabetes, researchers are studying what triggers the immune system to attack the pancreas and how to stop it. For type 2 diabetes, efforts at early prevention and detection are key. Regular screenings are recommended for everyone over age 45 and for younger people with two or more risk factors. Lifestyle changes also make a difference.

Over 90 percent of the 25 million people with diabetes in the United States have type 2 diabetes, and one-third don't even know it. Half of the people diagnosed with type 2 already have a complication of diabetes on the day of diagnosis, such as numbness, tingling or pain in the feet (due to nerve damage) or early damage of the blood vessels in the eyes, leading to poor vision.

What if your blood glucose test is higher than normal but not high enough to be diabetes? Or what if you've had gestational diabetes? How can you keep from developing diabetes later in life? Studies show that making modest lifestyle changes can cut your risk of developing diabetes by at least one-half. Certain medications may also reduce your risk.

LIFESTYLE CHANGES MAKE A DIFFERENCE

- Five days a week, get 30 to 60 minutes of mild aerobic exercise such as brisk walking.
- Lose 5 to 7 percent of your starting weight. For someone who weighs 200 pounds, that is losing 10 to 14 pounds. Keeping it off can be a significant benefit as well.
- Eat less total fat, particularly saturated fat.
- Increase your intake of whole grains, vegetables, fruits and fiber.

Get the whole family involved. Incorporating positive habits into kids' lives early—at home and in school—makes diabetes prevention more effective. Diabetes screening and lifestyle changes offer hope that fewer people will have to live with diabetes in the future. Now that's a goal worth striving for!

DIABETES TYPE 2 RISK FACTORS

Check out this list of factors that may increase your risk of type 2 diabetes.

- Family history of type 2 diabetes.
- Being overweight.
- Rarely physically active.
- High blood pressure.
- Polycystic ovary syndrome (PCOS).
- Ever had a high glucose level.
- Over age 45.
- Black or African-American, Hispanic or Latino, Asian American, Native Hawaiian or other Pacific Islander, Native American or Alaska Native.
- Diabetes during pregnancy or a baby weighing more than 9 pounds at birth.
- Heart disease or abnormal cholesterol or triglycerides.
- Smoker.

2
Carbohydrate
Choices

Breakfast Panini

PREP TIME: 10 min • **START TO FINISH:** 10 min • 2 panini

1 PANINI: Calories 260
(Calories from Fat 60);
Total Fat 7g (Saturated
Fat 2.5g; Trans Fat 0g);
Cholesterol 220mg;
Sodium 410mg; Total
Carbohydrate 32g
(Dietary Fiber 2g; Sugars
5g); Protein 15g

% DAILY VALUE:
Vitamin A 10%; Vitamin
C 4%; Calcium 15%;
Iron 15%

EXCHANGES: 2 Starch,
½ Very Lean Meat,
1 Medium-Fat Meat

2   eggs, beaten
½   teaspoon salt-free
    seasoning blend
2   tablespoons chopped
    fresh chives
2   whole wheat thin bagels
2   slices tomato
2   thin slices onion
4   ultra-thin slices reduced-
    sodium deli ham
2   thin slices reduced-fat
    Cheddar cheese

1   Spray 8-inch skillet with cooking spray; heat skillet
    over medium heat. In medium bowl, beat eggs,
    seasoning and chives with fork or whisk until well
    mixed. Pour into skillet. As eggs begin to set at
    bottom and side, gently lift cooked portions with
    spatula so that thin, uncooked portion can flow to
    bottom. Avoid constant stirring. Cook 3 to 4 minutes
    or until eggs are thickened throughout but still moist
    and creamy; remove from heat.

2   Meanwhile, heat closed contact grill or panini maker
    5 minutes.

3   For each panini, divide cooked eggs evenly between
    bottom halves of bagels. Top each with 1 slice each
    tomato and onion, 2 ham slices, 1 cheese slice and top
    half of bagel. Transfer filled panini to heated grill. Close
    cover, pressing down lightly. Cook 2 to 3 minutes or
    until browned and cheese is melted. Serve immediately.

Diabetes Team Tip Breakfast eaters usually eat better
overall than those who skip—it's
so important to eat early in the
day. Even when you're in a hurry,
take time to grab a slice of toast,
a container of yogurt and a small
piece of fruit on your way out the
door. —Diane Reader, Dietitian

Betty's Success Tip For a little variety, change the
fillings by using turkey instead
of ham and Swiss cheese
instead of Cheddar.

0
Carbohydrate
Choices

Bacon and Tomato Frittata

PREP TIME: 20 min • **START TO FINISH:** 20 min • 4 servings

1 SERVING: Calories 110 (Calories from Fat 35); Total Fat 4g (Saturated Fat 1g; Trans Fat 0g); Cholesterol 5mg; Sodium 400mg; Total Carbohydrate 4g (Dietary Fiber 1g; Sugars 2g); Protein 15g

% DAILY VALUE: Vitamin A 35%; Vitamin C 4%; Calcium 10%; Iron 15%

EXCHANGES: ½ Starch, 1 Very Lean Meat, 1 Lean Meat

1 carton (16 oz) fat-free egg product

¼ teaspoon salt-free garlic-and-herb seasoning

2 teaspoons canola oil

4 medium green onions, sliced (¼ cup)

½ cup sliced celery

2 large plum (Roma) tomatoes, sliced

¼ cup shredded sharp reduced-fat Cheddar cheese (2 oz)

2 tablespoons real bacon pieces (from 2.8-oz package)

2 tablespoons light sour cream, if desired

1 In medium bowl, mix egg product and garlic-and-herb seasoning; set aside.

2 In 10-inch nonstick ovenproof skillet, heat oil over medium heat. Add onions and celery; cook and stir 1 minute. Reduce heat to medium-low. Pour in egg mixture. Cook 6 to 9 minutes, gently lifting edges of cooked portions with spatula so that uncooked egg mixture can flow to bottom of skillet, until set.

3 Set oven control to broil. Top frittata with tomatoes, cheese and bacon. Broil with top 4 inches from heat 1 to 2 minutes or until cheese is melted. Top each serving with sour cream.

Betty's Success Tip
If you don't have an ovenproof skillet, just wrap the skillet handle in a double layer of heavy-duty foil.

Raspberry Lemonade Smoothies

PREP TIME: 10 min • **START TO FINISH:** 10 min • 4 servings (1 cup each)

3
Carbohydrate
Choices

1 cup refrigerated raspberry lemonade

2 ripe bananas, thickly sliced

1½ cups fresh raspberries

2 containers (6 oz each) raspberry fat-free yogurt

1 In blender or food processor, place all ingredients.

2 Cover; blend on high speed about 1 minute or until smooth and creamy. Pour into glasses. Serve immediately.

1 SERVING: Calories 190 (Calories from Fat 10); Total Fat 1.5g (Saturated Fat 0.5g; Trans Fat 0g); Cholesterol 5mg; Sodium 45mg; Total Carbohydrate 42g (Dietary Fiber 4g; Sugars 28g); Protein 3g

% DAILY VALUE: Vitamin A 8%; Vitamin C 15%; Calcium 10%; Iron 4%

EXCHANGES: 1 Starch, 2 Other Carbohydrate

Diabetes Team Tip
Because blood glucose levels can vary at different times of the day, test your blood sugar throughout the day, not just in the morning. Good times to check it are before lunch or two hours after dinner. —Dr. Bergenstal

Betty's Success Tip
Don't have the fresh raspberries? Use frozen raspberries that are slightly thawed instead. Float a few fresh raspberries on top of each smoothie.

2½
Carbohydrate
Choices

Crunchy-Topped Strawberry-Kiwi Parfaits

PREP TIME: 10 min • **START TO FINISH:** 20 min • 4 parfaits

1 PARFAIT: Calories 230 (Calories from Fat 40); Total Fat 4.5g (Saturated Fat 0.5g; Trans Fat 0g); Cholesterol 5mg; Sodium 150mg; Total Carbohydrate 41g (Dietary Fiber 3g; Sugars 25g); Protein 5g

% DAILY VALUE: Vitamin A 15%; Vitamin C 60%; Calcium 20%; Iron 20%

EXCHANGES: 1½ Starch, ½ Fruit, ½ Other Carbohydrate, 1 Fat

2 cups Banana Nut Cheerios® cereal

¼ cup sliced almonds

1½ cups creamy vanilla or creamy peach fat-free yogurt

1 cup sliced fresh strawberries

2 medium kiwifruit, peeled, cut into chunks

1 Heat oven to 350°F. In ungreased 13×9-inch pan, place cereal and almonds. Bake 6 to 10 minutes, stirring occasionally, until light brown. Cool about 5 minutes.

2 In each of 4 parfait glasses, alternate layers of yogurt, strawberries, kiwifruit and toasted cereal mixture. Serve immediately.

Betty's Success Tip
Strawberries provide vitamin C, also called ascorbic acid. Choosing vitamin C–rich foods keeps gums and blood vessels healthy.

Triple-Berry Oatmeal Muesli

PREP TIME: 25 min • **START TO FINISH:** 40 min • 6 servings

3
Carbohydrate
Choices

2¾ cups old-fashioned oats or rolled barley

½ cup sliced almonds

2 containers (6 oz each) banana crème or French vanilla fat-free yogurt

1½ cups milk

¼ cup ground flaxseed or flaxseed meal

½ cup fresh blueberries

½ cup fresh raspberries

½ cup sliced fresh strawberries

1 Heat oven to 350°F. On cookie sheet, spread oats and almonds. Bake 18 to 20 minutes, stirring occasionally, until light golden brown; cool 15 minutes.

2 In large bowl, mix yogurt and milk until well blended. Stir in oats, almonds and flaxseed. Divide muesli evenly among 6 bowls. Top each serving with berries.

1 SERVING: Calories 320 (Calories from Fat 90); Total Fat 10g (Saturated Fat 2g; Trans Fat 0g); Cholesterol 5mg; Sodium 65mg; Total Carbohydrate 46g (Dietary Fiber 7g; Sugars 15g); Protein 11g

% DAILY VALUE: Vitamin A 8%; Vitamin C 10%; Calcium 20%; Iron 15%

EXCHANGES: 2 Starch, 1 Other Carbohydrate, 1 Very Lean Meat, 1½ Fat

Betty's Success Tip

For the best flavor and nuttiest texture, use old-fashioned oats— not the quick type—for this recipe.

2
Carbohydrate
Choices

Tropical Fruit 'n Ginger Oatmeal

PREP TIME: 15 min • **START TO FINISH:** 45 min • 4 servings

1 SERVING: Calories 200 (Calories from Fat 50); Total Fat 6g (Saturated Fat 2g; Trans Fat 0g); Cholesterol 0mg; Sodium 110mg; Total Carbohydrate 31g (Dietary Fiber 4g; Sugars 16g); Protein 5g

% DAILY VALUE: Vitamin A 8%; Vitamin C 25%; Calcium 10%; Iron 6%

EXCHANGES: ½ Starch, 1 Fruit, ½ Skim Milk, 1 Fat

2¼ cups water

¾ cup steel-cut oats

2 teaspoons finely chopped gingerroot

⅛ teaspoon salt

½ medium banana, mashed

1 container (6 oz) vanilla low-fat yogurt

1 medium mango, pitted, peeled and chopped (1 cup)

½ cup sliced fresh strawberries

2 tablespoons shredded coconut, toasted*

2 tablespoons chopped walnuts

1 In 1½-quart saucepan, heat water to boiling. Stir in oats, gingerroot and salt. Reduce heat; simmer gently uncovered 25 to 30 minutes, without stirring, until oats are tender yet slightly chewy; stir in banana. Divide oatmeal evenly among 4 bowls.

2 Top each serving with yogurt, mango, strawberries, coconut and walnuts. Serve immediately.

*To toast coconut, heat oven to 350°F. Spread coconut in shallow pan. Bake uncovered 5 to 7 minutes, stirring occasionally, until golden brown.

Betty's Success Tip

To speed cooking time, substitute 1½ cups quick-cooking oats for the steel-cut oats, cooking as directed on the oats package.

2
Carbohydrate Choices

Upside-Down Date-Bran Muffins

PREP TIME: 20 min • **START TO FINISH:** 40 min • 12 muffins

1 MUFFIN: Calories 230 (Calories from Fat 70); Total Fat 8g (Saturated Fat 2g; Trans Fat 0g); Cholesterol 25mg; Sodium 210mg; Total Carbohydrate 35g (Dietary Fiber 4g; Sugars 20g); Protein 3g

% DAILY VALUE: Vitamin A 0%; Vitamin C 0%; Calcium 6%; Iron 8%

EXCHANGES: 1 Starch, 1 Other Carbohydrate, 1½ Fat

MUFFINS

1	cup Fiber One® cereal
1	cup buttermilk
¼	cup canola oil
1	teaspoon vanilla
1	egg
1¼	cups whole wheat flour
¾	cup chopped dates
½	cup packed brown sugar
1	teaspoon baking soda
¼	teaspoon salt

TOPPING

3	tablespoons packed brown sugar
2	tablespoons butter or margarine, melted
1	tablespoon light corn syrup

1 Heat oven to 400°F. Grease bottoms and sides of 12 regular-size muffin cups with shortening or cooking spray (do not use paper baking cups).

2 In blender or food processor, place cereal, buttermilk, oil, vanilla and egg. Cover; let stand 10 minutes. Meanwhile, in small bowl, stir topping ingredients until well mixed. Place 1 teaspoon of the topping in bottom of each muffin cup.

3 In blender, blend cereal mixture on medium speed until smooth; set aside. In medium bowl, stir flour, dates, ½ cup brown sugar, the baking soda and salt until well mixed. Pour cereal mixture over flour mixture; stir just until moistened (batter will be thick). Divide batter evenly among muffin cups.

4 Bake 14 to 18 minutes or until toothpick inserted in center comes out clean. Immediately place cookie sheet upside down on muffin pan; turn cookie sheet and pan over to remove muffins. Serve warm if desired.

Betty's Success Tip

You can make jumbo muffins, similar to the ones you see in the bakery. To make, just grease 6 jumbo muffin cups with shortening or cooking spray (do not use paper baking cups). Place 2 teaspoons of the topping in each cup before adding batter. Bake as directed.

Double-Berry Muffins

PREP TIME: 15 min • **START TO FINISH:** 40 min • 12 muffins

2
Carbohydrate
Choices

¼ cup packed brown sugar

½ teaspoon ground cinnamon

1 cup fat-free (skim) milk

¼ cup unsweetened applesauce

2 tablespoons canola oil

½ teaspoon vanilla

1 egg or ¼ cup fat-free egg product

2 cups all-purpose flour

⅓ cup granulated sugar

3 teaspoons baking powder

½ teaspoon salt

½ cup fresh or frozen (thawed and drained) raspberries

½ cup fresh or frozen (thawed and drained) blueberries

1 Heat oven to 400°F. Place paper baking cup in each of 12 regular-size muffin cups, or grease bottoms only with shortening. In small bowl, mix brown sugar and cinnamon; set aside.

2 In large bowl, beat milk, applesauce, oil, vanilla and egg with fork or whisk. Stir in flour, granulated sugar, baking powder and salt all at once just until flour is moistened (batter will be lumpy). Fold in raspberries and blueberries. Divide batter evenly among muffin cups. Sprinkle brown sugar mixture evenly over tops of muffins.

3 Bake 20 to 25 minutes or until golden brown. Immediately remove from pan to cooling rack. Serve warm if desired.

1 MUFFIN: Calories 160 (Calories from Fat 25); Total Fat 3g (Saturated Fat 0g; Trans Fat 0g); Cholesterol 20mg; Sodium 240mg; Total Carbohydrate 30g (Dietary Fiber 1g; Sugars 12g); Protein 3g

% DAILY VALUE: Vitamin A 0%; Vitamin C 0%; Calcium 10%; Iron 6%

EXCHANGES: 1 Starch, 1 Other Carbohydrate, ½ Fat

Betty's Success Tip

Choose a wide variety of fruits and vegetables to be sure you're getting all the nutrients these foods offer.

2

Carbohydrate Choices

Carrot-Lemon Bread

PREP TIME: 20 min • **START TO FINISH:** 2 hr 45 min • 1 loaf (16 slices)

1 SLICE: Calories 210 (Calories from Fat 60); Total Fat 7g (Saturated Fat 0.5g; Trans Fat 0g); Cholesterol 25mg; Sodium 270mg; Total Carbohydrate 32g (Dietary Fiber 4g; Sugars 10g); Protein 4g

% DAILY VALUE:
Vitamin A 60%; Vitamin C 4%; Calcium 8%; Iron 15%

EXCHANGES: 1½ Starch, ½ Other Carbohydrate, 1½ Fat

1½	cups Fiber One® cereal
2⅔	cups all-purpose flour
⅓	cup granulated sugar
⅓	cup packed brown sugar
2	teaspoons baking powder
2	teaspoons pumpkin pie spice
½	teaspoon salt
½	teaspoon baking soda
½	cup chopped walnuts
⅓	cup lemon juice
¼	cup canola oil
1	teaspoon grated lemon peel
2	eggs or ½ cup fat-free cholesterol-free egg product
2	cans (8 oz each) julienne-cut carrots, undrained

1 Heat oven to 350°F. Grease bottom and sides of 9×5-inch loaf pan with shortening. Place cereal in plastic bag or between sheets of waxed paper; finely crush with rolling pin (or crush cereal in blender or food processor); set aside.

2 In large bowl, mix flour, sugars, baking powder, pumpkin pie spice, salt and baking soda. Stir in cereal and walnuts.

3 In small bowl, beat remaining ingredients with spoon until well mixed. Stir into cereal mixture just until moistened. Pour into pan. Bake about 1 hour 10 minutes or until toothpick inserted in center comes out clean.

4 Cool 15 minutes; remove from pan to cooling rack. Cool completely, about 1 hour, before slicing.

Diabetes Team Tip At 4 grams per slice, this bread is a great source of fiber. Fiber can help with blood glucose management. Fruits, vegetables and whole grains, along with beans and other legumes, contain good amounts of fiber. —Diane Reader, Dietitian

21 GREAT 1 CARBOHYDRATE CHOICE SNACKS

Having great snacks readily available is a valuable key to following your meal plan. Keep these on hand and reach for them whenever you need a quick, healthy snack. Check the package label to confirm that each one counts as 1 Carbohydrate Choice.

- 1 (1-ounce) granola bar
- 3 graham cracker squares with 1 tablespoon of peanut butter
- 3 cups popped popcorn (no fat added) with seasoned salt
- 6 animal crackers
- 10 seasoned mini rice or mini popcorn cakes
- 15 mini-pretzel twists dipped in 1 tablespoon of cheese sauce
- 10 to 15 tortilla chips (1 ounce) with ¼ cup salsa
- 2 to 5 whole grain snack crackers or small pita triangles with 1 tablespoon of hummus
- 6 saltine cracker squares plus 1 ounce of reduced-fat cheese
- ¾ cup mix-and-match unsweetened cereals
- 1 small muffin or 3-inch cookie
- ½ cup sugar-free pudding
- 1 cup artificially sweetened hot cocoa
- 1 medium apple, orange or pear
- 12 to 15 cherries or grapes
- ¼ cup raisins or other dried fruit
- 3 cups baby carrots, broccoli, cauliflower, cherry tomatoes, celery, cucumber, pea pods, bell peppers, radishes, tomatoes or zucchini with 1 tablespoon of low-fat dip
- 1½ cups tomato or vegetable juice
- ½ cup light ice cream or 1 ice-cream bar
- ¾ to 1 cup yogurt, artificially sweetened (light) or plain
- 1 cup low-fat soymilk

CHAPTER 2

Smart Snacks and Breads

1

Carbohydrate
Choice

Onion–Poppy Seed Scones

PREP TIME: 15 min • **START TO FINISH:** 40 min • 12 scones

1 SCONE: Calories
130 (Calories from
Fat 40); Total Fat 4.5g
(Saturated Fat 0g; Trans
Fat 0g); Cholesterol
0mg; Sodium 240mg;
Total Carbohydrate 20g
(Dietary Fiber 1g; Sugars
3g); Protein 3g

% DAILY VALUE:
Vitamin A 0%; Vitamin
C 0%; Calcium 10%;
Iron 8%

EXCHANGES: 1 Starch,
½ Fat

3	tablespoons canola oil
¼	cup chopped onion
1¾	cups white whole wheat flour
½	cup old-fashioned oats
2	tablespoons sugar
1	tablespoon poppy seed
3	teaspoons baking powder
1	teaspoon ground mustard
½	teaspoon salt
½	cup buttermilk
¼	cup fat-free egg product
1	tablespoon fat-free egg product

1 Heat oven to 400°F. Spray cookie sheet with cooking spray or line with cooking parchment paper.

2 In 8-inch skillet, heat 1 tablespoon of the oil over medium-high heat. Add onion to oil; cook 3 to 4 minutes, stirring frequently, until tender and just beginning to brown; remove from heat.

3 In large bowl, stir flour, oats, sugar, poppy seed, baking powder, mustard and salt; set aside. In small bowl, stir together buttermilk, ¼ cup egg product, the cooked onions and remaining 2 tablespoons oil. Add flour mixture to onion mixture, all at once; stir just until moistened.

4 On lightly floured surface, knead dough 10 times. On cookie sheet, lightly roll or pat dough into 8-inch round about ¾ inch thick. Cut round into 12 wedges with sharp knife that has been dipped in flour. Carefully pull wedges out about ½ inch to create small amount of space between each scone. Brush scones with 1 tablespoon egg product. Bake 15 to 18 minutes or until golden brown. Immediately transfer from cookie sheet to cooling rack; cool 5 minutes. Serve warm.

**Betty's
Success
Tip**

To keep scones tender, handle dough as little as possible. After kneading a few times, dough should hold its shape, but may still look a bit rough.

1/2
Carbohydrate Choice

Three-Seed Flatbread

PREP TIME: 10 min • **START TO FINISH:** 1 hr 15 min • 12 servings

1 SERVING: Calories 70 (Calories from Fat 20); Total Fat 2g (Saturated Fat 0g; Trans Fat 0g); Cholesterol 0mg; Sodium 220mg; Total Carbohydrate 9g (Dietary Fiber 1g; Sugars 2g); Protein 3g

% DAILY VALUE: Vitamin A 0%; Vitamin C 0%; Calcium 4%; Iron 4%

EXCHANGES: ½ Starch, ½ Fat

6   frozen unbaked large whole wheat rolls (from 48-oz package)

2   teaspoons olive or canola oil

3   cloves garlic, finely chopped

1   teaspoon ground flaxseed or flaxseed meal

½   teaspoon black sesame seed or poppy seed

½   teaspoon white sesame seed

½   teaspoon salt

¼   teaspoon dried basil leaves

2   tablespoons shredded Parmesan cheese

1 On microwavable plate, place frozen rolls. Cover with microwavable plastic wrap; microwave on High 25 seconds. Turn rolls over; rotate plate one half turn. Microwave on High 25 seconds longer to thaw.

2 Spray 13×9-inch pan with cooking spray. On lightly floured surface, knead roll dough together. Pat dough in bottom of pan; brush with oil. Sprinkle with remaining ingredients.

3 Cover; let rise in warm place about 40 minutes or until slightly puffy.

4 Heat oven to 350°F. Bake 20 to 22 minutes or until golden brown. Cut into 12 squares.

Diabetes Team Tip
Nuts and seeds are great little nuggets of nutrients, but adding them in moderation is wise because they can be high in fat. Fortunately a little goes a long way in terms of flavor. —Diane Reader, Dietitian

Betty's Success Tip
Olive oil is a great choice for this three-seed bread. It contains monounsaturated fat. A simple change, like replacing butter with olive oil, may help to lower cholesterol.

Mini Rosemary Scones

PREP TIME: 25 min • **START TO FINISH:** 55 min • 18 mini scones

1 Carbohydrate Choice

1 cup all-purpose flour

1 cup whole wheat flour

2 tablespoons sugar

2 teaspoons baking powder

½ teaspoon baking soda

½ teaspoon salt

2 teaspoons grated lemon peel

1 tablespoon finely chopped fresh or 1 teaspoon dried rosemary leaves, crushed

3 tablespoons cold butter or margarine

½ cup fat-free sour cream

¼ cup canola oil

1 tablespoon lemon juice

1 Heat oven to 400°F. Spray cookie sheet with cooking spray.

2 In medium bowl, mix flours, sugar, baking powder, baking soda, salt, lemon peel and rosemary. Cut in butter, using pastry blender or fork, until mixture looks like fine crumbs. Stir in sour cream, oil and lemon juice.

3 On lightly floured surface, knead dough lightly 10 times. Divide dough into thirds. On cookie sheet, pat each third of dough into 5-inch round. Cut each round into 6 wedges, using sharp knife, but do not separate wedges.

4 Bake 12 to 17 minutes or until edges are golden brown. Immediately transfer from cookie sheet to cooling rack. Carefully separate wedges. Cool 5 to 10 minutes. Serve warm.

1 MINI SCONE: Calories 110 (Calories from Fat 45); Total Fat 5g (Saturated Fat 1.5g; Trans Fat 0g); Cholesterol 5mg; Sodium 180mg; Total Carbohydrate 13g (Dietary Fiber 1g; Sugars 2g); Protein 2g

% DAILY VALUE: Vitamin A 0%; Vitamin C 0%; Calcium 4%; Iron 4%

EXCHANGES: 1 Starch, 1 Fat

Diabetes Team Tip

If you haven't already, consider an activity that has an impact on your body to help strengthen your bones, such as walking, jogging or dancing; try anything where you're on your feet, working against gravity.

—Diane Reader, Dietitian

Blueberry-Almond Brown Bread

PREP TIME: 10 min • **START TO FINISH:** 3 hr 10 min • 1 loaf (16 slices)

1 SLICE: Calories 170 (Calories from Fat 25); Total Fat 3g (Saturated Fat 0.5g; Trans Fat 0g); Cholesterol 0mg; Sodium 250mg; Total Carbohydrate 30g (Dietary Fiber 2g; Sugars 11g); Protein 4g

% DAILY VALUE: Vitamin A 0%; Vitamin C 0%; Calcium 6%; Iron 8%

EXCHANGES: 1 Starch, 1 Other Carbohydrate, ½ Fat

2½	cups white whole wheat flour
½	cup old-fashioned oats
⅓	cup ground flaxseed or flaxseed meal
½	cup packed dark brown sugar
¼	cup chopped blanched slivered almonds
1	teaspoon baking soda
1	teaspoon salt
½	cup dried blueberries or currants
1⅔	cups buttermilk
2	teaspoons vanilla
1	tablespoon old-fashioned oats

1 Heat oven to 375°F (350°F for dark or nonstick pan). Spray 9×5-inch loaf pan with cooking spray.

2 In large bowl, stir flour, ½ cup oats, the flaxseed, brown sugar, almonds, baking soda and salt. Add blueberries; stir to coat in flour mixture. Stir in buttermilk and vanilla just until mixed. Spread in pan; sprinkle with 1 tablespoon oats.

3 Bake 45 to 50 minutes or until toothpick inserted in center comes out clean and top is golden brown. Cool 5 minutes. Loosen sides of loaf from pan; remove from pan and place top side up on cooling rack. Cool completely, about 2 hours, before slicing.

Betty's Success Tip

Brown breads have a classic crispy crust that has a tendency to make testing for doneness tricky (the crust can cause the toothpick to look clean as it is pulled out). When checking for doneness on this bread, the toothpick should be dry rather than having a sticky or moist feeling to it.

1½ Carbohydrate Choices

Chocolate Chip–Cherry Scones

PREP TIME: 20 min • **START TO FINISH:** 40 min • 16 scones

1 SCONE: Calories 130 (Calories from Fat 35); Total Fat 4g (Saturated Fat 2.5g; Trans Fat 0g); Cholesterol 10mg; Sodium 200mg; Total Carbohydrate 22g (Dietary Fiber 1g; Sugars 9g); Protein 2g

% DAILY VALUE: Vitamin A 2%; Vitamin C 0%; Calcium 6%; Iron 6%

EXCHANGES: 1 Starch, ½ Other Carbohydrate, ½ Fat

2	cups all-purpose flour
¼	cup sugar
2	teaspoons baking powder
½	teaspoon baking soda
½	teaspoon salt
¼	cup cold butter or margarine
¾	cup plain or vanilla fat-free yogurt
½	cup dried cherries or cherry-flavored dried cranberries
¼	cup semisweet chocolate chips
2	teaspoons coarse sugar

1 Heat oven to 400°F. Spray cookie sheet with cooking spray.

2 In medium bowl, mix flour, sugar, baking powder, baking soda and salt. Cut in butter, using pastry blender or fork, until mixture looks like fine crumbs. Stir in yogurt, cherries and chocolate chips (dough will seem dry and crumbly).

3 On lightly floured surface, shape dough into a ball. Knead dough lightly 10 times. Divide dough in half. On cookie sheet, pat each half of dough into 6-inch round. Cut each round into 8 wedges, using sharp knife, but do not separate wedges. Sprinkle with coarse sugar.

4 Bake 12 to 14 minutes or until golden brown. Immediately transfer from cookie sheet to cooling rack. Carefully separate wedges. Cool 5 minutes. Serve warm.

Betty's Success Tip

These great-tasting scones have the best of both worlds: flavor and texture that only a little butter can provide, plus the nutrition of yogurt. Yum!

Creamy Apple-Cinnamon Quesadilla

PREP TIME: 15 min • **START TO FINISH:** 20 min • 4 servings (2 wedges each)

1 tablespoon granulated sugar

½ teaspoon ground cinnamon

¼ cup reduced-fat cream cheese (from 8-oz container)

1 tablespoon packed brown sugar

2 whole wheat tortillas (8 inch)

½ small apple, cut into ¼-inch slices (½ cup)

Cooking spray

1   In small bowl, mix granulated sugar and ¼ teaspoon of the cinnamon; set aside. In another small bowl, mix cream cheese, brown sugar and remaining ¼ teaspoon cinnamon with spoon.

2   Spread cream cheese mixture over tortillas. Place apple slices on cream cheese mixture on 1 tortilla. Top with remaining tortilla, cheese side down. Spray both sides of quesadilla with cooking spray; sprinkle with cinnamon-sugar mixture.

3   Heat 10-inch nonstick skillet over medium heat. Add quesadilla; cook 2 to 3 minutes or until bottom is brown and crisp. Turn quesadilla; cook 2 to 3 minutes longer or until bottom is brown and crisp.

4   Transfer quesadilla from skillet to cutting board; let stand 2 to 3 minutes. Cut into 8 wedges to serve.

1 SERVING: Calories 110 (Calories from Fat 25); Total Fat 3g (Saturated Fat 1.5g; Trans Fat 0g); Cholesterol 10mg; Sodium 170mg; Total Carbohydrate 19g (Dietary Fiber 2g; Sugars 9g); Protein 3g

% DAILY VALUE: Vitamin A 4%; Vitamin C 0%; Calcium 4%; Iron 4%

EXCHANGES: 1 Starch, ½ Fat

Betty's Success Tip

If your family isn't used to whole wheat tortillas, ask them to try something new—they may just like (or love) the new flavor!

1
Carbohydrate
Choice

Sweet Potato Oven Fries with Spicy Sour Cream

PREP TIME: 10 min • **START TO FINISH:** 45 min • 4 servings (½ cup potatoes and 2 tablespoons dip each)

1 SERVING: Calories 120 (Calories from Fat 35); Total Fat 4g (Saturated Fat 2.5g; Trans Fat 0g); Cholesterol 10mg; Sodium 140mg; Total Carbohydrate 20g (Dietary Fiber 3g; Sugars 7g); Protein 2g

% DAILY VALUE: Vitamin A 340%; Vitamin C 15%; Calcium 6%; Iron 4%

EXCHANGES: 1 Starch, 1 Vegetable, 1 Fat

1   teaspoon salt-free southwest chipotle seasoning
2   large dark-orange sweet potatoes (1 lb), peeled, cut into ½-inch-thick slices
　　Olive oil cooking spray
½   cup reduced-fat sour cream
1   tablespoon sriracha sauce
1   tablespoon chopped fresh cilantro

1 Heat oven to 425°F. Spray large cookie sheet with cooking spray. Place ¾ teaspoon of the seasoning in 1-gallon resealable food-storage plastic bag; add potatoes. Seal bag; shake until potatoes are evenly coated. Place potatoes in single layer on cookie sheet; spray lightly with cooking spray. Bake 20 minutes or until bottoms are golden brown. Turn potatoes; bake 10 to 15 minutes longer or until tender and bottoms are golden brown.

2 Meanwhile, in small bowl, stir sour cream, sriracha sauce, cilantro and remaining ¼ teaspoon seasoning; refrigerate until ready to serve.

3 Serve fries warm with spicy sour cream.

Diabetes Team Tip
If you love seasoned sweet potato fries but don't want the fat, then you will like this easy recipe for making them in the oven. They're delicious and full of beta-carotene. —Diane Reader, Dietitian

Betty's Success Tip
Sweet potatoes aren't as evenly shaped as other potatoes. If possible, choose those that don't have long, pointy ends. For evenly baked fries, cut off and discard any narrow ends.

0
Carbohydrate
Choices

Greek Salad Kabobs

PREP TIME: 15 min • **START TO FINISH:** 15 min • 24 servings (1 kabob and ½ tablespoon dip each)

1 SERVING: Calories 15 (Calories from Fat 0); Total Fat 0.5g (Saturated Fat 0g; Trans Fat 0g); Cholesterol 0mg; Sodium 70mg; Total Carbohydrate 2g (Dietary Fiber 0g; Sugars 1g); Protein 0g

% DAILY VALUE: Vitamin A 0%; Vitamin C 2%; Calcium 2%; Iron 0%

EXCHANGES: Free

DIP

¾	cup plain fat-free yogurt
2	teaspoons honey
2	teaspoons chopped fresh dill weed
2	teaspoons chopped fresh oregano leaves
¼	teaspoon salt
1	small clove garlic, finely chopped

KABOBS

24	cocktail picks or toothpicks
24	pitted kalamata olives
24	small grape tomatoes
12	slices (½ inch) English (seedless) cucumber, cut in half crosswise

1 In small bowl, mix dip ingredients; set aside.

2 On each cocktail pick, thread 1 olive, 1 tomato and 1 half-slice cucumber. Serve kabobs with dip.

Diabetes Team Tip
Do you drink enough water? Quench your thirst with water or carbohydrate-free beverages like herbal teas. Juices and milk contain carbohydrates, so limit portions to 4 to 8 ounces. —Dr. Bergenstal

Betty's Success Tip
A regular cucumber can be substituted for the English variety. If the skin is thick or has been coated with a vegetable coating, you may want to peel it.

Roasted Carrot and Herb Spread

PREP TIME: 20 min • **START TO FINISH:** 1 hr 20 min • 16 servings (2 tablespoons spread and 2 crackers each)

1
Carbohydrate Choice

1   lb ready-to-eat baby-cut carrots

1   dark orange sweet potato, peeled, cut into 1-inch pieces (2½ cups)

1   small onion, cut into 8 wedges, separated

2   tablespoons olive oil

1   clove garlic, finely chopped

1   tablespoon chopped fresh or 1 teaspoon dried thyme leaves

¼   teaspoon salt

⅛   teaspoon freshly ground pepper

    Assorted whole-grain crackers or vegetable chips

1   Heat oven to 350°F. Spray 15×10×1-inch pan with cooking spray. Place carrots, sweet potato and onion in pan; drizzle with oil. Sprinkle with garlic, thyme, salt and pepper; stir to coat.

2   Bake uncovered about 1 hour, stirring occasionally, until vegetables are tender.

3   In food processor, place vegetable mixture. Cover; process until blended. Spoon into serving bowl. Serve warm, or cover and refrigerate until serving. Serve with crackers.

1 SERVING: Calories 90 (Calories from Fat 30); Total Fat 3.5g (Saturated Fat 0g; Trans Fat 0g); Cholesterol 0mg; Sodium 125mg; Total Carbohydrate 12g (Dietary Fiber 2g; Sugars 3g); Protein 1g

% DAILY VALUE: Vitamin A 160%; Vitamin C 4%; Calcium 2%; Iron 4%

EXCHANGES: ½ Other Carbohydrate, 1 Vegetable, ½ Fat

Betty's Success Tip

Red garnet sweet potatoes—or any of the deep-orange variety—help give this dip its intense color, flavor and nutritional value, but you can use any kind of sweet potato that you like.

1½
Carbohydrate Choices

Smoky Spinach Hummus with Popcorn Chips

PREP TIME: 10 min • **START TO FINISH:** 10 min • 12 servings (10 chips and 2 tablespoons hummus each)

1 SERVING: Calories 140 (Calories from Fat 35); Total Fat 3.5g (Saturated Fat 0g; Trans Fat 0g); Cholesterol 0mg; Sodium 270mg; Total Carbohydrate 22g (Dietary Fiber 3g; Sugars 0g); Protein 4g

% DAILY VALUE: Vitamin A 10%; Vitamin C 6%; Calcium 4%; Iron 10%

EXCHANGES: 1½ Starch, ½ Fat

1   can (15 oz) chickpeas (garbanzo beans), drained, liquid reserved
1   cup chopped fresh spinach leaves
2   tablespoons lemon juice
2   tablespoons sesame tahini paste (from 16-oz. jar)
2   teaspoons smoked Spanish paprika
1   teaspoon ground cumin
½   teaspoon salt
2   tablespoons chopped red bell pepper, if desired
6   oz popcorn snack chips

1   In food processor, place chickpeas, ¼ cup of the reserved liquid, spinach, lemon juice, tahini paste, paprika, cumin and salt. Cover; process 30 seconds, using quick on-and-off motions; scrape side.

2   Add additional reserved bean liquid, 1 tablespoon at a time, covering and processing, using quick on-and-off motions, until smooth and desired dipping consistency. Garnish with bell pepper. Serve with popcorn snack chips.

Betty's Success Tip

Tahini is a thick paste made from ground sesame seed and is a typical ingredient in hummus. Look for it in the ethnic section of your grocery store near the peanut butter, in food co-ops or at Asian markets.

0 Carbohydrate Choices

Vegetable Kabobs with Mustard Dip

PREP TIME: 35 min • **START TO FINISH:** 1 hr 35 min • 9 servings (about 9 vegetable pieces and 2 tablespoons dip each)

1 SERVING: Calories 60 (Calories from Fat 30); Total Fat 3.5g (Saturated Fat 0g; Trans Fat 0g); Cholesterol 0mg; Sodium 180mg; Total Carbohydrate 6g (Dietary Fiber 1g; Sugars 3g); Protein 2g

% DAILY VALUE: Vitamin A 6%; Vitamin C 15%; Calcium 4%; Iron 2%

EXCHANGES: 1 Vegetable, ½ Fat

DIP

⅔ cup plain fat-free yogurt

⅓ cup fat-free sour cream

1 tablespoon finely chopped fresh parsley

1 teaspoon onion powder

1 teaspoon garlic salt

1 tablespoon Dijon mustard

KABOBS

1 medium bell pepper, cut into 6 strips, then cut into thirds

1 medium zucchini, cut diagonally into ½-inch slices

1 package (8 oz) fresh whole mushrooms

9 large cherry tomatoes

2 tablespoons olive or vegetable oil

1 In small bowl, mix dip ingredients. Cover; refrigerate at least 1 hour.

2 Heat gas or charcoal grill. On 5 (12-inch) metal skewers, thread vegetables so that one kind of vegetable is on the same skewer (use 2 skewers for mushrooms); leave space between each piece. Brush vegetables with oil.

3 Place skewers of bell pepper and zucchini on grill over medium heat. Cover grill; cook 2 minutes. Add skewers of mushrooms and tomatoes. Cover grill; cook 4 to 5 minutes, carefully turning every 2 minutes, until vegetables are tender. Transfer vegetables from skewers to serving plate. Serve with dip.

Betty's Success Tip

No metal skewers? Grill the vegetable pieces in a wire basket. Place the bell pepper and zucchini in the basket first and grill as directed, then add the mushrooms and cherry tomatoes.

Ginger and Mint Dip with Fruit

PREP TIME: 20 min • **START TO FINISH:** 35 min • 6 servings (2 heaping tablespoons dip and 2 skewers each)

1
Carbohydrate Choice

DIP

1¼	cups plain fat-free yogurt
¼	cup packed brown sugar
2	teaspoons chopped fresh mint leaves
2	teaspoons grated gingerroot
½	teaspoon grated lemon peel

FRUIT SKEWERS

12	bamboo skewers (6 inch)
1	cup fresh raspberries
2	cups melon cubes (cantaloupe and/or honeydew)

1 In small bowl, mix dip ingredients with whisk until smooth. Cover; refrigerate at least 15 minutes to blend flavors.

2 On each skewer, alternately thread 3 raspberries and 2 melon cubes. Serve with dip.

1 SERVING: Calories 100 (Calories from Fat 0); Total Fat 0g (Saturated Fat 0g; Trans Fat 0g); Cholesterol 0mg; Sodium 50mg; Total Carbohydrate 20g (Dietary Fiber 2g; Sugars 17g); Protein 3g

% DAILY VALUE: Vitamin A 35%; Vitamin C 45%; Calcium 10%; Iron 2%

EXCHANGES: ½ Fruit, ½ Other Carbohydrate, ½ Very Lean Meat

Betty's Success Tip

Increasing the chilling time to 30 minutes or more heightens the flavor of this terrific dip. And if you have any leftovers, it's even more flavorful the next day.

½
Carbohydrate Choice

Spicy Cajun Onion Dip

PREP TIME: 15 min • **START TO FINISH:** 30 min • 5 servings (¼ cup dip, 4 pepper strips, 12 pea pods and 4 shrimp each)

1 SERVING: Calories 110 (Calories from Fat 35); Total Fat 4g (Saturated Fat 2.5g; Trans Fat 0g); Cholesterol 60mg; Sodium 430mg; Total Carbohydrate 9g (Dietary Fiber 2g; Sugars 6g); Protein 9g

% DAILY VALUE: Vitamin A 30%; Vitamin C 100%; Calcium 15%; Iron 10%

EXCHANGES: ½ Starch, ½ Vegetable, 1 Lean Meat

DIP

¾ cup plain low-fat yogurt

½ cup reduced-fat sour cream

3 medium green onions, chopped (3 tablespoons)

1½ teaspoons Cajun seasoning

2 cloves garlic, finely chopped

VEGETABLES AND SHRIMP

1 medium red bell pepper, cut into 20 strips

½ lb fresh sugar snap pea pods, strings removed

20 cooked deveined peeled large (21 to 30 count) shrimp, thawed if frozen

1 In small bowl, mix dip ingredients with whisk until smooth. Cover; refrigerate at least 15 minutes to blend flavors.

2 Serve dip with bell pepper, pea pods and shrimp.

Betty's Success Tip

Low-fat dairy ingredients and seasonings give you a flavorful dip. Combining the dip with veggies and shrimp, you get a nice hit of vitamins, calcium and iron for less than 1 Carb Choice per serving.

Crunchy Chicken Chunks with Thai Peanut Sauce

1 Carbohydrate Choice

PREP TIME: 10 min • **START TO FINISH:** 30 min • 8 servings

1½ cups cornflakes cereal, crushed (½ cup)

½ cup Original Bisquick® mix

¾ teaspoon paprika

¼ teaspoon salt

¼ teaspoon pepper

1 lb boneless skinless chicken breasts, cut into 1-inch pieces

Cooking spray

THAI PEANUT SAUCE

½ cup plain fat-free yogurt

¼ cup creamy peanut butter

½ cup fat-free (skim) milk

1 tablespoon soy sauce

⅛ teaspoon ground red pepper (cayenne), if desired

1 Heat oven to 400°F. Line 15×10×1-inch pan with foil.

2 Mix cereal, Bisquick®, paprika, salt and pepper in 2-quart resealable food-storage plastic bag. Shake about 6 chicken pieces at a time in bag until coated. Shake off any extra crumbs. Place chicken pieces in pan. Spray with cooking spray.

3 Bake uncovered 20 to 25 minutes or until coating is crisp and chicken is no longer pink in center.

4 Meanwhile, mix sauce ingredients in 10-inch nonstick skillet. Cook over medium heat 3 to 4 minutes, stirring occasionally, until mixture begins to thicken. Serve sauce with chicken.

1 SERVING: Calories 190 (Calories from Fat 60); Total Fat 7g (Saturated Fat 2g; Trans Fat 0g); Cholesterol 35mg; Sodium 400mg; Total Carbohydrate 15g (Dietary Fiber 1g; Sugars 5g); Protein 16g

% DAILY VALUE: Vitamin A 6%; Vitamin C 0%; Calcium 6%; Iron 15%

EXCHANGES: 1 Starch, 2 Lean Meat

Diabetes Team Tip
Snacks are not required just because you have diabetes, since they often add extra calories and fat. Check with your doctor or diabetes educator to determine if you need between-meal snacks. —Dr. Bergenstal

Betty's Success Tip
Rich in vitamins, minerals and heart-healthy fat, peanut butter, enjoyed in moderation, provides satisfaction. A modest amount may actually prevent you from overindulging in other foods.

0
Carbohydrate
Choices

Vietnamese Meatball Lollipops with Dipping Sauce

PREP TIME: 50 min • **START TO FINISH:** 50 min • 12 servings (2 meatballs and 1 tablespoon sauce each)

1 SERVING: Calories 80 (Calories from Fat 25); Total Fat 2.5g (Saturated Fat 0.5g; Trans Fat 0g); Cholesterol 30mg; Sodium 440mg; Total Carbohydrate 5g (Dietary Fiber 0g; Sugars 3g); Protein 10g

% DAILY VALUE: Vitamin A 0%; Vitamin C 0%; Calcium 0%; Iron 4%

EXCHANGES: ½ Vegetable, 1 Very Lean Meat, ½ Lean Meat

MEATBALLS

1¼ lb lean (at least 90%) ground turkey

¼ cup chopped water chestnuts (from 8-oz can), drained

¼ cup chopped fresh cilantro

1 tablespoon cornstarch

2 tablespoons fish sauce

½ teaspoon pepper

3 cloves garlic, finely chopped

DIPPING SAUCE

¼ cup water

¼ cup reduced-sodium soy sauce

2 tablespoons packed brown sugar

2 tablespoons chopped fresh chives or green onions

2 tablespoons lime juice

2 cloves garlic, finely chopped

½ teaspoon crushed red pepper

About 24 (6-inch) bamboo skewers

1 Heat oven to 400°F. Line cookie sheet with foil; spray with cooking spray (or use nonstick foil).

2 In large bowl, combine all meatball ingredients until well mixed. Shape into 1¼-inch meatballs. On cookie sheet, place meatballs 1 inch apart. Bake 20 minutes, turning halfway through baking, until thermometer inserted in center of meatballs reads at least 165°F.

3 Meanwhile, in 1-quart saucepan, heat all dipping sauce ingredients over low heat until sugar is dissolved; set aside.

4 Insert bamboo skewers into cooked meatballs; place on serving plate. Serve with warm dipping sauce.

Betty's Success Tip

Use plastic gloves when mixing ground meat mixtures with your hands to distribute ingredients evenly while keeping your hands clean.

½
Carbohydrate Choice

Caramelized Onion–Shrimp Spread

PREP TIME: 30 min • **START TO FINISH:** 30 min • 18 servings (2 tablespoons spread and 2 crackers each)

1 SERVING: Calories 90 (Calories from Fat 35); Total Fat 4g (Saturated Fat 2g; Trans Fat 0g); Cholesterol 25mg; Sodium 140mg; Total Carbohydrate 10g (Dietary Fiber 1g; Sugars 3g); Protein 3g

% DAILY VALUE:
Vitamin A 4%; Vitamin C 0%; Calcium 2%; Iron 4%

EXCHANGES: ½ Starch, 1 Fat

1	tablespoon butter (do not use margarine)
½	medium onion, thinly sliced (about ½ cup)
1	clove garlic, finely chopped
¼	cup apple jelly
1	container (8 oz) reduced-fat cream cheese, softened
1	bag (4 oz) frozen cooked salad shrimp, thawed, well drained (about 1 cup)
1	teaspoon chopped fresh chives
36	whole-grain crackers

1 In 1-quart saucepan, melt butter over medium-low heat. Add onion; cook 15 minutes, stirring frequently. Add garlic; cook 1 minute, stirring occasionally, until onion and garlic are tender and browned. Stir in apple jelly. Cook, stirring constantly, until melted. Remove from heat. Let stand 5 minutes to cool.

2 Meanwhile, in small bowl, stir together cream cheese and shrimp. On 8-inch plate, spread shrimp mixture into a 5-inch round.

3 Spoon onion mixture over shrimp mixture. Sprinkle with chives. Serve with crackers.

Betty's Success Tip

This is an easy appetizer to tote to a gathering. Just pack the shrimp mixture, onion mixture and chives in separate containers and take the plate—assemble when you get there.

SNACKING SAVVY

Snacks may be part of a diabetes food plan. Snacking during the day or evening is a good way to manage blood glucose levels and spread calories and carbohydrates over the course of the day. Remember to always carry a carb snack with you if you take insulin or other medications that lower glucose. The key to snacking well is to plan good-for-you, delicious snacks with total carbohydrates and calories that fit into your food plan. Consider these great "fast" snacks:

- Whole grain granola bars, fruit-and-grain bars, cereal snack mixes, ready-to-eat cereal and light popcorn are good to carry with you or bring to work.

- Fresh fruits and vegetables provide many needed nutrients. Keep baby carrots, celery sticks, grapes, bananas, apples, kiwifruit or other favorites on hand.

- String cheese, cheese slices or chunks provide necessary calcium and do not effect glucose levels. Whenever possible, choose the low-fat or nonfat versions.

- Cereal and yogurt are nutrient powerhouses. Choose a high-fiber cereal, such as Fiber One®, and a light yogurt. Or layer the two for a parfait!

- Lower-fat crackers and pretzels and baked tortilla chips can be spread with hummus, roasted vegetable dip or salsa. If your food plan allows, enjoy with low-fat cheese or peanut butter.

- Peanuts or roasted soy nuts are great munchies, but their calories and fat can add up quickly. Mix with low-fat popcorn or mini pretzels, or sprinkle with savory herb blends.

- Dried fruits are packed with important vitamins, but they're concentrated sources of carbohydrate, so keep the portions small. Dried plums, apricots, dates and raisins are good choices. Stretch them by mixing with pretzels, low-fat popcorn, ready-to-eat cereal or nuts.

- Whole-wheat sandwiches of lean turkey breast, beef, ham, tuna or low-fat cheese make more substantial snacks. Mustard and other nonfat condiments are great add-ons, but keep the mayo to a minimum. Load them up with your favorite raw veggies, such as lettuce, spinach, tomatoes, peppers or jicama.

- Yogurt smoothies with fruit can be a delicious treat as well as an excellent source of calcium, vitamins and other important nutrients. Blend your favorite light yogurt with cut-up fresh or frozen fruit.

- Small low-fat cookies, cakes or miniature candy bars may fit occasionally as a snack, but look at the Nutrition Facts label for the total number of carbohydrates per serving. Then, adjust the serving to fit your food plan.

CHAPTER 3

Pleasing Poultry, Fish and Meat

2
Carbohydrate
Choices

Buffalo Chicken Pizza

PREP TIME: 10 min • **START TO FINISH:** 20 min • 6 servings

1 SERVING: Calories 230 (Calories from Fat 50); Total Fat 6g (Saturated Fat 3g; Trans Fat 0g); Cholesterol 25mg; Sodium 640mg; Total Carbohydrate 27g (Dietary Fiber 3g; Sugars 3g); Protein 16g

% DAILY VALUE:
Vitamin A 4%; Vitamin C 8%; Calcium 20%; Iron 10%

EXCHANGES:
1½ Starch, ½ Other Carbohydrate, ½ Very Lean Meat, 1 Lean Meat, ½ Fat

1   ready-to-serve whole wheat pizza crust (10 oz)
¼   cup fat-free ranch dressing
¼   cup finely chopped celery
1   cup cut-up cooked chicken breast
3   tablespoons Buffalo wing sauce
¾   cup green and red bell pepper strips
¾   cup shredded reduced-fat mozzarella cheese (3 oz)
1   tablespoon crumbled blue cheese

1   Heat oven to 400°F. On large cookie sheet, place pizza crust. Spread ranch dressing over crust. Sprinkle with celery.

2   In small bowl, stir together chicken and wing sauce; arrange over crust. Top with bell pepper strips and cheeses.

3   Bake 10 minutes or until mozzarella cheese is melted and just beginning to brown. To serve, cut into wedges.

Betty's Success Tip   Serve this tasty pizza with additional fresh veggies or a green salad and fat-free ranch dressing.

1½
Carbohydrate
Choices

Mandarin Chicken Salad

PREP TIME: 20 min • **START TO FINISH:** 2 hr 20 min • 6 servings

1 SERVING: Calories 210 (Calories from Fat 30); Total Fat 3.5g (Saturated Fat 1g; Trans Fat 0g); Cholesterol 60mg; Sodium 260mg; Total Carbohydrate 22g (Dietary Fiber 2g; Sugars 12g); Protein 23g

% DAILY VALUE: Vitamin A 20%; Vitamin C 20%; Calcium 8%; Iron 8%

EXCHANGES: 1½ Fruit, 2½ Very Lean Meat

3 cups cut-up cooked chicken

¾ cup sliced green grapes

2 medium stalks celery, thinly sliced (1 cup)

2 green onions, thinly sliced

1 can (11 oz) mandarin orange segments, drained

1 can (8 oz) sliced water chestnuts, drained

1 container (6 oz) lemon fat-free yogurt

2 tablespoons reduced-sodium soy sauce

Mixed salad greens

1 In large bowl, mix chicken, grapes, celery, onions, orange segments and water chestnuts. In small bowl, mix yogurt and soy sauce. Pour over chicken mixture; toss until combined.

2 Cover and refrigerate at least 2 hours or until chilled. Serve on salad greens.

Betty's Success Tip

Look for a variety of mixed greens combinations in the produce department—they're all packaged and ready to go. Or, you can make your own mix with favorite garden greens.

Baked Chicken Dijon

PREP TIME: 25 min • **START TO FINISH:** 55 min • 6 servings (about 1 cup each)

2
Carbohydrate
Choices

3 cups uncooked bow-tie (farfalle) pasta (6 oz)

2 cups frozen broccoli cuts (from 12-oz bag)

2 cups cubed cooked chicken

⅓ cup diced roasted red bell peppers (from 7-oz jar)

1 can (10.75 oz) condensed cream of chicken or cream of mushroom soup

⅓ cup reduced-sodium chicken broth (from 32-oz carton)

3 tablespoons Dijon mustard

1 tablespoon finely chopped onion

½ cup shredded Parmesan cheese

1 Heat oven to 375°F. Spray 2½-quart casserole with cooking spray.

2 Cook pasta as directed on package, adding broccoli for the last 2 minutes of cooking time; drain. In casserole, mix chicken and roasted peppers. In small bowl, mix soup, broth, mustard and onion; stir into chicken mixture. Stir in pasta and broccoli. Sprinkle with cheese.

3 Cover; bake about 30 minutes or until hot in center and cheese is melted.

1 SERVING: Calories 290 (Calories from Fat 80); Total Fat 9g (Saturated Fat 3g; Trans Fat 0g); Cholesterol 50mg; Sodium 770mg; Total Carbohydrate 29g (Dietary Fiber 3g; Sugars 2g); Protein 24g

% DAILY VALUE: Vitamin A 15%; Vitamin C 15%; Calcium 15%; Iron 10%

EXCHANGES: 2 Starch, 2½ Lean Meat

Betty's Success Tip

Fresh broccoli can be used instead of frozen. Cut into 1- to 1½-inch pieces and add to the boiling pasta during the last 2 to 3 minutes of cooking time.

1½ Carbohydrate Choices

Greek Chicken Burgers with Tzatziki Sauce

PREP TIME: 30 min • **START TO FINISH:** 30 min • 4 sandwiches

1 SANDWICH: Calories 260 (Calories from Fat 80); Total Fat 8g (Saturated Fat 2g; Trans Fat 0g); Cholesterol 65mg; Sodium 460mg; Total Carbohydrate 25g (Dietary Fiber 3g; Sugars 6g); Protein 20g

% DAILY VALUE: Vitamin A 25%; Vitamin C 6%; Calcium 10%; Iron 15%

EXCHANGES: 1 Starch, ½ Other Carbohydrate, ½ Vegetable, 1 Very Lean Meat, 1½ Lean Meat, ½ Fat

TZATZIKI SAUCE

1 medium peeled or unpeeled cucumber

½ cup plain Greek yogurt (from 6-oz container)

2 tablespoons chopped onion

2 teaspoons chopped fresh mint

BURGERS

1 lb lean ground chicken

1 cup chopped fresh spinach

¼ cup chopped pitted kalamata olives

1 tablespoon cornstarch

1 tablespoon chopped fresh oregano leaves

2 cloves garlic, chopped

¼ teaspoon salt

¼ teaspoon pepper

2 whole-grain pita breads (6 inch), cut in half to form pockets

½ cup chopped fresh tomato

1 Set oven control to broil. Chop enough cucumber to equal ½ cup; place in small bowl (cut 12 thin slices from remaining cucumber for sandwiches; set aside). Stir in remaining sauce ingredients; refrigerate until ready to use.

2 In large bowl, mix chicken, spinach, olives, cornstarch, oregano, garlic, salt and pepper. Shape into 4 oval patties, each about ½ inch thick. On broiler pan, place patties. Broil with tops about 5 inches from heat 10 to 12 minutes, turning once, until thermometer inserted in center of burgers reads at least 165°F.

3 Place burgers in pita pocket halves. To serve, top each burger with tomato, cucumber slices and about 3 tablespoons sauce.

Betty's Success Tip

Serve with a lemon wedge to squeeze over the filling in the pita pocket halves. Lemon juice enhances the flavor of food without adding salt or carbs.

3
Carbohydrate
Choices

Jerk Chicken Casserole

PREP TIME: 15 min • **START TO FINISH:** 1 hr • 6 servings

1 SERVING: Calories 330 (Calories from Fat 80); Total Fat 8g (Saturated Fat 2g; Trans Fat 0g); Cholesterol 45mg; Sodium 550mg; Total Carbohydrate 43g (Dietary Fiber 9g; Sugars 16g); Protein 21g

% DAILY VALUE: Vitamin A 200%; Vitamin C 10%; Calcium 10%; Iron 20%

EXCHANGES: 2½ Starch, ½ Other Carbohydrate, 1½ Very Lean Meat, 1 Fat

1¼ teaspoons salt
½ teaspoon pumpkin pie spice
¾ teaspoon ground allspice
¾ teaspoon dried thyme leaves
¼ teaspoon ground red pepper (cayenne)
6 boneless skinless chicken thighs
1 tablespoon vegetable oil
1 can (15 oz) black beans, drained, rinsed
1 large sweet potato (1 lb), peeled, cubed (3 cups)
¼ cup honey
¼ cup lime juice
2 teaspoons cornstarch
2 tablespoons sliced green onions (2 medium)

1 Heat oven to 375°F. Spray 8-inch square (2-quart) glass baking dish with cooking spray. In small bowl, mix salt, pumpkin pie spice, allspice, thyme and red pepper. Rub mixture on all sides of chicken. In 12-inch nonstick skillet, heat oil over medium-high heat. Cook chicken in oil 2 to 3 minutes per side, until brown.

2 In baking dish, layer beans and sweet potato. Top with browned chicken. In small bowl, mix honey, lime juice and cornstarch; add to skillet. Heat to boiling, stirring constantly. Pour over chicken in baking dish.

3 Bake 35 to 45 minutes or until juice of chicken is clear when center of thickest part is cut (165°F) and sweet potatoes are fork-tender. Sprinkle with green onions.

Betty's Success Tip

If a dry jerk seasoning or rub is available, use it to save a few minutes. This is a mild jerk seasoning rub; an authentic jerk rub will be spicier. You can substitute ¼ teaspoon ground cinnamon, ⅛ teaspoon ground ginger and ⅛ teaspoon ground nutmeg for the pumpkin pie spice.

Wild Rice and Turkey Casserole

PREP TIME: 10 min • **START TO FINISH:** 1 hr 15 min • 6 servings

2
Carbohydrate Choices

2 cups cut-up cooked turkey or chicken

2¼ cups boiling water

⅓ cup fat-free (skim) milk

4 medium green onions, sliced (¼ cup)

1 can (10.75 oz) condensed 98% fat-free cream of mushroom soup

1 package (6 oz) original long-grain and wild rice mix

Additional green onions, if desired

1 Heat oven to 350°F. In ungreased 2-quart casserole, mix all ingredients, including seasoning packet from rice mix.

2 Cover; bake 45 to 50 minutes or until rice is tender. Uncover; bake 10 to 15 minutes longer or until liquid is absorbed. Sprinkle with additional green onions.

1 SERVING: Calories 220 (Calories from Fat 40); Total Fat 4.5g (Saturated Fat 1g; Trans Fat 0g); Cholesterol 45mg; Sodium 740mg; Total Carbohydrate 27g (Dietary Fiber 1g; Sugars 2g); Protein 17g

% DAILY VALUE: Vitamin A 0%; Vitamin C 0%; Calcium 6%; Iron 15%

EXCHANGES: 2 Starch, ½ Very Lean Meat, 1 Lean Meat

Betty's Success Tip

If you don't have cream of mushroom soup on hand, you can use cream of chicken or cream of celery instead. But be sure to choose the 98% fat-free versions when you shop.

1
Carbohydrate
Choice

Asian Mushroom-Chicken Soup

PREP TIME: 30 min • **START TO FINISH:** 30 min • 6 servings

1 SERVING: Calories 150 (Calories from Fat 35); Total Fat 4g (Saturated Fat 0.5g; Trans Fat 0g); Cholesterol 20mg; Sodium 490mg; Total Carbohydrate 16g (Dietary Fiber 3g; Sugars 3g); Protein 11g

% DAILY VALUE: Vitamin A 8%; Vitamin C 15%; Calcium 4%; Iron 8%

EXCHANGES: ½ Starch, 1½ Vegetable, 1 Very Lean Meat, ½ Fat

1½	cups water
1	package (1 oz) dried portabella or shiitake mushrooms
1	tablespoon canola oil
¼	cup thinly sliced green onions (4 medium)
2	tablespoons gingerroot, peeled, minced
3	cloves garlic, minced
1	jalapeño chile, seeded, minced
1	cup fresh snow pea pods, sliced diagonally
3	cups reduced-sodium chicken broth
1	can (8 oz) sliced bamboo shoots, drained
2	tablespoons low-sodium soy sauce
½	teaspoon sriracha sauce
1	cup shredded cooked chicken breast
1	cup cooked brown rice
4	teaspoons lime juice
½	cup thinly sliced fresh basil leaves

1 In medium microwavable bowl, heat water uncovered on High 30 seconds or until hot. Add mushrooms; let stand 5 minutes or until tender. Drain mushrooms (reserve liquid). Slice any mushrooms that are large. Set aside.

2 In 4-quart saucepan, heat oil over medium heat. Add 2 tablespoons of the green onions, the gingerroot, garlic and chile to oil. Cook about 3 minutes, stirring occasionally, until vegetables are tender. Add snow pea pods; cook 2 minutes, stirring occasionally. Stir in mushrooms, reserved mushroom liquid and the remaining ingredients, except lime juice and basil. Heat to boiling; reduce heat. Cover and simmer 10 minutes or until hot. Stir in lime juice.

3 Divide soup evenly among 6 bowls. Top servings with basil and remaining green onions.

Betty's Success Tip
Cooked boneless skinless chicken breasts are great to use in this recipe. Purchased rotisserie chicken often contains extra sodium and fat, so it is not the best choice.

2
Carbohydrate
Choices

Asian Turkey Burgers

PREP TIME: 25 min • **START TO FINISH:** 25 min • 5 sandwiches

1 SANDWICH:
Calories 300 (Calories from Fat 60); Total Fat 7g (Saturated Fat 1.5g; Trans Fat 0.5g); Cholesterol 60mg; Sodium 560mg; Total Carbohydrate 32g (Dietary Fiber 9g; Sugars 8g); Protein 26g

% DAILY VALUE:
Vitamin A 15%; Vitamin C 8%; Calcium 10%; Iron 20%

EXCHANGES: 2 Starch, ½ Vegetable, 2½ Very Lean Meat, 1 Fat

1   cup Fiber One® original bran cereal
1   lb lean (at least 90%) ground turkey
⅓   cup finely chopped onion
¼   cup reduced-sodium teriyaki marinade and sauce
¼   cup chopped fresh parsley
½   teaspoon ground ginger
⅛   teaspoon pepper
5   whole wheat burger buns, split
5   leaves leaf lettuce
5   tomato slices

1   Heat gas or charcoal grill.* Place cereal in resealable food-storage plastic bag; seal bag and crush with rolling pin or meat mallet.

2   In large bowl, mix cereal and all remaining ingredients except buns, lettuce and tomato until well mixed. Shape mixture into five 4-inch patties.

3   When ready to grill, carefully oil grill rack. Place patties on grill over medium heat. Cover grill; cook 11 to 15 minutes, turning once, until meat thermometer inserted in center of patties reads 165°F.

4   For each sandwich, place 1 lettuce leaf and 1 tomato slice on bottom half of bun; top with patty and top half of bun.

*To broil patties, set oven control to broil. Place patties on broiler pan; broil with tops about 5 inches from heat, using times above as a guide, turning once.

Betty's Success Tip   Look for teriyaki marinade and sauce in the Asian foods section in your supermarket. Don't confuse the baste and glaze, which is thick like molasses, with teriyaki marinade and sauce, which is watery.

Turkey–Butternut Squash Ragout

PREP TIME: 15 min • **START TO FINISH:** 7 hr 15 min • 4 servings

3
Carbohydrate
Choices

1½ lb turkey thighs (about 2 medium), skin removed

1 small butternut squash (about 2 lb), peeled, seeded, cut into 1½-inch pieces (3 cups)

1 medium onion, cut in half, then cut into slices

1 can (16 oz) baked beans, undrained

1 can (14.5 oz) diced tomatoes with Italian herbs, undrained

2 tablespoons chopped fresh parsley

1 Spray 3- to 4-quart slow cooker with cooking spray. In slow cooker, mix all ingredients except parsley.

2 Cover; cook on Low heat setting 7 to 8 hours.

3 Transfer turkey from slow cooker to cutting board. Remove meat from bones; discard bones. Return turkey to slow cooker and stir to reheat. Just before serving, sprinkle with parsley.

1 SERVING: Calories 410 (Calories from Fat 60); Total Fat 6g (Saturated Fat 2g; Trans Fat 0g); Cholesterol 155mg; Sodium 690mg; Total Carbohydrate 41g (Dietary Fiber 7g; Sugars 16g); Protein 46g

% DAILY VALUE: Vitamin A 220%; Vitamin C 30%; Calcium 15%; Iron 35%

EXCHANGES: 1 Starch, 1 Other Carbohydrate, 2 Vegetable, 4½ Very Lean Meat, 1 Lean Meat

Betty's Success Tip

Butternut squash, rich in color, is an excellent source of vitamin A. It's often available pre-cut in the produce department—look for it when you want a great time-saver!

2½
Carbohydrate Choices

Quinoa Pilaf with Salmon and Asparagus

PREP TIME: 30 min • **START TO FINISH:** 30 min • 4 servings (1¾ cups each)

1 SERVING: Calories 380 (Calories from Fat 110); Total Fat 12g (Saturated Fat 2.5g; Trans Fat 0g); Cholesterol 70mg; Sodium 600mg; Total Carbohydrate 37g (Dietary Fiber 6g; Sugars 7g); Protein 32g

% DAILY VALUE: Vitamin A 30%; Vitamin C 10%; Calcium 8%; Iron 30%

EXCHANGES: 2 Starch, 1½ Vegetable, 3½ Lean Meat

1	cup uncooked quinoa
6	cups water
1	vegetable bouillon cube
1	lb salmon fillets
2	teaspoons butter or margarine
20	stalks fresh asparagus, cut diagonally into 2-inch pieces (2 cups)
4	medium green onions, sliced (¼ cup)
1	cup frozen sweet peas (from 1-lb bag), thawed
½	cup halved grape tomatoes
½	cup vegetable or chicken broth
1	teaspoon lemon-pepper seasoning
2	teaspoons chopped fresh or ½ teaspoon dried dill weed

1 Rinse quinoa thoroughly by placing in a fine-mesh strainer and holding under cold running water until water runs clear; drain well.

2 In 2-quart saucepan, heat 2 cups of the water to boiling over high heat. Add quinoa; reduce heat to low. Cover; simmer 10 to 12 minutes or until water is absorbed.

3 Meanwhile, in 12-inch skillet, heat remaining 4 cups water and the bouillon cube to boiling over high heat. Add salmon, skin side up; reduce heat to low. Cover; simmer 10 to 12 minutes or until fish flakes easily with fork. Transfer with slotted spoon to plate; let cool. Discard water. Remove skin from salmon; break into large pieces.

4 Meanwhile, rinse and dry skillet. Melt butter in skillet over medium heat. Add asparagus; cook 5 minutes, stirring frequently. Stir in onions; cook 1 minute, stirring frequently. Stir in peas, tomatoes and broth; cook 1 minute.

5 Gently stir quinoa, salmon, lemon-pepper seasoning and dill weed into asparagus mixture. Cover; cook about 2 minutes or until hot.

Betty's Success Tip

High in fiber and protein, quinoa is an ancient grain that is delicious and cooks fairly quickly—look for it with the rice or pasta at the grocery store.

Grilled Fish with Jicama Salsa

PREP TIME: 15 min • **START TO FINISH:** 2 hr 15 min • 6 servings

½
Carbohydrate
Choice

JICAMA SALSA

- **2** cups chopped peeled jicama (¾ lb)
- **1** medium cucumber, peeled, chopped (1 cup)
- **1** medium orange, peeled, chopped (¾ cup)
- **1** tablespoon chopped fresh cilantro or parsley
- **½** teaspoon chili powder
- **¼** teaspoon salt
- **1** tablespoon lime juice

FISH

- **1½** lb swordfish, tuna or marlin steaks, ¾ to 1 inch thick
- **2** tablespoons olive or canola oil
- **1** tablespoon lime juice
- **¼** teaspoon salt
- **⅛** teaspoon crushed red pepper

1 In medium bowl, mix salsa ingredients. Cover and refrigerate at least 2 hours to blend flavors.

2 If fish steaks are large, cut into 6 serving pieces. Mix oil, lime juice, salt and red pepper in shallow glass or plastic dish or heavy-duty resealable food-storage plastic bag. Add fish; turn to coat with marinade. Cover dish or seal bag; refrigerate 30 minutes.

3 Heat charcoal or gas grill for direct heat. Remove fish from marinade; reserve marinade. Cover and grill fish 5 to 6 inches from medium heat about 10 minutes, brushing 2 or 3 times with marinade and turning once, until fish flakes easily with fork. Discard any remaining marinade. Serve fish with salsa.

1 SERVING: Calories 200 (Calories from Fat 90); Total Fat 10g (Saturated Fat 2g; Trans Fat 0g); Cholesterol 60mg; Sodium 250mg; Total Carbohydrate 7g (Dietary Fiber 3g; Sugars 2g); Protein 20g

% DAILY VALUE: Vitamin A 6%; Vitamin C 20%; Calcium 2%; Iron 6%

EXCHANGES:
1 Vegetable, 2½ Lean Meat, ½ Fat

Betty's Success Tip

Low-fat salsas, relishes and chutneys can turn humble foods into taste sensations. Featuring the flavors of lime, orange, cucumber and jicama, this salsa adds a splash of flavor to your grilled fish.

2
Carbohydrate
Choices

Citrus-Glazed Salmon

PREP TIME: 10 min • **START TO FINISH:** 25 min • 4 servings (1 piece of fish and 3 tablespoons sauce)

1 SERVING: Calories 320 (Calories from Fat 70); Total Fat 8g (Saturated Fat 2.5g; Trans Fat 0g); Cholesterol 95mg; Sodium 680mg; Total Carbohydrate 30g (Dietary Fiber 3g; Sugars 23g); Protein 31g

% DAILY VALUE: Vitamin A 6%; Vitamin C 25%; Calcium 6%; Iron 8%

EXCHANGES: ½ Fruit, 1½ Other Carbohydrate, 2½ Very Lean Meat, 2 Lean Meat

2	medium limes
1	small orange
⅓	cup agave syrup
1	teaspoon salt
1	teaspoon pepper
4	cloves garlic, finely chopped
1¼	lb salmon fillet, cut into 4 pieces
2	tablespoons sliced green onions
1	lime slice, cut into 4 wedges
1	orange slice, cut into 4 wedges
	Hot cooked orzo pasta or rice, if desired

1 Heat oven to 400°F. Line 15×10×1-inch pan with cooking parchment paper or foil. In small bowl, grate lime peel from limes. Squeeze enough lime juice to equal 2 tablespoons; add to peel in bowl. Grate orange peel from oranges into bowl. Squeeze enough orange juice to equal 2 tablespoons; add to peel mixture. Stir in agave syrup, salt, pepper and garlic. In small cup, measure ¼ cup citrus mixture for salmon (reserve remaining citrus mixture).

2 Place salmon fillets in pan, skin side down. Using ¼ cup citrus mixture, brush tops and sides of salmon. Bake 13 to 17 minutes or until fish flakes easily with fork. Lift salmon pieces from skin with metal spatula onto serving plate. Sprinkle with green onions. Top each fish fillet with lime and orange wedges. Serve each fillet with 3 tablespoons reserved sauce and rice.

Diabetes Team Tip
Salmon is a super source of vitamin B$_{12}$ which is needed for all body cells to function properly. Salmon also contains omega-3 fats, the good-for-you fats that are so beneficial for your heart and overall health. —Dr. Bergenstal

Betty's Success Tip
Made from the nectar of a succulent plant called the agave and native to Mexico, agave syrup is a liquid sweetener that's used in all types of foods. Honey can be substituted for the agave syrup.

0
Carbohydrate
Choices

Halibut with Lime and Cilantro

PREP TIME: 30 min • **START TO FINISH:** 45 min • 2 servings

1 SERVING: Calories 190 (Calories from Fat 40); Total Fat 4.5g (Saturated Fat 1g; Trans Fat 0g); Cholesterol 90mg; Sodium 600mg; Total Carbohydrate 6g (Dietary Fiber 0g; Sugars 2g); Protein 32g

% DAILY VALUE:
Vitamin A 10%; Vitamin C 4%; Calcium 2%; Iron 4%

EXCHANGES:
1 Vegetable, 4½ Very Lean Meat

2 tablespoons lime juice
1 tablespoon chopped fresh cilantro
1 teaspoon olive or canola oil
1 clove garlic, finely chopped
2 halibut or salmon steaks (about ¾ lb)
   Freshly ground pepper to taste
½ cup chunky-style salsa

1 In shallow glass or plastic dish or in resealable food-storage plastic bag, mix lime juice, cilantro, oil and garlic. Add halibut, turning several times to coat with marinade. Cover; refrigerate 15 minutes, turning once.

2 Heat gas or charcoal grill. Remove halibut from marinade; discard marinade.

3 Place halibut on grill over medium heat. Cover grill; cook 10 to 20 minutes, turning once, until halibut flakes easily with fork. Sprinkle with pepper. Serve with salsa.

Diabetes Team Tip
Eating fish at least once or twice a week is recommended by health experts because most fish is low in fat and calories and contains heart-healthy nutrients. —Dr. Bergenstal

Betty's Success Tip
You may want to consider using a grill basket when grilling delicate fish that can break apart easily. Be sure to lightly brush the basket with vegetable oil before adding the fish.

Roasted Tilapia and Vegetables

PREP TIME: 15 min • **START TO FINISH:** 40 min • 4 servings

½ lb fresh asparagus spears, trimmed, halved

2 small zucchini, halved lengthwise, cut into ½-inch pieces

1 red bell pepper, cut into ½-inch strips

1 large onion, cut into ½-inch wedges

1 tablespoon olive oil

2 teaspoons Montreal steak seasoning

4 tilapia fillets (about 1½ lb)

2 teaspoons butter or margarine, melted

½ teaspoon paprika

1 Heat oven to 450°F. In large bowl, toss asparagus, zucchini, bell pepper, onion and oil. Sprinkle with 1 teaspoon of the steak seasoning; toss to coat. Spread vegetables in ungreased 15×10×1-inch pan. Place on lower oven rack; roast 5 minutes.

2 Meanwhile, spray 13×9-inch (3-quart) glass baking dish with cooking spray. Pat tilapia fillets dry with paper towels. Brush with butter; sprinkle with remaining 1 teaspoon steak seasoning and the paprika. Place in baking dish.

3 Place baking dish on middle oven rack. Roast fish and vegetables 17 to 18 minutes longer or until fish flakes easily with fork and vegetables are tender.

1 SERVING: Calories 250 (Calories from Fat 70); Total Fat 8g (Saturated Fat 2.5g; Trans Fat 0g); Cholesterol 95mg; Sodium 160mg; Total Carbohydrate 10g (Dietary Fiber 3g; Sugars 5g); Protein 35g

% DAILY VALUE: Vitamin A 35%; Vitamin C 45%; Calcium 6%; Iron 15%

EXCHANGES: 2 Vegetable, 4½ Very Lean Meat, 1 Fat

Betty's Success Tip

Any firm or medium-firm fish fillets with mild flavor will work in this recipe. Try cod, haddock or red snapper. Baking time will vary depending on the thickness of the fillets.

½
Carbohydrate
Choice

Cobia with Lemon-Caper Sauce

PREP TIME: 25 min • **START TO FINISH:** 25 min • 4 servings

1 SERVING: Calories 230 (Calories from Fat 80); Total Fat 9g (Saturated Fat 1.5g; Trans Fat 0g); Cholesterol 75mg; Sodium 400mg; Total Carbohydrate 9g (Dietary Fiber 0g; Sugars 0g); Protein 28g

% DAILY VALUE: Vitamin A 2%; Vitamin C 4%; Calcium 2%; Iron 6%

EXCHANGES: ½ Starch, 3½ Very Lean Meat, ½ Lean Meat, 1 Fat

⅓	cup all-purpose flour
¼	teaspoon salt
¼	teaspoon pepper
1¼	lb cobia or sea bass fillets, cut into 4 pieces
2	tablespoons olive oil
⅓	cup dry white wine
½	cup reduced-sodium chicken broth
2	tablespoons lemon juice
1	tablespoon capers, rinsed, drained
1	tablespoon chopped fresh parsley

1 In shallow dish, stir flour, salt and pepper. Coat cobia pieces in flour mixture (reserve remaining flour mixture). In 12-inch nonstick skillet, heat oil over medium-high heat. Place coated cobia in oil. Cook 8 to 10 minutes, turning halfway through cooking, until fish flakes easily with fork; remove from heat. Lift fish from skillet to serving platter with slotted spatula (do not discard drippings); keep warm.

2 Heat skillet (with drippings) over medium heat. Stir in 1 tablespoon reserved flour mixture; cook and stir 30 seconds. Stir in wine; cook about 30 seconds or until thickened and slightly reduced. Stir in chicken broth and lemon juice; cook and stir 1 to 2 minutes until sauce is smooth and slightly thickened. Stir in capers.

3 Serve sauce over cobia; sprinkle with parsley.

Betty's Success Tip

This dish would be delicious served with a rice blend. Look for one with wild and whole grain brown rice that doesn't include sodium. To keep sodium low, consider making rice by substituting dry white wine or low-sodium chicken broth for half the liquid and omitting the butter and salt.

2½
Carbohydrate
Choices

Calypso Shrimp with Black Bean Salsa

PREP TIME: 25 min • **START TO FINISH:** 25 min • 4 servings

1 SERVING: Calories 300 (Calories from Fat 45); Total Fat 5g (Saturated Fat 0.5g; Trans Fat 0g); Cholesterol 160mg; Sodium 190mg; Total Carbohydrate 37g (Dietary Fiber 12g; Sugars 7g); Protein 26g

% DAILY VALUE: Vitamin A 25%; Vitamin C 35%; Calcium 10%; Iron 30%

EXCHANGES: 2 Starch, 1½ Vegetable, 2½ Very Lean Meat, ½ Fat

SHRIMP

½ teaspoon grated lime peel

1 tablespoon lime juice

1 tablespoon canola oil

1 teaspoon finely chopped gingerroot

1 clove garlic, finely chopped

1 lb uncooked deveined peeled large shrimp, thawed if frozen

SALSA

1 can (15 oz) black beans, drained, rinsed

1 medium mango, peeled, pitted and chopped (1 cup)

1 small red bell pepper, chopped (½ cup)

2 medium green onions, sliced (2 tablespoons)

1 tablespoon chopped fresh cilantro

½ teaspoon grated lime peel

1 to 2 tablespoons lime juice

1 tablespoon red wine vinegar

¼ teaspoon ground red pepper (cayenne)

1 In medium glass or plastic bowl, mix lime peel, lime juice, oil, gingerroot and garlic. Stir in shrimp; let stand 15 minutes.

2 Meanwhile, in medium bowl, mix salsa ingredients.

3 In 10-inch skillet, cook shrimp over medium-high heat about 5 minutes, turning once, until pink. Serve with salsa.

Betty's Success Tip

If you don't have a fresh mango, look for jars of cut-up mango in juice. It's perfect to use in the salad.

Spicy Shrimp Fajitas

PREP TIME: 30 min • **START TO FINISH:** 30 min • 6 fajitas

2
Carbohydrate
Choices

MARINADE

- 1 tablespoon lime juice
- 1 tablespoon olive or canola oil
- ¼ teaspoon salt
- 1 teaspoon chili powder
- 1 teaspoon ground cumin
- 2 cloves garlic, crushed
  Pinch ground red pepper (cayenne)

FAJITAS

- 2 lb uncooked deveined peeled medium shrimp, thawed if frozen, tail shells removed
- 2 medium red bell peppers, cut into strips (2 cups)
- 1 medium red onion, sliced (2 cups)
  Olive oil cooking spray
- 6 flour tortillas (8 inch)
- ¾ cup refrigerated guacamole (from 14-oz package)

1 Heat gas or charcoal grill. In 1-gallon resealable food-storage plastic bag, mix marinade ingredients. Add shrimp; seal bag and toss to coat. Set aside while grilling vegetables, turning bag once.

2 In medium bowl, place bell peppers and onion; spray with cooking spray. Place vegetables in grill basket (grill "wok"). Wrap tortillas in foil; set aside.

3 Place basket on grill rack over medium heat. Cover grill; cook 10 minutes, turning vegetables once.

4 Drain shrimp; discard marinade. Add shrimp to grill basket. Cover grill; cook 5 to 7 minutes longer, turning shrimp and vegetables once, until shrimp are pink. Place wrapped tortillas on grill. Cook 2 minutes, turning once, until warm.

5 On each tortilla, place shrimp, vegetables and guacamole; fold tortilla over filling.

1 FAJITA: Calories 310 (Calories from Fat 90); Total Fat 10g (Saturated Fat 2g; Trans Fat 1g); Cholesterol 215mg; Sodium 770mg; Total Carbohydrate 29g (Dietary Fiber 2g; Sugars 4g); Protein 27g

% DAILY VALUE: Vitamin A 30%; Vitamin C 45%; Calcium 15%; Iron 30%

EXCHANGES: 1½ Starch, 1 Vegetable, 3 Very Lean Meat, 1½ Fat

Betty's Success Tip

Don't marinate the shrimp longer than 20 minutes or they'll start to "cook" in the marinade.

2
Carbohydrate
Choices

Slow Cooker Chipotle Beef Stew

PREP TIME: 25 min • **START TO FINISH:** 8 hr 25 min • 6 servings (1⅓ cups each)

1 SERVING: Calories 310 (Calories from Fat 90); Total Fat 10g (Saturated Fat 3g; Trans Fat 0g); Cholesterol 60mg; Sodium 580mg; Total Carbohydrate 30g (Dietary Fiber 5g; Sugars 10g); Protein 25g

% DAILY VALUE: Vitamin A 25%; Vitamin C 45%; Calcium 6%; Iron 20%

EXCHANGES: 1½ Starch, 1½ Vegetable, 2½ Lean Meat, ½ Fat

STEW

1 package (12 oz) frozen whole kernel corn

1 lb boneless beef top sirloin, trimmed of fat, cut into 1-inch cubes

1 chipotle chile in adobo sauce (from 7-oz can), finely chopped

2 large onions, chopped (2 cups)

2 poblano chiles, seeded, diced

3 cloves garlic, chopped

2 cans (14.5 oz each) diced tomatoes, undrained

1½ teaspoons ground cumin

½ teaspoon salt

¼ teaspoon cracked black pepper

TOPPINGS

1 avocado, pitted, peeled cut into 12 wedges

12 baked tortilla chips, crushed

6 small cilantro sprigs, coarsely chopped

6 tablespoons reduced-fat sour cream

1 Spray 4- to 5-quart slow cooker with cooking spray. In small microwavable bowl, microwave corn uncovered on High 2 minutes or until thawed. In slow cooker, place corn and all remaining stew ingredients; mix well. Cover and cook on Low heat setting 8 to 10 hours (or High heat setting 4 to 5 hours).

2 Divide stew evenly among 6 bowls. To serve, top with avocado, tortilla chips, cilantro and sour cream.

Diabetes Team Tip Beef is a super source of the mineral zinc, which is important for growth, wound healing and your ability to taste foods. —Diane Reader, Dietitian

Betty's Success Tip Top sirloin is an extra-lean cut of beef widely available at the supermarket. If you prefer, flank steak may be substituted. Be sure to look at labels when choosing meat, as many "stew cuts" can be quite fatty and may not meet recipe guidelines for people with diabetes.

1½
Carbohydrate
Choices

Broiled Dijon Burgers

PREP TIME: 25 min • **START TO FINISH:** 25 min • 6 burgers

1 BURGER: Calories 250 (Calories from Fat 70); Total Fat 8g (Saturated Fat 3g; Trans Fat 1g); Cholesterol 45mg; Sodium 450mg; Total Carbohydrate 23g (Dietary Fiber 3g; Sugars 5g); Protein 22g

% DAILY VALUE:
Vitamin A 4%; Vitamin C 0%; Calcium 8%; Iron 20%

EXCHANGES: 1½ Starch, 2½ Lean Meat

¼　cup fat-free egg product or 2 egg whites

2　tablespoons fat-free (skim) milk

2　teaspoons Dijon mustard or horseradish sauce

¼　teaspoon salt

⅛　teaspoon pepper

1　cup soft bread crumbs (about 2 slices bread)

1　small onion, finely chopped (⅓ cup)

1　lb extra-lean (at least 90%) ground beef

6　whole-grain burger buns, split, toasted

1 Set oven control to broil. Spray broiler pan rack with cooking spray.

2 In medium bowl, mix egg product, milk, mustard, salt and pepper. Stir in bread crumbs and onion. Stir in beef. Shape mixture into 6 patties, each about ½ inch thick. Place patties on rack in broiler pan.

3 Broil with tops of patties about 5 inches from heat 6 minutes. Turn; broil until meat thermometer inserted in center of patties reads 160°F, 4 to 6 minutes longer. Serve patties in buns.

Diabetes Team Tip
Broiling, braising and roasting are healthy, low-fat techniques to use when cooking meats. Grilling is another great method, as it allows the fat to drip away from the meat.
—Diane Reader, Dietitian

Betty's Success Tip
These meaty sandwiches prove that the best burgers don't have to be loaded with fat and calories to be delicious! The place to pile it on is with the veggies: try lettuce leaves, sliced tomatoes, dill pickles, sliced onions or green peppers, or your favorites, and a little ketchup and mustard.

Swiss Steak Casserole

PREP TIME: 20 min • **START TO FINISH:** 2 hr 5 min • 6 servings (1 cup each)

1
Carbohydrate
Choice

3 tablespoons all-purpose flour

½ teaspoon salt

1 teaspoon paprika

½ teaspoon pepper

1 lb boneless beef round steak, cut into ¾-inch cubes

2 tablespoons canola oil

2 cups sliced fresh mushrooms

1 cup frozen pearl onions

1 clove garlic, finely chopped

4 cups sliced carrots (8 medium)

1 can (14.5 oz) stewed tomatoes, undrained

1 Heat oven to 350°F. In medium bowl, mix flour, salt, paprika and pepper. Add beef; toss to coat. In 12-inch skillet, heat 1 tablespoon of the oil over medium-high heat. Add beef, reserving remaining flour mixture. Cook beef on all sides. Spoon into ungreased 2½-quart casserole.

2 To same skillet, add remaining 1 tablespoon oil, the mushrooms, onions and garlic. Cook 2 to 3 minutes, stirring constantly, until browned; add to casserole. Stir in carrots, tomatoes and reserved flour mixture until well mixed.

3 Cover casserole. Bake 1 hour 30 minutes to 1 hour 45 minutes or until beef and vegetables are tender.

1 SERVING: Calories 260 (Calories from Fat 80); Total Fat 9g (Saturated Fat 2g; Trans Fat 0g); Cholesterol 55mg; Sodium 660mg; Total Carbohydrate 20g (Dietary Fiber 4g; Sugars 10g); Protein 25g

% DAILY VALUE: Vitamin A 290%; Vitamin C 15%; Calcium 4%; Iron 20%

EXCHANGES: 1 Starch, 1½ Vegetable, 2½ Lean Meat

Diabetes Team Tip
Although protein will not raise your blood glucose levels, it's still wise to eat only 1 serving of 3 to 4 ounces per meal to control your total calorie and fat intake. —Diane Reader, Dietitian

Betty's Success Tip
Take some help from the grocery store. Look for packages of sliced carrots and mushrooms in the produce section to save time.

2
Carbohydrate Choices

Beef Roast with Onions and Potatoes

PREP TIME: 30 min • **START TO FINISH:** 9 hr 45 min • 6 servings

1 SERVING: Calories 480 (Calories from Fat 90); Total Fat 10g (Saturated Fat 3.5g; Trans Fat 0g); Cholesterol 165mg; Sodium 750mg; Total Carbohydrate 29g (Dietary Fiber 3g; Sugars 4g); Protein 70g

% DAILY VALUE:
Vitamin A 0%; Vitamin C 10%; Calcium 4%; Iron 40%

EXCHANGES: 2 Starch, 1 Vegetable, 9 Lean Meat, ½ Fat

1	large sweet onion, cut in half, then cut into thin slices
1	boneless beef bottom round roast (3 lb), trimmed of excess fat
3	baking potatoes, cut into 1½- to 2-inch cubes
2	cloves garlic, finely chopped
1¾	cups beef-flavored broth
1	package (1 oz) onion soup mix (from 2-oz box)
¼	cup all-purpose flour

1 Spray 5- to 6-quart slow cooker with cooking spray. In slow cooker, place onion. If beef roast comes in netting or is tied, remove netting or strings. Place beef on onion. Place potatoes and garlic around beef. In small bowl, mix 1¼ cups of the broth and the dry soup mix; pour over beef. (Refrigerate remaining broth.)

2 Cover; cook on Low heat setting 9 to 10 hours.

3 Remove beef and vegetables from slow cooker; place on serving platter. Cover to keep warm.

4 In small bowl, mix remaining ½ cup broth and the flour; gradually stir into juices in slow cooker. Increase heat setting to High. Cover; cook about 15 minutes, stirring occasionally, until sauce has thickened. Serve sauce over beef and vegetables.

Diabetes Team Tip
Beef is a great source of vitamin B_{12} and the mineral iron. Both of these are important for proper body function. —Diane Reader, Dietitian

Betty's Success Tip
To save precious time in the morning, cut the onion and chop the garlic the night before and refrigerate.

Flank Steak with Smoky Honey Mustard Sauce

1½ Carbohydrate Choices

PREP TIME: 30 min • **START TO FINISH:** 30 min • 6 servings

SAUCE

- ¼ cup fat-free honey mustard or honey Dijon dressing
- 1 tablespoon frozen (thawed) orange juice concentrate
- 1 tablespoon water
- 1 clove garlic, finely chopped
- 1 chipotle chile in adobo sauce (from 7-oz can), finely chopped

STEAK

- 1 beef flank steak (about 1½ lb)
- 6 flour tortillas for burritos (8 inch), heated as directed on package

1 Heat gas or charcoal grill. In small bowl, mix sauce ingredients. On both sides of beef, make cuts about ½ inch apart and ⅛ inch deep in diamond pattern. Brush 2 tablespoons of the sauce on both sides of beef.

2 Place beef on grill over medium heat. Cover grill; cook 17 to 20 minutes, turning once, until beef is of desired doneness.

3 Cut beef across grain into thin slices. Serve with tortillas and remaining sauce.

1 SERVING: Calories 310 (Calories from Fat 80); Total Fat 9g (Saturated Fat 2.5g; Trans Fat 1g); Cholesterol 85mg; Sodium 380mg; Total Carbohydrate 22g (Dietary Fiber 0g; Sugars 2g); Protein 36g

% DAILY VALUE: Vitamin A 0%; Vitamin C 4%; Calcium 6%; Iron 25%

EXCHANGES: 1½ Starch, 2½ Very Lean Meat, 2 Lean Meat

Diabetes Team Tip
You don't have to avoid all red meat if you're trying to lose weight. By selecting lean cuts, trimming all visible fat and eating small portions, you can enjoy meat as part of a healthy diet. —Diane Reader, Dietitian

Betty's Success Tip
Chipotle chiles are dried, smoked jalapeños. They have wrinkled, dark brown skin and a smoky, sweet, almost chocolaty flavor. Canned chipotles in adobo sauce are spicy as well as smoky.

0 Carbohydrate Choices

Sirloin Steaks with Cilantro Chimichurri

PREP TIME: 25 min • **START TO FINISH:** 25 min • 4 servings

1 SERVING: Calories 270 (Calories from Fat 80); Total Fat 9g (Saturated Fat 2.5g; Trans Fat 0g); Cholesterol 110mg; Sodium 350mg; Total Carbohydrate 3g (Dietary Fiber 0g; Sugars 0g); Protein 45g

% DAILY VALUE: Vitamin A 6%; Vitamin C 4%; Calcium 2%; Iron 30%

EXCHANGES: ½ Vegetable, 6½ Very Lean Meat, 1 Fat

1 cup loosely packed fresh cilantro

1 small onion, cut into quarters

2 cloves garlic, cut in half

1 jalapeño chile, cut in half, seeded

2 teaspoons lime juice

2 teaspoons canola oil

½ teaspoon salt

2 teaspoons ground cumin

½ teaspoon pepper

4 beef sirloin steaks, 1 inch thick (about 1½ lb)

1 Heat gas or charcoal grill. In food processor, place cilantro, onion, garlic, chile, lime juice, oil and ¼ teaspoon of the salt. Cover; process until finely chopped. Blend in 2 to 3 teaspoons water to make sauce thinner, if desired. Transfer to small bowl; set aside until serving time.

2 In small bowl, mix cumin, pepper and remaining ¼ teaspoon salt; rub evenly over steaks. Place steaks on grill over medium heat. Cover grill; cook 7 to 10 minutes for medium-rare (145°F), turning once halfway through cooking.

3 Serve 2 tablespoons chimichurri over each steak.

Betty's Success Tip

For the freshest flavor, purchase whole cumin seed and grind in a mortar and pestle or spice grinder just before using.

Asian Steak Salad

PREP TIME: 20 min • **START TO FINISH:** 20 min • 6 servings

1½ Carbohydrate Choices

1 lb cut-up lean beef for stir-fry

1 package (3 oz) Oriental-flavor ramen noodle soup mix

½ cup low-fat Asian marinade and dressing

1 bag (10 oz) romaine and leaf lettuce mix

1 cup fresh snow pea pods

½ cup matchstick-cut carrots (from 10-oz bag)

1 can (11 oz) mandarin orange segments, drained

1 Spray 12-inch skillet with cooking spray; heat over medium-high heat. Place beef in skillet; sprinkle with 1 teaspoon seasoning mix from soup mix. (Discard remaining seasoning mix.) Cook beef 4 to 5 minutes, stirring occasionally, until brown. Stir in 1 tablespoon of the dressing.

2 Break block of noodles from soup mix into small pieces. Mix noodles, lettuce, pea pods, carrots, and orange segments in large bowl. Add remaining dressing; toss until well coated. Divide mixture among 6 serving plates. Top with beef.

1 SERVING: Calories 240 (Calories from Fat 60); Total Fat 7g (Saturated Fat 2.5g; Trans Fat 1g); Cholesterol 30mg; Sodium 990mg; Total Carbohydrate 25g (Dietary Fiber 2g; Sugars 14g); Protein 19g

% DAILY VALUE: Vitamin A 130%; Vitamin C 30%; Calcium 4%; Iron 15%

EXCHANGES: 1½ Starch, 1 Vegetable, 2 Lean Meat

Diabetes Team Tip

Just the colors of fruits and vegetables tell us that they are good for us, so choose the most colorful ones. Fruits and veggies contain vitamins and minerals, which are good for our bodies in many ways.
—Diane Reader, Dietitian

2

Carbohydrate Choices

Pork Chops with Raspberry-Chipotle Sauce and Herbed Rice

PREP TIME: 25 min • **START TO FINISH:** 25 min • 4 servings

1 SERVING: Calories 370 (Calories from Fat 110); Total Fat 12g (Saturated Fat 3.5g; Trans Fat 0g); Cholesterol 85mg; Sodium 140mg; Total Carbohydrate 34g (Dietary Fiber 0g; Sugars 12g); Protein 31g

% DAILY VALUE: Vitamin A 2%; Vitamin C 0%; Calcium 4%; Iron 10%

EXCHANGES: 1 Starch, 1 Other Carbohydrate, 2½ Very Lean Meat, 1½ Lean Meat, 1 Fat

PORK CHOPS

- 4 bone-in pork rib chops, about ¾ inch thick
- ½ teaspoon garlic-pepper blend
- 1 tablespoon canola oil

RASPBERRY-CHIPOTLE SAUCE

- ⅓ cup all-fruit raspberry spread
- 1 tablespoon water
- 1 tablespoon raspberry-flavored vinegar
- 1 large or 2 small chipotle chiles in adobo sauce, finely chopped (from 7-oz can)

HERBED RICE

- 1 package (8.8 oz) quick-cooking (ready in 90 seconds) whole-grain brown rice
- ¼ teaspoon salt-free garlic-herb blend
- ½ teaspoon lemon peel
- 1 tablespoon chopped fresh cilantro

1 Sprinkle pork with garlic pepper. In 12-inch nonstick skillet, heat oil over medium-high heat. Add pork to oil. Cook 8 to 10 minutes, turning once, until pork is no longer pink and meat thermometer inserted in center reads 145°F. Remove from skillet to serving platter (reserve pork drippings); keep warm.

2 Meanwhile, in small bowl, stir raspberry spread, water, vinegar and chile; set aside. Make rice as directed on package. Stir in remaining rice ingredients; keep warm.

3 In skillet with pork drippings, pour raspberry mixture. Cook and stir over low heat about 1 minute or until sauce is bubbly and slightly thickened. Serve pork chops with sauce and rice.

Betty's Success Tip

Substitute other flavors of fruit spread for the raspberry, such as apricot or peach, and use cider vinegar instead of raspberry vinegar.

3
Carbohydrate Choices

Slow-Cooked Pork Burrito Bowls

PREP TIME: 15 min • **START TO FINISH:** 8 hr 15 min • 10 servings

1 SERVING: Calories 460 (Calories from Fat 150); Total Fat 17g (Saturated Fat 7g; Trans Fat 0g); Cholesterol 75mg; Sodium 1030mg; Total Carbohydrate 48g (Dietary Fiber 5g; Sugars 4g); Protein 30g

% DAILY VALUE: Vitamin A 10%; Vitamin C 6%; Calcium 25%; Iron 15%

EXCHANGES: 3 Starch, ½ Vegetable, 2½ Very Lean Meat, 3 Fat

1	boneless pork shoulder (2 lb), trimmed of excess fat
1	can (15 to 16 oz) pinto beans, drained, rinsed
1	package (1 oz) 40% less-sodium taco seasoning mix
1	can (4.5 oz) diced green chiles, undrained
2	packages (7.6 oz each) Spanish rice mix
5	cups water
1½	cups shredded Mexican cheese blend (6 oz)
3	cups shredded lettuce
¾	cup chunky-style salsa

1 Spray 3- to 4-quart slow cooker with cooking spray. If pork comes in netting or is tied, remove netting or strings. Place pork in slow cooker. Pour beans around pork. Sprinkle taco seasoning mix over pork. Pour chiles over beans.

2 Cover; cook on Low heat setting 8 to 10 hours.

3 About 45 minutes before serving, in 3-quart saucepan, make rice mixes as directed on package, using water and omitting butter.

4 Remove pork from slow cooker; place on cutting board. Use 2 forks to pull pork into shreds. Return pork to slow cooker; gently stir to mix with beans.

5 To serve, spoon rice into each of 10 serving bowls; top each with pork mixture, cheese, lettuce and salsa.

Betty's Success Tip

You'll find that boneless pork shoulder also may be called pork butt, shoulder blade roast, Boston roast or Boston butt.

Couscous and Sweet Potatoes with Pork

PREP TIME: 20 min • **START TO FINISH:** 20 min • 5 servings

3
Carbohydrate
Choices

1¼ cups uncooked couscous

1 lb pork tenderloin, thinly sliced

1 medium sweet potato, peeled, cut into julienne strips

1 cup chunky-style salsa

½ cup water

2 tablespoons honey

¼ cup chopped fresh cilantro

1 Cook couscous as directed on package.

2 While couscous is cooking, spray 12-inch skillet with cooking spray. Cook pork in skillet over medium heat 2 to 3 minutes, stirring occasionally, until brown.

3 Stir sweet potato, salsa, water and honey into pork. Heat to boiling; reduce heat to medium. Cover and cook 5 to 6 minutes, stirring occasionally, until potato is tender. Sprinkle with cilantro. Serve pork mixture over couscous.

1 SERVING: Calories 320 (Calories from Fat 35); Total Fat 4g (Saturated Fat 1.5g; Trans Fat 0g); Cholesterol 40mg; Sodium 420mg; Total Carbohydrate 48g (Dietary Fiber 3g; Sugars 11g); Protein 23g

% DAILY VALUE: Vitamin A 100%; Vitamin C 4%; Calcium 2%; Iron 6%

EXCHANGES: 3 Starch, 1 Very Lean Meat, 1 Lean Meat

Betty's Success Tip

Want a little crunch with this quick pasta and pork dinner? Try baby-cut carrots, apple wedges, bell pepper strips or celery sticks.

3
Carbohydrate Choices

Pork Mole Quesadillas

PREP TIME: 35 min • **START TO FINISH:** 35 min • 4 quesadillas

1 QUESADILLA:
Calories 450 (Calories from Fat 160); Total Fat 17g (Saturated Fat 6g; Trans Fat 1g); Cholesterol 45mg; Sodium 810mg; Total Carbohydrate 50g (Dietary Fiber 4g; Sugars 8g); Protein 23g

% DAILY VALUE:
Vitamin A 40%; Vitamin C 60%; Calcium 25%; Iron 25%

EXCHANGES: 2½ Starch, ½ Other Carbohydrate, 1 Vegetable, 2 Very Lean Meat, 3 Fat

2   teaspoons canola oil

½   lb boneless pork loin chops, trimmed of fat, cut into thin strips

1   medium green bell pepper, thinly sliced

1   medium red bell pepper, thinly sliced

1   medium onion, thinly sliced

3   cloves garlic, finely chopped

1   tablespoon chili powder

1   teaspoon all-purpose flour

1   teaspoon ground cumin

¼   teaspoon salt

¼   teaspoon ground cinnamon

¼   cup reduced-sodium chicken broth

2   tablespoons semisweet chocolate chips

4   fat-free flour tortillas (10 inch)

     Cooking spray

½   cup chopped tomato

4   teaspoons chopped fresh cilantro

½   cup shredded reduced-fat Monterey Jack cheese (2 oz)

1 In 12-inch nonstick skillet, heat 1 teaspoon of the oil over medium-high heat. Add pork to oil. Cook 4 to 5 minutes, stirring frequently, until pork is no longer pink; remove from skillet.

2 In same skillet, heat remaining 1 teaspoon oil over medium heat. Add bell peppers, onion and garlic to oil. Cook 3 to 5 minutes, stirring occasionally, until bell peppers are crisp-tender. Stir in chili powder, flour, cumin, salt and cinnamon; cook 30 seconds. Stir in chicken broth; heat to boiling. Cook about 30 seconds, stirring constantly, until thickened and bubbly. Remove from heat; stir in chocolate chips until melted. Stir in pork.

3 Spray 1 side of each tortilla with cooking spray. On work surface, place tortillas, sprayed side down. Arrange pork mixture, tomato, cilantro and cheese evenly over half of each tortilla. Fold tortilla over filling, pressing gently.

4 Heat 12-inch skillet over medium heat until hot. Cook 2 quesadillas 3 to 4 minutes, turning once, until tortillas begin to brown; remove quesadillas from pan. Keep warm. Repeat with remaining 2 quesadillas.

5 To serve, cut into wedges, beginning from center of folded side.

Betty's Success Tip

Mole sauces originated from various regions of Mexico and differ from cook to cook. The common element among moles is a little touch of chocolate.

Pork Medallions with Cherry Sauce

PREP TIME: 25 min • **START TO FINISH:** 35 min • 4 servings

1 SERVING: Calories 330 (Calories from Fat 60); Total Fat 7g (Saturated Fat 2g, Trans Fat 0g); Cholesterol 50mg; Sodium 170mg; Total Carbohydrate 44g (Dietary Fiber 1g, Sugars 30g); Protein 23g

% DAILY VALUE: Vitamin A 0%; Vitamin C 6%; Calcium 2%; Iron 6%

EXCHANGES: 1 Starch, 2 Other Carbohydrate, 1 Very Lean Meat, 2 Lean Meat

1   pork tenderloin (1 to 1¼ lb), cut into ½-inch slices

½   teaspoon garlic-pepper blend

2   teaspoons olive oil

¾   cup cherry preserves

2   tablespoons chopped shallots

1   tablespoon Dijon mustard

1   tablespoon balsamic vinegar

1   clove garlic, finely chopped

1   Sprinkle both sides of pork with garlic-pepper blend.

2   In 12-inch skillet, heat 1 teaspoon of the oil over medium-high heat. Add pork; cook 6 to 8 minutes, turning once, until pork is browned and meat thermometer inserted in center reads 145°F. Remove pork from skillet; keep warm.

3   In same skillet, mix remaining teaspoon oil, the preserves, shallots, mustard, vinegar and garlic, scraping any brown bits from bottom of skillet. Heat to boiling. Reduce heat; simmer uncovered 10 minutes or until reduced to about ½ cup. Serve sauce over pork slices.

Betty's Success Tip   For easy slicing, freeze the pork for 15 to 30 minutes before cutting.

Sick Days

Any illness, even a simple cold, puts extra stress on your body, which can raise blood glucose levels.

On days when you are ill:

- Check your blood glucose every two to four hours, and record the results.

- Keep taking your diabetes medications even if you can't keep food down. Your body will still make glucose, and you need your medicines to keep it in check. Call your doctor to ask if you need to change doses.

- Drink at least 1 cup of water or other sugar-free, caffeine-free liquids every hour while you're awake.

- Eat foods with carbohydrate such as saltine crackers, frozen popsicles or soup with noodles if you can't eat your usual foods. Sip on liquids like regular soda pop or juice if you can't eat.

- Eating will be easier if you're eating foods that you like, even if it means eating for breakfast what you normally would eat for dinner. If the food is appealing to you, enjoy it.

- Test your urine for ketones (a buildup of acids in the blood) every two to four hours, or anytime your blood glucose is over 250 mg/dL.

Call your doctor right away if:

- Most of your blood glucose readings are higher than 250 mg/dL for 2 days in a row.

- You are vomiting or have persistent diarrhea.

- Your blood glucose level falls too low more than once during your illness.

- You have moderate to high amounts of ketones in your urine.

CHAPTER 4

Stand-Out Meatless Meals

2
Carbohydrate Choices

Asian-Stuffed Portabellas

PREP TIME: 55 min • **START TO FINISH:** 1 hr 10 min • 4 servings

1 SERVING: Calories 250 (Calories from Fat 80); Total Fat 9g (Saturated Fat 1g; Trans Fat 0g); Cholesterol 0mg; Sodium 560mg; Total Carbohydrate 35g (Dietary Fiber 6g; Sugars 5g); Protein 7g

% DAILY VALUE:
Vitamin A 15%; Vitamin C 15%; Calcium 4%; Iron 10%

EXCHANGES: 2 Starch, 1 Vegetable, 1½ Fat

¾	cup uncooked regular brown rice
1½	cups water
4	large portabella mushrooms (4 to 5 inches in diameter), stems removed
1	tablespoon canola oil
1½	cups shredded coleslaw mix
½	cup cut-up snow pea pods
¼	cup sliced green onions (4 medium)
1	tablespoon finely chopped gingerroot
1	clove garlic, finely chopped
¼	cup reduced-sodium soy sauce
2	teaspoons sesame oil
4	teaspoons sesame seed

1 Heat oven to 400°F. Spray 15×10×1-inch pan with cooking spray. In 1½-quart saucepan, heat brown rice and water to boiling; reduce heat. Cover and simmer 45 to 50 minutes or until water is absorbed.

2 Meanwhile, place mushrooms in pan, gill side down. Bake 5 minutes or until tender and beginning to brown.

3 In 10-inch nonstick skillet, heat canola oil over medium-high heat. Add coleslaw mix, snow pea pods, green onions, gingerroot and garlic to oil. Cook 2 to 3 minutes, stirring frequently, until coleslaw mix is wilted and vegetables are crisp-tender. Stir in cooked rice; sprinkle with soy sauce and sesame oil. Cook rice mixture, tossing gently with soy sauce and oil, until thoroughly heated; remove from heat.

4 In pan, turn mushrooms gill side up. For each serving, spoon about ¾ cup rice mixture onto mushroom and sprinkle with 1 teaspoon sesame seed. Bake 13 to 15 minutes or until sesame seed begins to turn brown.

Betty's Success Tip
Keep sodium under control by cooking rice in water instead of broth and don't add the salt. The soy sauce provides plenty of flavor.

Caramelized Onion, Potato and Polenta Pizza

PREP TIME: 50 min • **START TO FINISH:** 2 hr 20 min • 6 servings

1 SERVING: Calories 310 (Calories from Fat 130); Total Fat 15g (Saturated Fat 7g; Trans Fat 0g); Cholesterol 30mg; Sodium 880mg; Total Carbohydrate 37g (Dietary Fiber 3g; Sugars 6g); Protein 8g

% DAILY VALUE: Vitamin A 10%; Vitamin C 6%; Calcium 15%; Iron 10%

EXCHANGES: 2 Starch, 1 Vegetable, 3 Fat

CRUST

1	cup plus 1 tablespoon yellow cornmeal
¾	cup water
3¼	cups boiling water
1½	teaspoons salt
1	tablespoon olive oil

TOPPING

2	tablespoons butter
1	large sweet onion (Maui or Walla Walla), cut in half, thinly sliced (3 cups)
1	tablespoon sugar
1	cup refrigerated home-style sliced potatoes (from 20-oz bag)
1	tablespoon olive oil
⅛	teaspoon salt
⅛	teaspoon pepper
½	cup pizza sauce
1	cup shredded fontina cheese (4 oz)
1	tablespoon chopped fresh oregano

1 Spray large cookie sheet with cooking spray; sprinkle with 1 tablespoon cornmeal. In 2-quart saucepan, mix 1 cup cornmeal and ¾ cup water. Stir in 3¼ cups boiling water and salt. Cook over medium heat about 4 minutes, stirring constantly, until mixture thickens and boils.

2 Reduce heat; cover and simmer about 10 minutes, stirring occasionally, until very thick. Remove from heat. Stir in olive oil until smooth. Spread hot polenta in 11-inch round on cookie sheet. Cover with plastic wrap; refrigerate at least 1 hour or until very firm.

3 Meanwhile, in 10-inch nonstick skillet, melt butter over medium heat. Add onion and sugar; cook 15 to 20 minutes, stirring frequently, until deep golden brown and caramelized. In 7-inch skillet, cook potatoes in oil as directed on package; season with the salt and pepper.

4 Heat oven to 450°F. Bake crust 20 minutes. Spread pizza sauce over crust; spoon onions evenly over sauce. Top with potatoes and cheese. Bake 8 to 10 minutes longer or until cheese is melted and potatoes are tender. Sprinkle with oregano before serving.

Betty's Success Tip

Polenta as a crust adds flavor and texture to this great pizza. If you like, you can make the crust as directed up to 24 hours before you plan to bake it.

Stir-Fried Tofu with Almonds

PREP TIME: 30 min • **START TO FINISH:** 30 min • 4 servings

2
Carbohydrate
Choices

4 oz uncooked spinach fettuccine or fettuccine, broken into 3-inch pieces

½ cup vegetable broth

⅓ cup dry white wine or vegetable broth

1 tablespoon cornstarch

3 tablespoons hoisin sauce

⅛ teaspoon pepper

1 package (14 oz) firm or extra-firm tofu, drained if needed

1 tablespoon canola oil

1½ cups small fresh cauliflower florets

1 large red or green bell pepper, cut into ¼-inch strips

2 cloves garlic, finely chopped

¼ cup sliced almonds, toasted*

1 Cook and drain fettuccine as directed on package. Meanwhile, in small bowl, mix broth, wine, cornstarch, hoisin sauce and pepper; set aside.

2 Place tofu between 2 layers of paper towels; press gently to remove as much water as possible. Cut into ¾-inch cubes; set aside.

3 Heat wok or 12-inch skillet over high heat. Add 1 teaspoon of the oil; rotate wok to coat side. Cook and stir cauliflower and bell pepper in oil about 4 minutes or until crisp-tender. Remove vegetables from wok.

4 Add remaining 2 teaspoons oil to wok; rotate wok to coat side. Cook tofu and garlic in oil over high heat 5 minutes, stirring gently. Stir in reserved broth mixture; cook and stir about 1 minute or until thickened. Stir in vegetables and fettuccine; cook until thoroughly heated. Sprinkle with almonds.

*To toast almonds, sprinkle in ungreased heavy skillet. Cook over medium heat 5 to 7 minutes, stirring frequently until almonds begin to brown, then stirring constantly until light brown.

1 SERVING: Calories 340 (Calories from Fat 130); Total Fat 14g (Saturated Fat 2g; Trans Fat 0g); Cholesterol 20mg; Sodium 370mg; Total Carbohydrate 35g (Dietary Fiber 4g; Sugars 5g); Protein 15g

% DAILY VALUE: Vitamin A 25%; Vitamin C 60%; Calcium 25%; Iron 20%

EXCHANGES: 2 Starch, 1 Vegetable, 1 Lean Meat, 2 Fat

Diabetes Team Tip
Tofu is a great alternative to meat. Made from soybeans, it provides protein, iron and calcium, but it's a bit high in carbohydrates, so plan accordingly. —Diane Reader, Dietitian

Betty's Success Tip
Uniquely flavored hoisin sauce can best be described as an Asian barbecue sauce, yet it's nothing like its American counterpart! It can be found near the other Asian sauces.

3
Carbohydrate Choices

Mushroom-Spinach Stroganoff

PREP TIME: 45 min • **START TO FINISH:** 45 min • 4 servings (1⅔ cups each)

1 SERVING: Calories 320 (Calories from Fat 110); Total Fat 12g (Saturated Fat 5g; Trans Fat 0g); Cholesterol 55mg; Sodium 430mg; Total Carbohydrate 42g (Dietary Fiber 3g; Sugars 9g); Protein 12g

% DAILY VALUE: Vitamin A 40%; Vitamin C 10%; Calcium 15%; Iron 15%

EXCHANGES: 2 Starch, 2½ Vegetable, 2 Fat

4   cups wide or dumpling egg noodles (8 oz)
3   tablespoons chopped fresh parsley
2   teaspoons olive oil
½   cup chopped onion (1 medium)
1   lb mixed fresh mushrooms (such as cremini, portabella and regular white), cut into ¼-inch slices
2   cloves garlic, finely chopped
2   tablespoons tomato paste
2   cups fresh spinach leaves
1   container (8 oz) reduced-fat sour cream
¾   cup fat-free (skim) milk
½   teaspoon salt
¼   teaspoon pepper

1   Cook noodles as directed on package; drain. Toss with 2 tablespoons of the parsley; place in serving dish. Cover to keep warm.

2   Meanwhile, in 10-inch skillet, heat oil over medium-high heat. Add onion and mushrooms; cook 10 minutes, stirring occasionally. Add garlic; cook 1 minute, stirring occasionally. Reduce heat to medium. Stir in tomato paste. Stir in spinach; cook 1 to 2 minutes or until spinach is wilted. Gently fold in sour cream, milk, salt and pepper. Cook just until hot, stirring constantly. Cover; remove from heat.

3   Pour onion-mushroom mixture over noodles. Sprinkle with remaining 1 tablespoon parsley.

Betty's Success Tip

Tomato paste is now available in a tube—a convenient way to use just a small amount, then store the rest of the tube, tightly covered, in the refrigerator for up to a year. If you use a can, freeze the rest of the tomato paste in 1-tablespoon portions. You can then add a frozen portion to a soup, stew or chili without thawing it first. Be sure to seal the tomato paste in an airtight container, label and date it.

Smashed Potato Stew

PREP TIME: 30 min • **START TO FINISH:** 30 min • 6 servings

2 Carbohydrate Choices

3½ cups fat-free (skim) milk

3 tablespoons all-purpose flour

1 tablespoon canola oil or butter

1 large onion, finely chopped (1 cup)

4 medium unpeeled potatoes (1½ lb), cut into ¼-inch pieces

1 teaspoon salt

¼ teaspoon black pepper

⅛ teaspoon ground red pepper (cayenne)

1½ cups shredded reduced-fat sharp Cheddar cheese (6 oz)

⅓ cup reduced-fat sour cream

8 medium green onions, sliced (½ cup)

1 Beat ½ cup of the milk and the flour with whisk until smooth; set aside. Heat oil in 4-quart Dutch oven over medium heat. Cook onion in oil about 2 minutes, stirring occasionally, until tender. Increase heat to high; stir in remaining 3 cups milk.

2 Stir in potatoes, salt, black pepper and red pepper. Heat to boiling; reduce heat. Simmer uncovered 15 to 16 minutes, stirring frequently, until potatoes are tender.

3 Beat in flour mixture with whisk. Cook about 2 minutes, stirring frequently, until thickened; remove from heat. Beat potato mixture with whisk until potatoes are slightly mashed. Stir in cheese, sour cream and green onions.

1 SERVING: Calories 250 (Calories from Fat 60); Total Fat 6g (Saturated Fat 2.5g; Trans Fat 0g); Cholesterol 15mg; Sodium 740mg; Total Carbohydrate 34g (Dietary Fiber 3g; Sugars 11g); Protein 15g

% DAILY VALUE: Vitamin A 10%; Vitamin C 10%; Calcium 40%; Iron 8%

EXCHANGES: 2 Starch, 1 Vegetable, 1 Medium-Fat Meat

Betty's Success Tip

This stew is so thick and creamy, you'll want to make it the star of your meal. At 2 carbohydrate choices, you could partner it with a slice of crusty French bread and a fresh garden salad for a delicious stick-to-your-ribs dinner.

2
Carbohydrate
Choices

Sweet Potato–Broccoli Soup

PREP TIME: 15 min • **START TO FINISH:** 45 min • 6 servings (1⅓ cups each)

1 SERVING: Calories 170 (Calories from Fat 40); Total Fat 4.5g (Saturated Fat 1.5g; Trans Fat 0g); Cholesterol 5mg; Sodium 590mg; Total Carbohydrate 29g (Dietary Fiber 4g; Sugars 13g); Protein 3g

% DAILY VALUE: Vitamin A 280%; Vitamin C 40%; Calcium 8%; Iron 6%

EXCHANGES: ½ Starch, 1 Other Carbohydrate, 1 Vegetable, 1 Fat

1 tablespoon olive oil

1 large onion, chopped (1 cup)

1 leek, cut in half lengthwise, rinsed, sliced thinly

3½ cups vegetable broth or reduced-sodium chicken broth

3 medium sweet potatoes, peeled, cut into 1-inch pieces (4 cups)

1 medium apple, peeled, cored, cut into 1-inch pieces

2 cups chopped fresh broccoli florets

1 tablespoon water

6 tablespoons reduced-fat sour cream

½ medium apple, cut into 12 thin slices

1 In 4-quart saucepan, heat oil over medium heat. Add onion and leek to oil; cook 4 minutes, stirring frequently, until soft. Stir in broth, sweet potatoes and apple pieces. Heat to boiling; reduce heat. Cover and simmer about 20 minutes or until sweet potatoes are tender.

2 Meanwhile, in small microwavable bowl, place broccoli and water. Cover with plastic wrap and microwave on High 1 minute 30 seconds or until crisp-tender; set aside.

3 In blender or food processor, place about one-third of soup mixture. Cover; blend on high speed until smooth, stopping blender to scrape side if necessary. Pour into large bowl. Repeat 2 times more with remaining soup mixture. Pour soup back into saucepan; stir in broccoli. Cover and heat over low heat about 10 minutes or until hot.

4 Divide soup evenly among 6 bowls. To serve, top each serving with 1 tablespoon sour cream and 2 apple slices.

Betty's Success Tip

Blending soups results in a wonderful consistency. Another way to puree soups is by using an immersion blender. The soup can be kept in its original pan; just make sure to keep the blender fully immersed to prevent the soup from splattering.

2½ Carbohydrate Choices

Italian Bean Soup with Greens

PREP TIME: 20 min • **START TO FINISH:** 1 hr 10 min • 8 servings (about 1⅓ cups each)

1 SERVING: Calories 270 (Calories from Fat 50); Total Fat 6g (Saturated Fat 2g, Trans Fat 0g); Cholesterol 0mg; Sodium 990mg; Total Carbohydrate 39g (Dietary Fiber 9g, Sugars 7g); Protein 15g

% DAILY VALUE: Vitamin A 100%; Vitamin C 20%; Calcium 25%; Iron 30%

EXCHANGES: 2 Starch, 1 Vegetable, 1 Medium-Fat Meat

2	tablespoons olive oil
2	medium carrots, peeled, sliced (1 cup)
1	large onion, chopped (1 cup)
1	stalk celery, chopped (⅓ cup)
2	cloves garlic, finely chopped
2	cans (15 to 15.5 oz each) great northern or cannellini (white kidney) beans, drained, rinsed
1	can (28 oz) diced tomatoes, undrained
2	teaspoons dried basil leaves
1	teaspoon dried oregano leaves
½	teaspoon salt
¼	teaspoon pepper
4	cups vegetable broth
4	cups packed fresh spinach leaves
½	cup shredded Parmesan cheese (2 oz)

1 In 5-quart Dutch oven or saucepan, heat oil over medium-high heat. Add carrots, onion, celery and garlic; cook about 5 minutes, stirring frequently, until onion is tender.

2 Stir in beans, tomatoes, basil, oregano, salt, pepper and broth. Cover; simmer 30 to 45 minutes or until vegetables are tender.

3 Increase heat to medium; stir in spinach. Cover; cook 3 to 5 minutes longer or until spinach is wilted. Ladle soup into bowls; top each with cheese.

Betty's Success Tip

Spinach will discolor if cooked in an aluminum saucepan and may also discolor the pan. For this recipe, use a Dutch oven or saucepan that is made of stainless steel, is porcelain covered, or made of other nonreactive material.

Mind and Body

A normal part of life, stress can be positive, such as getting ready for a vacation, or it can be negative, such as losing out on a promotion. Excess negative or ongoing stress may make it harder to control blood glucose levels. Fortunately, there are ways to manage stress and diabetes at the same time.

WHAT IS STRESS?

Stress is the body's response to the perception that you are somehow "under attack." That feeling may arise if you sense a threat to your physical or emotional well-being or your self-esteem. When the brain senses a threat, it signals the release of stress hormones that prepare the body for "fight or flight." These stress hormones release a burst of glucose that gives the body energy to deal with the threat at hand. This can cause your blood glucose levels to rise. Stress can also cause physical reactions that make it harder to fight infection and for cells to use insulin effectively.

HOW CAN STRESS BE PREVENTED?

When you become stressed or don't get enough sleep, you tax your immune system and can get sick. Prevent unnecessary physical or emotional stress by taking care of yourself. Here are some ways to de-stress:

- Get a good night's sleep, aiming for at least six to eight hours each night.

- Keep your individual self-management plan first and foremost. Follow your food plan and exercise regularly so you can better manage everyday physical and emotional stress.

- Plan your day and week so that you can control rushing around.

- Think positively to prevent the body's hormonal response to stress. Some people say to themselves, "I can handle this problem. It's not as bad as it seems at first glance."

- Go for a walk and talk things out with someone when you need extra support. Find a good friend, a support group or a counselor.

- Try yoga, the practice of balancing mind, body and spirit by deep breathing, stretching, strengthening and meditating; or progressive muscle relaxation, the process of tensing and relaxing muscle groups in a sequenced pattern. Both practices can help you relax.

- Enjoy a quiet moment of contemplation, mindfulness or meditation by closing your eyes, focusing on one thought, word, image or sound and allowing other thoughts to float away. Meditation can provide a sense of peacefulness and inner calm.

- Laugh out loud to keep your spirits up. Studies show that laughter has a calming effect. Having a smile on your face makes it easier to cope with stress.

2
Carbohydrate
Choices

Roasted Red Pepper Soup with Mozzarella

PREP TIME: 1 hr 10 min • **START TO FINISH:** 1 hr 10 min • 4 servings (1½ cups each)

1 SERVING: Calories 200 (Calories from Fat 50); Total Fat 6g (Saturated Fat 1.5g; Trans Fat 0g); Cholesterol 0mg; Sodium 620mg; Total Carbohydrate 29g (Dietary Fiber 6g; Sugars 13g); Protein 7g

% DAILY VALUE:
Vitamin A 90%; Vitamin C 160%; Calcium 10%; Iron 10%

EXCHANGES: 1½ Starch, 1½ Vegetable, 1 Fat

4	red bell peppers
1	tablespoon olive oil
2	large onions, chopped (2 cups)
3	cloves garlic, sliced
2	cups vegetable broth or reduced-sodium chicken broth
1	cup water
¼	teaspoon cracked black pepper
1	cup thinly sliced fresh basil leaves
½	yellow bell pepper, diced
8	small (cherry-size) mozzarella balls, quartered
4	slices crusty multigrain or whole wheat bread

1 Set oven control to broil. On rack in broiler pan, place red bell peppers. Broil with tops about 5 inches from heat for 10 to 15 minutes, turning occasionally, until skin is blistered and evenly browned. In large bowl, place roasted bell peppers; cover with plastic wrap. Let stand 15 minutes.

2 Meanwhile, in 4-quart saucepan, heat oil over medium-low heat. Add onions and garlic to oil. Cook 7 to 9 minutes, stirring occasionally, until onions begin to turn brown; remove from heat.

3 Remove skin, stems, seeds and membranes from roasted bell peppers; cut bell peppers into strips. Into onion mixture, stir bell pepper strips, broth, water and pepper. Heat to boiling; reduce heat. Simmer uncovered 10 minutes, stirring occasionally; stir in ½ cup of the basil.

4 In blender or food processor, place about one-third of the soup mixture. Cover; blend on high speed until smooth, stopping blender to scrape side if necessary. Pour into large bowl. Repeat 2 times more with remaining soup mixture.

5 Divide soup evenly among 4 bowls. To serve, top soup with diced yellow bell pepper and the mozzarella; sprinkle with remaining basil. Serve with bread.

Betty's Success Tip
If too much hot soup is added to the blender at one time, steam can build up during blending and cause the soup to pop out of the lid. It's easy to blend without problems if you do it in small batches with a towel held over the lid of blender. Take care when removing the lid, as the hot steam escapes.

4
Carbohydrate
Choices

Southwestern Bean Skillet

PREP TIME: 20 min • **START TO FINISH:** 20 min • 4 servings

1 SERVING: Calories 350 (Calories from Fat 50); Total Fat 5g (Saturated Fat 2g; Trans Fat 0g); Cholesterol 15mg; Sodium 500mg; Total Carbohydrate 57g (Dietary Fiber 18g; Sugars 5g); Protein 19g

% DAILY VALUE: Vitamin A 20%; Vitamin C 20%; Calcium 20%; Iron 25%

EXCHANGES: 3 Starch, 2½ Vegetable, ½ Very Lean Meat, ½ Fat

1 cup fresh corn kernels or frozen whole-kernel corn (from 12-oz bag)

2 tablespoons chopped fresh cilantro

1 small green bell pepper, chopped (½ cup)

1 small onion, chopped (¼ cup)

1 can (15 oz) chili beans in sauce, undrained

1 can (15 oz) black beans, drained, rinsed

½ cup shredded Cheddar-Jack with jalapeño chiles cheese blend (2 oz)

2 medium tomatoes, chopped (1½ cups)

1 In 12-inch skillet, mix all ingredients except cheese and tomatoes. Heat to boiling; reduce heat. Cover; simmer 5 minutes.

2 Uncover; simmer 5 to 10 minutes, stirring occasionally, until vegetables are tender. Add cheese and tomatoes; stir until cheese is melted.

Diabetes Team Tip Eating cheese is a tasty, satisfying way to get your calcium, a nutrient needed to maintain bone density. Good lower-fat choices are part-skim mozzarella and reduced-fat Cheddar cheese. —Diane Reader, Dietitian

Betty's Success Tip Keep with the Southwest-flavor theme by serving this meatless skillet meal with warmed tortillas or tortilla chips and sliced avocados and tomatoes.

Smoky Brown Rice–Stuffed Peppers

PREP TIME: 25 min • **START TO FINISH:** 1 hr 10 min • 6 servings

2 Carbohydrate Choices

½ cup uncooked brown rice

1⅓ cups water

1 teaspoon butter, if desired

6 large red or green bell peppers

2 tablespoons olive oil

1 medium onion, chopped (⅓ cup)

1 clove garlic, chopped

1 package (12 oz) frozen sausage-style soy-protein crumbles

1 can (14.5 oz) diced tomatoes, undrained

1 teaspoon dried basil leaves

½ teaspoon dried oregano leaves

½ teaspoon pepper

4 oz smoked Gouda cheese, shredded (1 cup)

1 Heat oven to 375°F. Spray 11×7-inch (2-quart) glass baking dish with cooking spray.

2 In 2-quart saucepan, mix rice, water and butter. Heat to boiling over medium-high heat. Reduce heat to medium-low; cover and simmer about 30 minutes or until water is absorbed.

3 Meanwhile, cut off top of each bell pepper, slicing evenly across top of pepper; remove seeds. If peppers will not sit upright, slice very thin strip off bottom but do not cut through. Arrange peppers, cut side up, in baking dish. Cut pepper flesh off pepper tops; chop. Discard stems.

4 In 10-inch skillet, heat oil over medium-high heat. Add onion, garlic and chopped pepper; cook 5 minutes, stirring frequently, until onion is tender. Stir in soy-protein crumbles, cooked rice, tomatoes, basil, oregano and pepper. Cook 5 to 7 minutes, stirring frequently, until hot. Remove from heat; stir in ½ cup of the cheese.

5 Spoon about 1 cup filling into each pepper shell, pressing very lightly with back of spoon.

6 Bake uncovered 35 to 40 minutes or until filling is hot and peppers are crisp-tender. Sprinkle remaining ½ cup cheese on top of peppers. Bake uncovered about 5 minutes longer or until cheese is melted.

Betty's Success Tip

Use either red or green bell peppers for this recipe, or choose both colors for an attractive presentation.

1 SERVING: Calories 320 (Calories from Fat 100); Total Fat 11g (Saturated Fat 4g; Trans Fat 0g); Cholesterol 20mg; Sodium 590mg; Total Carbohydrate 33g (Dietary Fiber 9g; Sugars 10g); Protein 21g

% DAILY VALUE: Vitamin A 110%; Vitamin C 190%; Calcium 25%; Iron 20%

EXCHANGES: 2 Starch, 1 Vegetable, 2 Lean Meat, ½ Fat

3½
Carbohydrate
Choices

Curried Lentils with Rice

PREP TIME: 20 min • **START TO FINISH:** 45 min • 4 servings (1¼ cups each)

1 SERVING: Calories 410 (Calories from Fat 120); Total Fat 13g (Saturated Fat 2.5g; Trans Fat 0g); Cholesterol 5mg; Sodium 430mg; Total Carbohydrate 54g (Dietary Fiber 11g; Sugars 5g); Protein 18g

% DAILY VALUE: Vitamin A 110%; Vitamin C 20%; Calcium 10%; Iron 30%

EXCHANGES: 3 Starch, 1½ Vegetable, 1 Lean Meat, 1½ Fat

1	tablespoon canola oil
1	cup coarsely chopped cauliflower
1	cup shredded carrots
1	large onion, chopped (1 cup)
2	teaspoons curry powder
2½	cups water
¾	cup dried red lentils, sorted, rinsed
½	cup uncooked long-grain rice
½	teaspoon salt
1	cup frozen shelled edamame (green soybeans)
2	teaspoons butter
¼	cup chopped dry-roasted peanuts

1 In 12-inch nonstick skillet, heat oil over medium-high heat. Add cauliflower, carrots and onion. Cook about 3 minutes, stirring occasionally, until softened. Stir in curry powder; cook and stir 1 minute.

2 Add water; heat to boiling. Stir in lentils, rice and salt; return to boiling. Reduce heat; cover and simmer 12 to 15 minutes or until lentils and rice are almost tender.

3 Stir in edamame; cook uncovered 5 to 10 minutes or until liquid is absorbed and lentils and rice are tender. Gently stir in butter until melted. Just before serving, sprinkle with peanuts.

Betty's Success Tip

Red lentils are reddish orange in color. While they are also known as European lentils, they are especially popular in Middle Eastern and Indian cooking. Look for these lentils in larger supermarkets or in those that specialize in Mideastern or Asian cuisines.

The Great Greek Sandwiches

PREP TIME: 25 min • **START TO FINISH:** 25 min • 4 sandwiches

2½ Carbohydrate Choices

4 slices eggplant,
  3 inches in diameter and
  ½ inch thick

2 teaspoons olive oil

⅛ teaspoon salt

4 ciabatta rolls (about
  3 inches in diameter),
  split

4 slices provolone cheese

4 thin slices red onion

4 slices tomato

4 teaspoons fat-free Greek
  vinaigrette dressing

¼ cup sliced kalamata olives

½ cup packed fresh spinach
  leaves

1 Heat gas or charcoal grill. Brush both sides of eggplant slices with oil; sprinkle with salt. Place on grill over medium heat. Cover grill; cook 8 to 10 minutes, turning once, until tender. During last minute of cooking, add rolls to grill, cut side down; cook about 1 minute or until toasted.

2 Place eggplant slices on bottom halves of buns. Top each with cheese, onion, tomato, dressing, olives and spinach. Cover with top halves of buns.

1 SANDWICH: Calories 310 (Calories from Fat 110); Total Fat 13g (Saturated Fat 5g; Trans Fat 0g); Cholesterol 20mg; Sodium 780mg; Total Carbohydrate 36g (Dietary Fiber 2g; Sugars 4g); Protein 12g

% DAILY VALUE: Vitamin A 15%; Vitamin C 10%; Calcium 25%; Iron 15%

EXCHANGES: 2 Starch, 1 Vegetable, ½ Medium-Fat Meat, 2 Fat

Betty's Success Tip

If your store offers only large ciabatta rolls, look for smaller take-and-bake ciabatta rolls in the bakery section of your supermarket.

3½
Carbohydrate Choices

Lentil-Corn Burgers

PREP TIME: 55 min • **START TO FINISH:** 1 hr 10 min • 6 burgers

1 BURGER: Calories 370 (Calories from Fat 80); Total Fat 9g (Saturated Fat 1.5g; Trans Fat 0g); Cholesterol 40mg; Sodium 630mg; Total Carbohydrate 55g (Dietary Fiber 10g; Sugars 9g); Protein 18g

% DAILY VALUE: Vitamin A 10%; Vitamin C 4%; Calcium 10%; Iron 30%

EXCHANGES: 3½ Starch, ½ Vegetable, 1 Very Lean Meat, 1 Fat

1½	cups water
1	cup dried brown lentils (8 oz), sorted, rinsed
¼	teaspoon salt
¾	cup unseasoned bread crumbs
2	teaspoons salt-free southwestern chipotle seasoning
1	can (11 oz) vacuum-packed whole-kernel corn with red and green peppers, drained
2	eggs, slightly beaten
1	tablespoon canola oil
6	lettuce leaves
6	round 100% whole wheat thin sandwich rolls (4 inch)
3	tablespoons light mayonnaise
6	tomato slices
6	thin onion slices

1 In 2-quart saucepan, heat water, lentils and salt to boiling. Reduce heat; cover and simmer 12 to 15 minutes, stirring occasionally, until lentils are tender yet hold their shape; drain. Spoon into large bowl; cool 15 minutes.

2 Into cooled lentils, lightly stir bread crumbs, seasoning, corn, and eggs. Form mixture into 6 patties about ½ inch thick and 3½ to 4 inches in diameter; place on platter or cookie sheet. Refrigerate 30 minutes (patties will firm up, making them easier to cook without falling apart).

3 In 12-inch nonstick skillet, heat 1½ teaspoons oil over medium heat. Cook 3 patties 6 to 8 minutes, turning halfway through cooking, until golden brown. Transfer from skillet to heatproof platter; cover and keep warm. Repeat with remaining 1½ teaspoons oil and patties.

4 Place lettuce leaf on bottom half of each roll; top with cooked patty. Spread each with 1½ teaspoons mayonnaise over patty; top with 1 slice tomato, 1 slice onion, and roll top.

Diabetes Team Tip
To reduce fat, calories and cholesterol, eat meatless meals often; aim for one or two times per week. Continue to count carbohydrates, as meatless meals often provide more carbohydrates than meat-based meals. —Diane Reader, Dietitian

Betty's Success Tip
If you can't find salt-free southwestern chipotle seasoning, substitute 1½ teaspoons salt-free Mexican seasoning and ½ teaspoon chipotle seasoning instead.

2½
Carbohydrate
Choices

Asian Sloppy Joes

PREP TIME: 15 min • **START TO FINISH:** 15 min • 6 sandwiches

1 SANDWICH:
Calories 290 (Calories
from Fat 45); Total
Fat 4.5g (Saturated
Fat 0.5g; Trans Fat
0g); Cholesterol 0mg;
Sodium 940mg; Total
Carbohydrate 40g
(Dietary Fiber 7g; Sugars
13g); Protein 21g

% DAILY VALUE:
Vitamin A 0%; Vitamin C
6%; Calcium 15%;
Iron 20%

EXCHANGES: 1½ Starch,
1 Other Carbohydrate,
2½ Very Lean Meat, ½ Fat

1	tablespoon canola oil
¼	cup chopped onion
¼	cup chopped green bell pepper
1	tablespoon finely chopped gingerroot
1	package (12 oz) frozen soy-protein crumbles
½	cup barbecue sauce
2	tablespoons reduced-sodium soy sauce
6	whole wheat burger buns, split

1 In 10-inch skillet, heat oil over medium heat.
Add onion, bell pepper and gingerroot; cook 3 to
4 minutes or until onion is softened.

2 Stir in soy-protein crumbles, barbecue sauce and soy
sauce. Heat to boiling. Reduce heat to low; simmer
uncovered about 2 minutes or until thoroughly
heated.

3 Spoon about ⅓ cup mixture into each bun.

**Betty's
Success
Tip**

Soy-protein crumbles come both
frozen and refrigerated. When
frozen, the crumbles do not
require thawing.

Falafel Sandwiches with Yogurt Sauce

PREP TIME: 1 hr • **START TO FINISH:** 1 hr • 8 sandwiches

2½ Carbohydrate Choices

SANDWICHES

¾ cup plus 3 tablespoons water

¼ cup uncooked bulgur

1 can (15 oz) chickpeas (garbanzo beans), drained, rinsed

¼ cup chopped fresh cilantro

¼ cup sliced green onions (4 medium)

1 tablespoon all-purpose flour

2 teaspoons ground cumin

¾ teaspoon baking powder

½ teaspoon salt

2 cloves garlic, finely chopped

2 tablespoons canola oil

4 pita (pocket) breads (6 inch), cut in half to form pockets

8 slices tomato

16 slices cucumber

SAUCE

1 cup plain fat-free yogurt

2 tablespoons chopped fresh mint leaves

¼ teaspoon ground cumin

1 In 1-quart saucepan, heat ¾ cup water to boiling. Stir in bulgur. Remove from heat; cover and let stand about 30 minutes or until tender. Drain; set aside.

2 Meanwhile, in food processor, place beans, cilantro, onions, flour, 3 tablespoons water, the cumin, baking powder, salt and garlic. Cover; process with on/off pulses 10 times or until well blended and coarsely chopped (mixture will be wet). Spoon mixture into large bowl.

3 Stir bulgur into bean mixture. Divide mixture into 8 equal portions, about ¼ cup each; shape each portion into ¼-inch-thick oval patty.

4 In 10-inch nonstick skillet, heat 1 tablespoon of the oil over medium heat. Place 4 patties in skillet; cook 8 minutes, turning once, until golden brown. Transfer patties to platter; cover with foil to keep warm. Repeat with remaining tablespoon oil and 4 patties.

5 Meanwhile, in small bowl, stir together sauce ingredients. Spread 2 tablespoons sauce in each pita pocket. Fill each with 1 tomato slice, 2 cucumber slices and falafel patty.

1 SANDWICH: Calories 240 (Calories from Fat 50); Total Fat 5g (Saturated Fat 1g; Trans Fat 0g); Cholesterol 0mg; Sodium 370mg; Total Carbohydrate 39g (Dietary Fiber 5g; Sugars 3g); Protein 10g

% DAILY VALUE: Vitamin A 6%; Vitamin C 4%; Calcium 15%; Iron 15%

EXCHANGES: 2½ Starch, ½ Vegetable, ½ Fat

Betty's Success Tip

Patties can be baked at 400°F for 20 minutes on a greased cookie sheet, turning once, but they won't have the crisp crust that comes from cooking on the stovetop.

3½ Carbohydrate Choices

Chipotle and Black Bean Burritos

PREP TIME: 20 min • START TO FINISH: 20 min • 4 burritos

1 BURRITO: Calories 370 (Calories from Fat 100); Total Fat 11g (Saturated Fat 2g; Trans Fat 0g); Cholesterol 10mg; Sodium 310mg; Total Carbohydrate 51g (Dietary Fiber 13g; Sugars 3g); Protein 16g

% DAILY VALUE: Vitamin A 10%; Vitamin C 10%; Calcium 20%; Iron 20%

EXCHANGES: 3 Starch, 1 Vegetable, ½ Lean Meat, 1½ Fat

2 tablespoons canola oil

1 large onion, chopped (1 cup)

6 cloves garlic, finely chopped

1 can (15 oz) black beans, drained, rinsed and mashed

1 to 2 teaspoons finely chopped drained chipotle chiles in adobo sauce (from 7-oz can)

4 fat-free flour tortillas for burritos (8 inch)

½ cup shredded reduced-fat mozzarella cheese (2 oz)

1 large tomato, chopped (1 cup)

Chunky-style salsa, if desired

Sour cream, if desired

1 In 10-inch nonstick skillet, heat oil over medium-high heat. Add onion and garlic; cook 6 to 8 minutes, stirring occasionally, until onion is tender. Stir in beans and chiles. Cook, stirring frequently, until hot.

2 Place one-fourth of the bean mixture on center of each tortilla. Top with cheese and tomato.

3 Fold one end of each tortilla up about 1 inch over filling; fold right and left sides over folded end, overlapping. Fold remaining end down. Place seam side down on serving platter or plate. Serve with salsa and sour cream.

Diabetes Team Tip A small increase in physical activity can have a big effect on your diabetes and your general health. It can help lower glucose levels and create a feeling of well being. —Dr. Bergenstal

Betty's Success Tip Chipotle chiles are dried, smoked jalapeño chiles and have a smoky, sweet flavor. They are available canned in adobo sauce, which is a spicy tomato-based sauce or dried and sold in cellophane bags.

Italian Veggie Sliders

PREP TIME: 45 min • **START TO FINISH:** 45 min • 6 servings (2 sandwiches each)

3 Carbohydrate Choices

1½ cups water

½ cup dried red lentils, sorted, rinsed

½ cup uncooked instant brown rice

¾ teaspoon salt

2 tablespoons olive or canola oil

½ cup chopped onion (1 medium)

½ cup finely chopped mushrooms

½ cup chopped red bell pepper

2 cloves garlic, finely chopped

¼ cup finely shredded Parmesan cheese

¼ cup plain bread crumbs

1 teaspoon Italian seasoning

½ teaspoon pepper

1 egg, slightly beaten

12 mini burger buns (about 2½ inches in diameter), split

¼ cup reduced-fat garlic and herb mayonnaise or garlic aioli

⅓ cup packed baby spinach leaves

1 In 2-quart saucepan, heat water, lentils, rice and salt to boiling. Reduce heat; cover and simmer 12 to 15 minutes, stirring occasionally, until lentils are tender but hold their shape and all water is absorbed. Spoon into large bowl; cool 15 minutes.

2 Meanwhile, in 10-inch nonstick skillet, heat 2 teaspoons of the oil over medium heat. Stir in onion, mushrooms, bell pepper and garlic; cook and stir 3 to 4 minutes or until vegetables are tender.

3 Add onion mixture to lentils and rice. Stir in cheese, bread crumbs, Italian seasoning, pepper and egg just until blended.

4 Wipe skillet clean with paper towel. In same skillet, heat 2 teaspoons of the oil over medium heat. Shape lentil mixture into 6 (2½-inch) patties, using about 2 rounded tablespoonfuls for each; place in skillet. Cook 6 to 8 minutes, turning once, until golden brown. Repeat with remaining 2 teaspoons oil and the lentil mixture, making 6 more patties.

5 Place patties on bottom halves of buns. Top each with 1 teaspoon mayonnaise and a few spinach leaves. Cover with top halves of buns.

1 SERVING: Calories 370 (Calories from Fat 110); Total Fat 13g (Saturated Fat 2.5g; Trans Fat 0g); Cholesterol 40mg; Sodium 650mg; Total Carbohydrate 49g (Dietary Fiber 6g; Sugars 5g); Protein 14g

% DAILY VALUE: Vitamin A 15%; Vitamin C 15%; Calcium 15%; Iron 20%

EXCHANGES: 3 Starch, ½ Vegetable, ½ Lean Meat, 2 Fat

Betty's Success Tip

If the lentil mixture is sticky, coat your hands with additional bread crumbs when shaping the patties.

2
Carbohydrate Choices

Veggie-Tofu Pizza

PREP TIME: 20 min • **START TO FINISH:** 1 hr 5 min • 6 servings

1 SERVING: Calories 300 (Calories from Fat 120); Total Fat 13g (Saturated Fat 4g; Trans Fat 0g); Cholesterol 10mg; Sodium 470mg; Total Carbohydrate 32g (Dietary Fiber 3g; Sugars 6g); Protein 13g

% DAILY VALUE:
Vitamin A 10%; Vitamin C 25%; Calcium 25%; Iron 15%

EXCHANGES: 2 Starch, ½ Vegetable, 1 Lean Meat, 2 Fat

8	oz firm tofu (from 14-oz package), cut into ½-inch cubes (1½ cups)
1	cup sliced fresh mushrooms
2	tablespoons red wine vinegar
1	tablespoon olive oil
2	teaspoons dried Italian seasoning
1	can (11 oz) refrigerated thin pizza crust
½	cup pizza sauce
½	cup sun-dried tomatoes in oil, drained, cut into small pieces
1	red bell pepper, thinly sliced
1	small onion, thinly sliced
1	tablespoon chopped fresh basil leaves
1	cup shredded reduced-fat mozzarella cheese (4 oz)

1 In medium bowl, stir tofu, mushrooms, vinegar, oil and Italian seasoning. Cover and refrigerate at least 30 minutes.

2 Meanwhile, move oven rack to lowest position. Heat oven to 375°F. Spray 15×10×1-inch pan with cooking spray. Unroll dough in pan. Bake about 10 minutes or just until edges are light golden brown.

3 Spread pizza sauce over crust. Drain marinade from tofu and mushrooms, discarding marinade. Top sauce with tofu, mushrooms, tomatoes, bell pepper, onion and basil.

4 Bake 10 minutes; sprinkle cheese over pizza. Bake about 10 minutes longer or until cheese is melted and crust is deep golden brown.

Diabetes Team Tip When picking out your pizza crust, think thin. The thicker crust type is much higher in carbohydrates per serving. —Diane Reader, Dietitian

Betty's Success Tip Firm and extra-firm tofu hold their shape while cooking and are an ideal choice for stir-frying and grilling. Soft tofu is used in Asian soups and can also be blended into foods. Silken tofu is creamy and can be used for making dips and spreads.

1½ Carbohydrate Choices

Homemade Veggie Pizza

PREP TIME: 15 min • **START TO FINISH:** 45 min • 8 servings

1 SERVING: Calories 190 (Calories from Fat 70); Total Fat 8g (Saturated Fat 3g, Trans Fat 0g); Cholesterol 10mg; Sodium 410mg; Total Carbohydrate 21g (Dietary Fiber 1g, Sugars 3g); Protein 10g

% DAILY VALUE: Vitamin A 15%; Vitamin C 20%; Calcium 25%; Iron 10%

EXCHANGES: 1½ Starch, ½ Lean Meat, 1 Fat

CRUST

1⅓	cups all-purpose flour
1	teaspoon baking powder
½	teaspoon salt
½	cup fat-free (skim) milk
2	tablespoons olive oil

TOPPING

1½	cups shredded reduced-fat mozzarella cheese (6 oz)
1	can (14.5 oz) diced tomatoes, drained
1	cup fresh baby spinach leaves, coarsely chopped
1	cup yellow or green bell pepper strips
¼	teaspoon dried oregano leaves
¼	teaspoon garlic powder
⅛	teaspoon pepper
2	tablespoons freshly shredded Parmesan cheese

1 Heat oven to 400°F. In medium bowl, mix flour, baking powder and salt. Stir in milk and oil until soft dough forms. (If dough is dry, stir in 1 to 2 tablespoons additional milk.) On lightly floured surface, knead dough 10 times. Shape dough into ball. Cover with bowl; let rest 10 minutes.

2 Place dough on ungreased cookie sheet; flatten slightly. Roll out to 12-inch round. Bake 8 minutes.

3 Sprinkle mozzarella cheese over crust; top with remaining topping ingredients. Bake 15 to 20 minutes longer or until crust is light golden brown and cheese begins to brown. Cut into wedges.

Betty's Success Tip

Once you've made this easy pizza crust, you'll make it again and again. Vary the veggies on top to suit your taste--sliced ripe olives, sliced mushrooms and green onions are all great toppers for pizza.

Activity Just Feels Good

Studies show that moderate physical activity helps control diabetes and even reduces the risk of developing diabetes by more than half! If you have diabetes, 30 to 60 minutes of physical activity each day will lower your blood glucose levels. Check it out with this simple exercise: Measure your blood glucose with a meter, then walk briskly for 20 minutes. Recheck your blood glucose; chances are good that it has dropped 30 to 50 points (mg/dL).

Try it! Seeing a nice drop in your blood glucose may motivate you to exercise.

Even short periods of moderate aerobic exercise over the course of the day can improve your health. If you spend close to 30 minutes being physically active on most days, you're already exercising! Regular and consistent activity helps your body use insulin more effectively, not just after exercise but all day. Best of all, you'll feel great!

COUNTDOWN TO A GREAT WORKOUT

You're more likely to continue exercising if you choose an activity you like. To enjoy a great workout:

- See your doctor for an evaluation before you begin exercising. Your doctor may ask you to do a treadmill or cardiac stress test to determine how vigorously you can work out. Stretching is great for flexibility, and mild weight training increases strength (and also lowers blood glucose).

- Buy supportive shoes and cotton socks. Examine your feet after exercising for calluses or blisters that indicate an improper fit.

- Measure your blood glucose level before and after exercise if you take insulin, and carry a carbohydrate snack with you in case your blood glucose level gets too low.

- Get a step counter and set your daily goal; 10,000 steps equals 5 miles!

- Find an activity you like and stick with it. Whether it's walking, swimming, yoga or playing a team sport, every activity counts. Can't pick a favorite? Even better. Combine a number of different activities to keep active just about every day of the week.

- Aim for at least 30 minutes of activity on most days. You can portion your exercise throughout the day if that's easier for your schedule. Remember, every little bit helps!

CHAPTER 5

Great Grains, Legumes and Pasta

3 Carbohydrate Choices

Brown Rice–Stuffed Butternut Squash

PREP TIME: 30 min • **START TO FINISH:** 1 hr 10 min • 4 servings

1 SERVING: Calories 350 (Calories from Fat 90); Total Fat 10g (Saturated Fat 2g; Trans Fat 0g); Cholesterol 35mg; Sodium 670mg; Total Carbohydrate 50g (Dietary Fiber 5g; Sugars 14g); Protein 14g

% DAILY VALUE:
Vitamin A 750%; Vitamin C 45%; Calcium 15%; Iron 20%

EXCHANGES: 3 Starch, 1 Vegetable, 2 Fat

2	small butternut squash (about 2 lb each)
4	teaspoons olive oil
¼	teaspoon salt
½	teaspoon freshly ground pepper
⅓	cup uncooked brown basmati rice
1¼	cups reduced-sodium chicken broth
1	thyme sprig
1	bay leaf
2	links (3 oz each) sweet Italian turkey sausage, casings removed
1	small onion, chopped (⅓ cup)
1	cup sliced cremini mushrooms
1	cup fresh baby spinach leaves
1	teaspoon chopped fresh or ¼ teaspoon dried sage leaves

1 Heat oven to 375°F. Cut each squash lengthwise in half; remove seeds and fibers. Drizzle cut sides with 3 teaspoons of the olive oil; sprinkle with salt and pepper. On cookie sheet, place squash, cut side down. Bake 35 to 40 minutes, until squash is tender at thickest portion when pierced with fork. When cool enough to handle, cut off long ends of squash to within ½ inch edge of cavities (peel and refrigerate ends for another use).

2 Meanwhile, in 1-quart saucepan, heat remaining 1 teaspoon oil over medium heat. Add rice to oil, stirring well to coat. Stir in chicken broth, thyme and bay leaf. Heat to boiling; reduce heat. Cover and simmer 30 to 35 minutes, until all liquid is absorbed and rice is tender. Remove from heat; discard thyme sprig and bay leaf.

3 In 10-inch nonstick skillet, cook sausage and onion over medium-high heat 8 to 10 minutes, stirring frequently, until sausage is thoroughly cooked. Add mushrooms. Cook 4 minutes or until mushrooms are tender. Stir in cooked rice, spinach and sage; cook about 3 minutes or until spinach is wilted and mixture is hot. Divide sausage-rice mixture between squash halves, pressing down on filling so it forms a slight mound over cavity.

Betty's Success Tip
Depending on the size squash you start with for this recipe, you'll have about 4½ cups cubed or 3 cups mashed squash left over. Freeze leftover cooked squash in freezer containers or resealable freezer plastic bags for up to 1 year.

2
Carbohydrate
Choices

Coconut-Ginger Rice

PREP TIME: 10 min • **START TO FINISH:** 25 min • 8 servings

1 SERVING: Calories 150 (Calories from Fat 20); Total Fat 2g (Saturated Fat 1.5g; Trans Fat 0g); Cholesterol 0mg; Sodium 340mg; Total Carbohydrate 30g (Dietary Fiber 0g; Sugars 1g); Protein 3g

% DAILY VALUE: Vitamin A 0%; Vitamin C 2%; Calcium 2%; Iron 8%

EXCHANGES: 1 Starch, 1 Other Carbohydrate, ½ Fat

2½ cups reduced-sodium chicken broth

⅔ cup reduced-fat (lite) coconut milk (not cream of coconut)

1 tablespoon grated gingerroot

½ teaspoon salt

1⅓ cups uncooked regular long-grain white rice

1 teaspoon grated lime peel

3 medium green onions, chopped (3 tablespoons)

3 tablespoons flaked coconut, toasted*

Lime slices

1 In 3-quart saucepan, heat broth, coconut milk, gingerroot and salt to boiling over medium-high heat. Stir in rice. Return to boiling. Reduce heat; cover and simmer about 15 minutes or until rice is tender and liquid is absorbed. Remove from heat.

2 Add lime peel and onions; fluff rice mixture lightly with fork to mix. Garnish with coconut and lime slices.

*To toast coconut, spread evenly on ungreased cookie sheet and bake at 350°F for 5 to 7 minutes, stirring occasionally, until golden brown.

Diabetes Team Tip
Choosing low-fat foods if you are trying to lose weight is a good rule to follow. Don't forget to balance your healthy eating habits with 30 to 60 minutes of aerobic exercise at least five times per week.
—Dr. Bergenstal

Betty's Success Tip
If you don't use fresh gingerroot quickly, tightly wrap and freeze it, unpeeled, up to 6 months. To use frozen gingerroot, slice off a piece and return the rest to the freezer.

Farmers' Market Barley Risotto

PREP TIME: 1 hr 15 min • **START TO FINISH:** 1 hr 15 min • 4 servings (1½ cups each)

3½
Carbohydrate
Choices

1 tablespoon olive oil

1 medium onion, chopped (½ cup)

1 medium bell pepper, coarsely chopped (1 cup)

2 cups chopped fresh mushrooms (4 oz)

1 cup frozen whole-kernel corn

1 cup uncooked medium pearled barley

¼ cup dry white wine or chicken broth

2 cups reduced-sodium chicken broth

3 cups water

1½ cups grape tomatoes, cut in half (if large, cut into quarters)

⅔ cup shredded Parmesan cheese

3 tablespoons chopped fresh or 1 teaspoon dried basil leaves

½ teaspoon pepper

1 In 4-quart Dutch oven or saucepan, heat oil over medium heat. Cook onion, bell pepper, mushrooms and corn in oil about 5 minutes, stirring frequently, until onion is crisp-tender. Add barley, stirring about 1 minute to coat.

2 Stir in wine and ½ cup of the broth. Cook 5 minutes, stirring frequently, until liquid is almost absorbed. Repeat with remaining broth and 3 cups water, adding ½ to ¾ cup of broth or water at a time and stirring frequently, until absorbed.

3 Stir in tomatoes, ¼ cup of the cheese, the basil and pepper. Cook until thoroughly heated. Sprinkle with remaining ¼ cup cheese.

Betty's Success Tip
Cooking grains in broth adds to the overall flavor of the dish. You can also cook grains, like the barley in this recipe, in apple juice or vegetable juice for added flavor.

Diabetes Team Tip
Risotto is traditionally made by stirring small amounts of broth into rice throughout the cook time to get the chewy texture. This recipe uses barley instead of rice. Barley is high in soluble fiber and may have the same cholesterol-lowering properties as oats. —Diane Reader, Dietitian

1 SERVING: Calories 370 (Calories from Fat 70); Total Fat 8g (Saturated Fat 3g; Trans Fat 0g); Cholesterol 10mg; Sodium 520mg; Total Carbohydrate 55g (Dietary Fiber 11g; Sugars 6g); Protein 15g

% DAILY VALUE: Vitamin A 20%; Vitamin C 35%; Calcium 20%; Iron 15%

EXCHANGES: 3 Starch, 2 Vegetable, 1½ Fat

½
Carbohydrate
Choice

Thai Beef Noodle Bowls

PREP TIME: 50 min • **START TO FINISH:** 50 min • 6 servings (about 1⅔ cups each)

1 SERVING: Calories 170 (Calories from Fat 50); Total Fat 5g (Saturated Fat 1g; Trans Fat 0g); Cholesterol 50mg; Sodium 590mg; Total Carbohydrate 7g (Dietary Fiber 2g; Sugars 2g); Protein 22g

% DAILY VALUE: Vitamin A 4%; Vitamin C 10%; Calcium 8%; Iron 15%

EXCHANGES: 1½ Vegetable, 1 Very Lean Meat, 1½ Lean Meat

1	tablespoon canola oil
1	lb beef top sirloin steak, thinly sliced across grain
½	teaspoon freshly ground pepper
¼	teaspoon salt
1	medium onion, thinly sliced (1 cup)
2	tablespoons finely chopped gingerroot
2	jalapeño chiles, seeded, chopped
2	large cloves garlic, finely chopped
3	cups water
3	cups reduced-sodium chicken broth
2	tablespoons reduced-sodium soy sauce
1½	cups thinly sliced Chinese (napa) cabbage
1	package (8 oz) tofu shirataki noodles, spaghetti style, drained, rinsed well
6	fresh mint leaves
2	tablespoons chopped fresh cilantro
6	tablespoons thinly sliced green onions (5 to 6 medium)
1	lime, cut into 6 pieces

1 In 5-quart Dutch oven or saucepan, heat oil over medium-high heat. Sprinkle beef with pepper and salt. Cook beef in oil, stirring occasionally, until brown on all sides. Using slotted spoon, transfer from pan to bowl (leave juices in pan). Cover and keep warm.

2 Reduce heat to medium. Add onion, gingerroot and chiles. Cook 5 to 7 minutes, stirring occasionally, until onion is tender. Add garlic; cook 1 minute, scraping up any beef bits on bottom of pan. Add water, chicken broth and soy sauce; heat to boiling. Add cabbage and noodles, stirring well to separate noodles. Add beef; cook uncovered, stirring occasionally, until heated through. Top each serving with 1 mint leaf, 1 teaspoon cilantro, 1 tablespoon onions and 1 piece lime.

Diabetes Team Tip A person with diabetes can drink alcohol in moderation. Alcohol temporarily lowers blood glucose however, so it's best to have just one glass of wine and have it with your meal. —Dr. Bergenstal

Betty's Success Tip Peeling fresh gingerroot requires nothing more than a cereal spoon. Use the inside of a spoon to scrape away thin skin, then thinly slice and mince.

3½
Carbohydrate Choices

African Squash and Chickpea Stew

PREP TIME: 30 min • **START TO FINISH:** 45 min • 4 servings (about 1¾ cups each)

1 SERVING: Calories 390 (Calories from Fat 110); Total Fat 13g (Saturated Fat 2g; Trans Fat 0g); Cholesterol 0mg; Sodium 650mg; Total Carbohydrate 54g (Dietary Fiber 12g; Sugars 11g); Protein 15g

% DAILY VALUE: Vitamin A 150%; Vitamin C 30%; Calcium 20%; Iron 35%

EXCHANGES: 2 Starch, ½ Other Carbohydrate, 3½ Vegetable, 2½ Fat

4	teaspoons olive oil
2	large onions, chopped (2 cups)
1	teaspoon ground coriander
1½	teaspoons ground cumin
½	teaspoon ground cinnamon
½	teaspoon ground turmeric
¼	teaspoon salt
¼	teaspoon ground red pepper (cayenne)
2	cups butternut squash, peeled, seeded, cut into 1-inch cubes
2	cups vegetable broth
1	can (14.5 oz) low-sodium diced tomatoes, undrained
1	can (15 oz) chickpeas (garbanzo beans), drained, rinsed
1½	cups thinly sliced okra
½	cup chopped fresh cilantro leaves
⅓	cup raw unsalted hulled pumpkin seeds (pepitas), toasted*

1 In 5-quart Dutch oven or saucepan, heat 3 teaspoons of the oil over medium heat. Add onions to oil; cook 10 minutes, stirring occasionally, until golden brown. Add all spices; stir until onions are well coated. Cook about 3 minutes, stirring frequently, until glazed and deep golden brown. Stir in squash; coat well with seasoned mixture. Stir in broth, tomatoes and chickpeas. Heat stew to boiling; reduce heat. Cover and simmer about 15 minutes or until squash is tender.

2 Meanwhile, in 8-inch skillet, heat remaining 1 teaspoon oil over medium-high heat; add okra to oil. Cook 3 to 5 minutes, stirring frequently, until tender and edges are golden brown; stir into stew.

3 Divide stew evenly among 4 bowls. For each serving, top stew with 2 tablespoons chopped cilantro and generous 1 tablespoon pumpkin seeds.

*To toast pumpkin seeds, in 8-inch skillet, heat pumpkin seeds over medium heat 3 to 5 minutes, stirring occasionally, until seeds are light brown. (Watch carefully; they can burn quickly.)

Diabetes Team Tip
Boost your fiber with beans. Filled with many other important nutrients, beans are an excellent source of fiber that's so important for good blood glucose management and to keep your digestive system moving. —Diane Reader, Dietitian

Betty's Success Tip
Okra is a common vegetable found in African cuisine available in grocery stores year-round and it's a great thickener. For the best texture and flavor, sauté it as we do in this recipe before adding to the stew. Choose fresh okra that is dry and firm.

2½
Carbohydrate
Choices

Sage and Garlic Vegetable Bake

PREP TIME: 30 min · **START TO FINISH:** 1 hr 45 min · 6 servings (1½ cups each)

1 SERVING: Calories 170 (Calories from Fat 0); Total Fat 0g (Saturated Fat 0g; Trans Fat 0g); Cholesterol 0mg; Sodium 410mg; Total Carbohydrate 37g (Dietary Fiber 8g; Sugars 9g); Protein 4g

% DAILY VALUE:
Vitamin A 150%; Vitamin C 30%; Calcium 8%; Iron 10%

EXCHANGES:
1½ Starch, 1½ Vegetable

1	medium butternut squash, peeled, cut into 1-inch pieces (3 cups)
2	medium parsnips, peeled, cut into 1-inch pieces (2 cups)
2	cans (14.5 oz each) stewed tomatoes, undrained
2	cups frozen cut green beans
1	medium onion, coarsely chopped (½ cup)
½	cup uncooked quick-cooking barley
½	cup water
1	teaspoon dried sage leaves
½	teaspoon seasoned salt
2	cloves garlic, finely chopped

1 Heat oven to 375°F. In ungreased 3-quart casserole, mix all ingredients, breaking up large pieces of tomatoes.

2 Cover; bake 1 hour to 1 hour 15 minutes or until vegetables and barley are tender.

Betty's Success Tip
Butternut squash is peanut shaped and has a peel that ranges in color from cream to yellow. Inside, the squash is bright orange, sweet and chock full of fiber and nutrients.

Veggies and Kasha with Balsamic Vinaigrette

1
Carbohydrate
Choice

PREP TIME: 15 min • **START TO FINISH:** 2 hr • 4 servings (1 cup each)

SALAD

1	cup water
½	cup uncooked buckwheat kernels or groats (kasha)
4	medium green onions, thinly sliced (¼ cup)
2	medium tomatoes, seeded, coarsely chopped (1½ cups)
1	medium unpeeled cucumber, seeded, chopped (1¼ cups)

VINAIGRETTE

2	tablespoons balsamic or red wine vinegar
1	tablespoon olive oil
2	teaspoons sugar
½	teaspoon salt
¼	teaspoon pepper
1	clove garlic, finely chopped

1 In 8-inch skillet, heat water to boiling. Add kasha; cook over medium-high heat 7 to 8 minutes, stirring occasionally, until tender. Drain if necessary.

2 In large bowl, mix kasha and remaining salad ingredients.

3 In tightly covered container, shake vinaigrette ingredients until blended. Pour vinaigrette over kasha mixture; toss. Cover; refrigerate 1 to 2 hours to blend flavors.

1 SERVING: Calories 120 (Calories from Fat 35); Total Fat 4g (Saturated Fat 0.5g; Trans Fat 0g); Cholesterol 0mg; Sodium 310mg; Total Carbohydrate 19g (Dietary Fiber 3g; Sugars 6g); Protein 2g

% DAILY VALUE: Vitamin A 15%; Vitamin C 10%; Calcium 2%; Iron 4%

EXCHANGES: 1 Starch, 1 Vegetable, 1 Fat

Betty's Success Tip

The color and crunch of the vegetables and the chewiness of the kasha create a salad that looks and tastes wonderful, perfect for family and friends.

3½ Carbohydrate Choices

Chicken–Wild Rice Salad with Dried Cherries

PREP TIME: 30 min • **START TO FINISH:** 30 min • 5 servings (1¼ cups each)

1 SERVING: Calories 380 (Calories from Fat 70); Total Fat 7g (Saturated Fat 1.5g; Trans Fat 0g); Cholesterol 45mg; Sodium 760mg; Total Carbohydrate 54g (Dietary Fiber 4g; Sugars 21g); Protein 24g

% DAILY VALUE: Vitamin A 15%; Vitamin C 20%; Calcium 8%; Iron 20%

EXCHANGES: 3 Starch, ½ Fruit, ½ Vegetable, 2 Very Lean Meat, 1 Fat

1 package (6.2 oz) fast-cooking long-grain and wild rice mix

2 cups chopped cooked chicken or turkey

1 medium unpeeled apple, chopped (1 cup)

1 medium green bell pepper, chopped (1 cup)

1 medium stalk celery, chopped (½ cup)

½ cup chopped dried apricots

⅓ cup chopped dried cherries

2 tablespoons reduced-sodium soy sauce

2 tablespoons water

2 teaspoons sugar

2 teaspoons cider vinegar

⅓ cup dry-roasted peanuts

1 Cook rice mix as directed on package, omitting butter. On large cookie sheet, spread rice evenly in thin layer. Let stand 10 minutes, stirring occasionally, until cool.

2 Meanwhile, in large bowl, mix chicken, apple, bell pepper, celery, apricots and cherries. In small bowl, mix soy sauce, water, sugar and vinegar until sugar is dissolved.

3 Add rice and soy sauce mixture to apple mixture; toss gently until coated. Add peanuts; toss gently.

Betty's Success Tip

This terrific main dish has a yummy combination of ingredients—turn up the heat by sprinkling in ¼ teaspoon of crushed red pepper flakes.

Chicken and Vegetables with Quinoa

PREP TIME: 25 min • **START TO FINISH:** 25 min • 4 servings (1 cup stir-fry and 1 cup quinoa each)

3
Carbohydrate
Choices

1⅓ cups uncooked quinoa

2⅔ cups water

⅔ cup chicken broth

2 cups 1-inch pieces fresh green beans

½ cup ready-to-eat baby-cut carrots, cut in half lengthwise

1 tablespoon olive oil

½ lb boneless skinless chicken breasts, cut into bite-size pieces

½ cup bite-size strips red bell pepper

½ cup sliced fresh mushrooms

½ teaspoon dried rosemary leaves

¼ teaspoon salt

2 cloves garlic, finely chopped

1 Rinse quinoa thoroughly by placing in a fine-mesh strainer and holding under cold running water until water runs clear; drain well.

2 In 2-quart saucepan, heat water to boiling. Add quinoa; return to boiling. Reduce heat to low. Cover; cook 12 to 16 minutes or until liquid is absorbed.

3 Meanwhile, in 12-inch nonstick skillet, heat broth to boiling over high heat. Add green beans and carrots. Reduce heat to medium-high. Cover; cook 5 to 7 minutes or until vegetables are crisp-tender.

4 Stir oil, chicken, bell pepper, mushrooms, rosemary, salt and garlic into vegetables. Cook over medium-high heat 8 to 9 minutes, stirring frequently, until chicken is no longer pink in center. Serve over quinoa.

1 SERVING: Calories 350 (Calories from Fat 80); Total Fat 9g (Saturated Fat 1.5g; Trans Fat 0g); Cholesterol 35mg; Sodium 380mg; Total Carbohydrate 46g (Dietary Fiber 6g; Sugars 6g); Protein 22g

% DAILY VALUE: Vitamin A 50%; Vitamin C 20%; Calcium 8%; Iron 35%

EXCHANGES: 2 Starch, ½ Other Carbohydrate, 1 Vegetable, 2 Very Lean Meat, 1½ Fat

Betty's Success Tip

Quinoa, pronounced KEEN-wah, was first grown in Peru. It contains all of the amino acids, making it a complete protein, and it is quick and easy to cook, making it a favorite grain. Quinoa's texture is light with a nutty flavor, perfect for main and side dishes.

2½ Carbohydrate Choices

Southwestern Quinoa Salad

PREP TIME: 15 min • **START TO FINISH:** 1 hr • 6 servings

1 SERVING: Calories 310 (Calories from Fat 110); Total Fat 12g (Saturated Fat 2g; Trans Fat 0g); Cholesterol 0mg; Sodium 170mg; Total Carbohydrate 38g (Dietary Fiber 9g; Sugars 5g); Protein 13g

% DAILY VALUE: Vitamin A 15%; Vitamin C 15%; Calcium 8%; Iron 20%

EXCHANGES: 2 Starch, 1½ Vegetable, ½ Very Lean Meat, 2 Fat

SALAD

- 1 cup uncooked quinoa
- 1 large onion, chopped (1 cup)
- 1½ cups reduced-sodium chicken broth
- 1 cup packed fresh cilantro leaves
- ¼ cup raw unsalted hulled pumpkin seeds (pepitas)
- 2 cloves garlic, sliced
- ⅛ teaspoon ground cumin
- 2 tablespoons chopped green chiles (from 4.5-oz can)
- 1 tablespoon olive oil
- 1 can (15 oz) no-salt-added black beans, drained, rinsed
- 6 medium plum (Roma) tomatoes, chopped (2 cups)
- 2 tablespoons lime juice

GARNISH

- 1 avocado, pitted, peeled, thinly sliced
- 4 small cilantro sprigs

1 Rinse quinoa thoroughly by placing in a fine-mesh strainer and holding under cold running water until water runs clear; drain well.

2 Spray 3-quart saucepan with cooking spray. Heat over medium heat. Add onion to pan; cook 6 to 8 minutes, stirring occasionally, until golden brown. Stir in quinoa and chicken broth. Heat to boiling; reduce heat. Cover and simmer 10 to 15 minutes or until all liquid is absorbed; remove from heat.

3 Meanwhile, in small food processor*, place cilantro, pumpkin seeds, garlic and cumin. Cover; process 5 to 10 seconds, using quick on-and-off motions; scrape side. Add chiles and oil. Cover; process, using quick on-and-off motions, until paste forms.

4 To cooked quinoa, add pesto mixture and the remaining salad ingredients. Refrigerate at least 30 minutes to blend flavors.

5 To serve, divide salad evenly among 4 plates; top each serving with 3 or 4 slices avocado and 1 sprig cilantro.

*If using blender to make pesto mixture, finely chop pumpkin seeds. Continue as directed above.

Betty's Success Tip

Quinoa is a wonderful, high-protein grain that has a unique nutty flavor. Before cooking, be sure to rinse quinoa well under running water in a fine-mesh strainer. Quinoa grains are sometimes coated with a natural substance that can result in a bitter-tasting, sticky consistency when cooked.

3½ Carbohydrate Choices

Spicy Couscous and Chickpea Salad

PREP TIME: 20 min • **START TO FINISH:** 20 min • 4 servings (1 cup each)

1 SERVING: Calories 370 (Calories from Fat 100); Total Fat 11g (Saturated Fat 1.5g; Trans Fat 0g); Cholesterol 0mg; Sodium 460mg; Total Carbohydrate 53g (Dietary Fiber 10g; Sugars 6g); Protein 16g

% DAILY VALUE: Vitamin A 8%; Vitamin C 10%; Calcium 10%; Iron 25%

EXCHANGES: 3 Starch, 1 Vegetable, ½ Very Lean Meat, 2 Fat

SALAD

½ cup uncooked whole wheat couscous

1½ cups water

¼ teaspoon salt

1 can (15 oz) chickpeas (garbanzo beans), drained, rinsed

1 can (14.5 oz) diced tomatoes with green chiles, undrained

½ cup frozen shelled edamame (green soybeans) or lima beans, thawed

2 tablespoons chopped fresh cilantro

Green bell peppers, halved, if desired

DRESSING

2 tablespoons olive oil

1 teaspoon ground coriander

½ teaspoon ground cumin

½ teaspoon ground cinnamon

1 Cook couscous in the water and salt as directed on package.

2 Meanwhile, in medium bowl, mix chickpeas, tomatoes, edamame and cilantro. In small bowl, mix dressing ingredients until well blended.

3 Add cooked couscous to salad; mix well. Pour dressing over salad; stir gently to mix. Spoon salad mixture into halved bell peppers. Serve immediately, or cover and refrigerate until serving time.

Betty's Success Tip

Edamame is the Japanese name for fresh green soybeans—tasty, bright little green gems that are high in protein. You can buy them frozen and shelled or in the pods.

Edamame-Tabbouleh Salad

PREP TIME: 20 min • **START TO FINISH:** 20 min • 6 servings (1 cup each)

SALAD

- 1 package (5.8 oz) roasted garlic and olive oil couscous mix
- 1¼ cups water
- 1 teaspoon olive or canola oil
- 1 bag (10 oz) refrigerated fully cooked ready-to-eat shelled edamame (green soybeans)
- 2 medium tomatoes, seeded, chopped (1½ cups)
- 1 small cucumber, peeled, chopped (1 cup)
- ¼ cup chopped fresh parsley

DRESSING

- 1 teaspoon grated lemon peel
- 2 tablespoons lemon juice
- 1 teaspoon olive or canola oil

1 Make couscous mix as directed on package, using the water and oil.

2 In large bowl, mix couscous and remaining salad ingredients. In small bowl, mix dressing ingredients. Pour dressing over salad; mix well. Serve immediately, or cover and refrigerate until serving time.

1 SERVING: Calories 200 (Calories from Fat 50); Total Fat 5g (Saturated Fat 0.5g; Trans Fat 0g); Cholesterol 0mg; Sodium 270mg; Total Carbohydrate 28g (Dietary Fiber 4g; Sugars 3g); Protein 10g

% DAILY VALUE: Vitamin A 15%; Vitamin C 15%; Calcium 8%; Iron 10%

EXCHANGES: 1½ Starch, 1 Vegetable, ½ Very Lean Meat, 1 Fat

Diabetes Team Tip
Soy foods like the edamame in this recipe or tofu contain high-fiber carbohydrates, low-fat protein and heart-healthy fat. —Diane Reader, Dietitian

Betty's Success Tip
You can use leftover tabbouleh salad to create a quick and easy lunch. Just spread the inside of a pita bread pocket with hummus and fill with salad.

3
Carbohydrate
Choices

Asiago Mac and Cheese

PREP TIME: 20 min • **START TO FINISH:** 20 min • 5 servings (1¼ cups each)

1 SERVING: Calories 400 (Calories from Fat 130); Total Fat 15g (Saturated Fat 5g; Trans Fat 0g); Cholesterol 20mg; Sodium 770mg; Total Carbohydrate 49g (Dietary Fiber 6g; Sugars 9g); Protein 17g

% DAILY VALUE:
Vitamin A 10%; Vitamin C 45%; Calcium 30%; Iron 15%

EXCHANGES: 3 Starch, 1 Vegetable, 1 Medium-Fat Meat, 1½ Fat

CRUMB TOPPING

2	teaspoons olive oil
¼	cup unseasoned panko bread crumbs

CASSEROLE

1½	cups uncooked whole-grain elbow macaroni
5	cups cauliflower florets
2	teaspoons olive oil
2	cups fat-free (skim) milk
¼	cup all-purpose flour
¾	cup shredded Asiago cheese
¼	teaspoon salt
⅛	teaspoon ground nutmeg
⅛	teaspoon pepper
1	jar (4 oz) diced pimientos, drained
2	tablespoons julienne-cut fresh basil leaves

1 In 8-inch skillet, heat oil over medium heat. Add bread crumbs to oil. Cook 2 to 3 minutes, stirring constantly, until golden brown; set aside.

2 In 5-quart Dutch oven or saucepan, cook macaroni as directed on package, except add cauliflower florets 5 minutes before end of cook time. Drain; return to Dutch oven.

3 Meanwhile, in 1½-quart saucepan, heat oil over medium heat. In small bowl, beat together milk and flour, using whisk, until smooth. Stir milk mixture into oil in saucepan. Cook, stirring constantly, until mixture thickens and bubbles. Remove from heat; cool 3 minutes. Stir in cheese, salt, nutmeg and pepper just until cheese melts; stir in pimientos and 1 tablespoon basil.

4 In Dutch oven, stir cheese mixture into cooked macaroni until well combined. For each serving, sprinkle macaroni with about 1 tablespoon crumb topping and about 1 teaspoon basil.

Betty's Success Tip

Real mac and cheese for people with diabetes? We've stretched the carbs by using less pasta, and then bulked it up with cauliflower! Cauliflower has such a mild taste that you barely notice it in the cheese sauce. Whether or not you choose to let your family know the secret is totally up to you.

4
Carbohydrate Choices

Slow Cooker Mediterranean Minestrone Casserole

PREP TIME: 20 min • **START TO FINISH:** 6 hr 40 min • 6 servings (about 1¼ cups each)

1 SERVING: Calories 340 (Calories from Fat 45); Total Fat 5g (Saturated Fat 2g; Trans Fat 0g); Cholesterol 5mg; Sodium 510mg; Total Carbohydrate 57g (Dietary Fiber 9g; Sugars 13g); Protein 16g

% DAILY VALUE: Vitamin A 130%; Vitamin C 30%; Calcium 20%; Iron 30%

EXCHANGES: 2½ Starch, 1 Other Carbohydrate, 1 Vegetable, 1 Very Lean Meat, ½ Fat

3 medium carrots, sliced (1½ cups)

1 medium onion, chopped (½ cup)

1 cup water

2 teaspoons sugar

1½ teaspoons dried Italian seasoning

¼ teaspoon pepper

1 can (28 oz) diced tomatoes, undrained

1 can (15 oz) chickpeas (garbanzo beans), drained, rinsed

1 can (6 oz) no-salt-added tomato paste

2 cloves garlic, finely chopped

1½ cups frozen cut green beans, thawed

1 cup uncooked elbow macaroni

½ cup shredded Parmesan cheese (2 oz)

1 In 3- to 4-quart slow cooker, mix all ingredients except green beans, macaroni and cheese.

2 Cover; cook on Low heat setting 6 to 8 hours.

3 About 20 minutes before serving, stir in green beans and macaroni. Increase heat setting to High. Cover; cook about 20 minutes or until beans and macaroni are tender. Sprinkle with cheese.

Betty's Success Tip

Eating plenty of fruits and vegetables every day is an important part of wellness. Choose from a variety of those that are bright and colorful. They are a treasure trove of vitamins and phytonutrients.

CONSIDER EATING MEDITERRANEAN-STYLE

Despite its name, there is no single "diet" for the people who live in the region that borders the Mediterranean Sea. What their menus have in common is less red meat, more fruits and veggies, healthier oils, fish, whole grains, beans and nuts. To eat more in a Mediterranean style, try these food tips.

- **Choose olive oil.**

   This monounsaturated fat, which is a staple in Mediterranean dishes, has been shown to lower total cholesterol and LDL (bad) cholesterol. Whenever possible, substitute olive oil for butter, vegetable oils and other saturated fats. Use olive oil in salads and stir-fries.

- **Eat red meat sparingly.**

   Limit portion sizes on any given day to 3 ounces, about the size of a cell phone. You won't feel deprived if you get creative and serve meat in casseroles, mix it into stir-fries, add it to soups or slice it thin and fan it atop a bed of mixed greens.

- **Focus on fish.**

   Enjoy fish and shellfish at least two times each week. Try to include fatty fish—such as mackerel, lake trout, herring, sardines, tuna and salmon, which are rich sources of omega-3 fatty acids—good for heart health.

- **Make fruits and veggies center stage.**

   Make veggies and fruits the centerpiece of the meal—and enjoy them in large portions. For peak flavor, serve fruits in season in many colors. Dress up veggies with olive oil, garlic, onions, herbs and spices—but keep them crisp and don't overcook them.

- **Eat more beans.**

   Add dry beans, peas and other legumes to soups, antipasti and salads. Beans provide texture and plenty of healthful fiber—as well as protein too.

- **Go nuts.**

   Almonds, pistachios, hazelnuts, cashews and walnuts make a quick snack—but choose unsalted nuts and keep portions small. Go for natural peanut butter and tahini (from ground sesame seeds) as a dip or spread for bread.

- **Choose whole grains.**

   Hearty grains and breads with fiber and the benefits of whole grains make better choices than refined grains. Include whole grains such as quinoa, amaranth, barley, bulgur wheat and brown rice in sides, soups and casseroles.

- **Eat slowly and enjoy your meal.**

   It's not a race. Sit back and relax. Even enjoying the occasional glass of wine with your meal can put you in a Mediterranean dining mood.

3
Carbohydrate
Choices

Whole Wheat Lasagna Wheels

PREP TIME: 50 min • **START TO FINISH:** 1 hr 20 min • 4 servings (2 wheels each)

1 SERVING: Calories 400 (Calories from Fat 100); Total Fat 11g (Saturated Fat 6g; Trans Fat 0g); Cholesterol 30mg; Sodium 740mg; Total Carbohydrate 50g (Dietary Fiber 6g; Sugars 17g); Protein 22g

% DAILY VALUE: Vitamin A 35%; Vitamin C 10%; Calcium 40%; Iron 15%

EXCHANGES: 1½ Starch, 1 Other Carbohydrate, 2 Vegetable, 2 Lean Meat, 1 Fat

8   uncooked whole wheat lasagna noodles

3   cups sliced cremini mushrooms

2   small zucchini, unpeeled, halved lengthwise and sliced

½   teaspoon pepper

1   cup part-skim ricotta cheese

½   cup shredded part-skim mozzarella cheese

¼   cup grated Parmesan cheese

½   cup chopped fresh basil leaves

1½   cups tomato pasta sauce

1   Heat oven to 350°F. Spray 13×9-inch (3-quart) glass baking dish with cooking spray. Cook noodles as directed on package. Drain; rinse with cold water to cool. Drain well; lay noodles flat.

2   Meanwhile, spray 10-inch skillet with cooking spray. Heat over medium-high heat. Add mushrooms and zucchini to skillet; sprinkle with pepper. Cook 5 to 8 minutes, stirring frequently, until vegetables are very tender. Remove from heat. Drain; return to skillet. Stir in ricotta cheese, mozzarella cheese, Parmesan cheese and basil until well blended.

3   In baking dish, spread ½ cup pasta sauce. For each lasagna wheel, spoon ⅓ cup vegetable mixture on center of each cooked noodle; spread to ends. Carefully roll up from short end, forming wheel. Place wheels, seam-side down, in baking dish. Spoon remaining 1 cup sauce evenly over tops of lasagna wheels.

4   Cover and bake 30 minutes or until sauce is bubbly. Serve warm, spooning sauce from baking dish over top of each lasagna wheel.

Betty's Success Tip

Be sure to read nutrition labels when choosing your pasta sauce, as many contain added fat and sugar. For this recipe, we used a sauce that contains 1.5 grams fat, 16 grams carbohydrates and 3 grams fiber per serving.

1
Carbohydrate Choice

Chunky Garden Noodles

PREP TIME: 30 min • **START TO FINISH:** 30 min • 6 servings (⅓ cup noodles and 1 cup sauce each)

1 SERVING: Calories 170 (Calories from Fat 70); Total Fat 8g (Saturated Fat 1.5g; Trans Fat 0g); Cholesterol 0mg; Sodium 760mg; Total Carbohydrate 18g (Dietary Fiber 5g; Sugars 9g); Protein 6g

% DAILY VALUE: Vitamin A 20%; Vitamin C 30%; Calcium 15%; Iron 8%

EXCHANGES: ½ Starch, 2 Vegetable, 1½ Fat

SAUCE

2   tablespoons olive oil

1   medium onion, chopped (1 cup)

1   green bell pepper, chopped

3   cups sliced cremini mushrooms

3   cloves garlic, chopped

1   can (28 oz) crushed tomatoes, undrained

½   cup pimiento-stuffed green olives, chopped

⅓   cup chopped fresh basil leaves

1   tablespoon chopped fresh oregano leaves

½   teaspoon crushed red pepper flakes

¼   teaspoon salt

NOODLES

2   packages (8 oz each) tofu shirataki noodles, spaghetti style drained

TOPPING

¼   cup grated Parmesan cheese

1 In 2-quart saucepan, heat oil over medium-high heat. Add onion and bell pepper to oil; cook about 5 minutes, stirring frequently, until onion is tender. Stir in mushrooms and garlic; cook about 5 minutes, stirring frequently, until mushrooms are tender and liquid evaporates. Add remaining sauce ingredients; reduce heat. Cover; simmer, stirring occasionally, while preparing noodles.

2 In 3-quart saucepan, heat 2 quarts water to boiling. Add noodles. Cook 2 to 3 minutes; drain. On heatproof plate lined with paper towels, place noodles (to prevent them from sticking together). Divide warm noodles evenly among 6 bowls. For each serving, top noodles with 1 cup sauce and sprinkle with 2 teaspoons Parmesan cheese.

Betty's Success Tip

Shirataki are very low-carb Japanese noodles, available in spaghetti, fettuccine and angel hair varieties. They come packed in liquid. You can find them near the refrigerated produce or tofu products at grocery or specialty food stores, or at Asian markets. If you like, cut the noodles into 2- to 3-inch pieces before cooking to make them easier to eat.

3
Carbohydrate Choices

Stuffed Pasta Shells

PREP TIME: 30 min • **START TO FINISH:** 55 min • 5 servings

1 SERVING: Calories 340 (Calories from Fat 70); Total Fat 8g (Saturated Fat 2g; Trans Fat 0g); Cholesterol 35mg; Sodium 770mg; Total Carbohydrate 44g (Dietary Fiber 3g; Sugars 13g); Protein 23g

% DAILY VALUE: Vitamin A 15%; Vitamin C 10%; Calcium 15%; Iron 15%

EXCHANGES: 2½ Starch, 1 Vegetable, 2 Lean Meat

15	uncooked jumbo pasta shells
½	lb lean (at least 90%) ground turkey
1	teaspoon dried Italian seasoning
½	teaspoon fennel seed
¼	teaspoon pepper
2	cups sliced fresh mushrooms
1	medium onion, chopped (½ cup)
4	cloves garlic, finely chopped
1	cup fat-free cottage cheese
¼	cup fat-free egg product
2	cups tomato pasta sauce
¼	cup shredded Parmesan cheese

1 Heat oven to 350°F. Cook and drain pasta as directed on package, omitting salt.

2 Meanwhile, in 10-inch nonstick skillet, cook turkey, Italian seasoning, fennel and pepper over medium heat 8 to 10 minutes, stirring occasionally, until turkey is no longer pink; remove turkey mixture from skillet.

3 In same skillet, cook mushrooms, onion and garlic over medium heat 6 to 8 minutes, stirring occasionally, until vegetables are tender. Stir turkey mixture, cottage cheese and egg product into mushroom mixture.

4 Spray 13×9-inch (3-quart) glass baking dish with cooking spray. Spoon about 1 tablespoon turkey mixture into each pasta shell. Place in baking dish. Spoon pasta sauce over shells.

5 Cover with foil. Bake 20 to 25 minutes or until hot. Sprinkle with Parmesan cheese.

Betty's Success Tip
For convenience, look for pre-sliced mushrooms in packages next to the whole mushrooms.

GREAT WHOLE GRAINS

How can whole grains help diabetes? Eating whole grain foods gives you fiber, vitamins, minerals and hundreds of phytonutrients (health-protective substances found in plant foods) that work together in powerful ways to help protect against heart disease and certain cancers. A diet rich in whole grains may contribute to preventing diabetes, too.

Q What are whole grains?

A Whole grains include all three parts of a grain: bran, germ and endosperm. By eating all three parts, you get the benefits of the entire package of nutrients.

Q How do I know if a food is made from whole grains?

A Read the ingredient list on the package. The word "whole" or "whole grain" before the name of the grain tells you that a food is made from the entire grain. Wheat, corn, oats and rice are the most common varieties of grains eaten in the United States. You'll find them in cereals, breads, crackers and pasta. Look for foods that include a statement on the package, called a health claim, or a whole-grain seal to ensure that you're getting a whole grain product. Branch out and try whole grains, such as amaranth, quinoa, barley and bulgur wheat, that may be less familiar to you.

Q How can I cook with whole grains—don't they take a long time to prepare?

A Some whole grains, such as wheat berries, brown rice and barley take a longer time to cook than other grains. However, if you have the time, it's worth the extra effort because they're delicious and good for you. Whole grains such as quinoa, bulgur wheat, quick-cooking barley and oats cook quickly. Baking with old-fashioned oats adds flavor, texture and nutrients to your baked goods.

GO WITH THE GRAIN

Choose three or more servings of whole grains daily. To get your grains:

- Eat whole-grain cereal or granola bars for breakfast or as a snack.
- Choose whole wheat or whole grain breads for toast and sandwiches. Breads with 3 grams of fiber or more per serving are good choices.
- Substitute old-fashioned oats, cooked bulgur or brown rice for the bread crumbs and one-third of the meat in meat loaves and meatballs.
- Add raw or cooked barley or brown rice to your favorite vegetable soup.
- Cook extra whole grains, then set aside half to make pilafs, toss in salads and use in soups or casseroles.
- Bake breads or muffins with oats, whole wheat flour and whole grain cornmeal. Choose recipes that include whole grains, or experiment by replacing about one-third of the regular flour with whole grain flour.

CHAPTER 6

Vital Vegetables and Salads

2
Carbohydrate Choices

Chipotle Twice-Baked Sweet Potatoes

PREP TIME: 20 min • **START TO FINISH:** 1 hr 25 min • 4 servings

1 SERVING: Calories 140 (Calories from Fat 15); Total Fat 1.5g (Saturated Fat 1g; Trans Fat 0g); Cholesterol 0mg; Sodium 400mg; Total Carbohydrate 27g (Dietary Fiber 4g; Sugars 9g); Protein 3g

% DAILY VALUE: Vitamin A 470%; Vitamin C 20%; Calcium 8%; Iron 6%

EXCHANGES: 2 Starch, ½ Fat

4	small sweet potatoes (about 1¾ lb)
¼	cup fat-free half-and-half
1	chipotle chile in adobo sauce (from 7-oz can), finely chopped
1	teaspoon adobo sauce (from can of chipotle chiles)
½	teaspoon salt
8	teaspoons reduced-fat sour cream
4	teaspoons chopped fresh cilantro

1 Heat oven to 375°F. Gently scrub potatoes but do not peel. Pierce potatoes several times with fork to allow steam to escape while potatoes bake. Bake about 45 minutes or until potatoes are tender when pierced in center with a fork.

2 When potatoes are cool enough to handle, cut lengthwise down through center of potato to within ½ inch of ends and bottom. Carefully scoop out inside, leaving thin shell. In medium bowl, mash potatoes, half-and-half, chile, adobo sauce and salt with potato masher or electric mixer on low speed until light and fluffy.

3 Increase oven temperature to 400°F. In 13×9-inch pan, place potato shells. Divide potato mixture evenly among shells. Bake uncovered 20 minutes or until potato mixture is golden brown and heated through.

4 Just before serving, top each potato with 2 teaspoons sour cream and 1 teaspoon cilantro.

Diabetes Team Tip Sweet potatoes, squash, carrots and other bright orange vegetables contain beta-carotene, which your body converts to vitamin A. It's vital for proper eyesight. —Dr. Bergenstal

Betty's Success Tip If the potato shells look a bit uneven after filling with the mashed mixture, gently pinch both ends at the same time; pull in opposite directions to pull back into shape.

½ Carbohydrate Choice

Broccoli and Squash Medley

PREP TIME: 30 min • **START TO FINISH:** 30 min • 14 servings (½ cup each)

1 SERVING: Calories 80 (Calories from Fat 35); Total Fat 4g (Saturated Fat 1g; Trans Fat 0g); Cholesterol 0mg; Sodium 125mg; Total Carbohydrate 10g (Dietary Fiber 2g; Sugars 5g); Protein 1g

% DAILY VALUE:
Vitamin A 50%; Vitamin C 30%; Calcium 4%; Iron 4%

EXCHANGES:
½ Other Carbohydrate, ½ Vegetable, 1 Fat

2 bags (12 oz each) frozen broccoli cuts

2 cups cubed (½ inch) peeled butternut squash (1½ lb)

½ cup orange juice

1 tablespoon butter or margarine, melted

½ cup sweetened dried cranberries

½ cup finely chopped pecans, toasted*

1 tablespoon grated orange peel

½ teaspoon salt

1 Cook broccoli as directed on bag; set aside.

2 Meanwhile, in 12-inch skillet, cook squash in orange juice over medium-low heat 8 to 10 minutes, stirring frequently, until tender but firm.

3 Stir in butter, broccoli, cranberries, pecans, orange peel and salt; toss to coat. Serve immediately.

*To toast pecans, sprinkle in ungreased heavy skillet. Cook over medium heat 5 to 7 minutes, stirring frequently until pecans begin to brown, then stirring constantly until light brown.

Diabetes Team Tip
Broccoli, part of the same vegetable family that includes Brussels sprouts, cabbage and cauliflower, is nutrient rich. These tasty gems are thought to help protect against diseases, particularly certain cancers.
—Dr. Bergenstal

Betty's Success Tip
Make it your way! Use your favorite nut, and vary the cranberries with raisins, golden raisins or even chopped dried apricots.

Asparagus-Pepper Stir-Fry

PREP TIME: 25 min • **START TO FINISH:** 25 min • 4 servings

0
Carbohydrate
Choices

1   lb fresh asparagus spears

1   teaspoon canola oil

1   medium red, yellow or orange bell pepper, cut into ¾-inch pieces

2   cloves garlic, finely chopped

1   tablespoon orange juice

1   tablespoon reduced-sodium soy sauce

½   teaspoon ground ginger

1   Break off tough ends of asparagus as far down as stalks snap easily. Cut into 1-inch pieces.

2   In 10-inch nonstick skillet or wok, heat oil over medium heat. Add asparagus, bell pepper and garlic; cook 3 to 4 minutes or until crisp-tender, stirring constantly.

3   In small bowl, mix orange juice, soy sauce and ginger until blended; stir into asparagus mixture. Cook and stir 15 to 30 seconds or until vegetables are coated.

1 SERVING: Calories 40 (Calories from Fat 10); Total Fat 1.5g (Saturated Fat 0g; Trans Fat 0g); Cholesterol 0mg; Sodium 135mg; Total Carbohydrate 6g (Dietary Fiber 2g; Sugars 3g); Protein 2g

% DAILY VALUE: Vitamin A 30%; Vitamin C 35%; Calcium 2%; Iron 8%

EXCHANGES:
1 Vegetable, ½ Fat

Diabetes Team Tip   Vegetables are loaded with the nutrients you need each day to be healthy. It's recommended to have three to five servings of veggies each day. —Diane Reader, Dietitian

Betty's Success Tip   Choose fresh asparagus that is firm and straight. It should be bright green with no signs of decay, and the tips should be firm and closed. Thinner spears will cook more quickly than the larger type.

1
Carbohydrate
Choice

Balsamic Green Beans and Fennel

PREP TIME: 20 min • **START TO FINISH:** 20 min • 4 servings (about ¾ cup each)

1 SERVING: Calories 80 (Calories from Fat 20); Total Fat 2.5g (Saturated Fat 0g; Trans Fat 0g); Cholesterol 0mg; Sodium 180mg; Total Carbohydrate 13g (Dietary Fiber 4g; Sugars 6g); Protein 1g

% DAILY VALUE: Vitamin A 8%; Vitamin C 8%; Calcium 6%; Iron 6%

EXCHANGES: 3 Vegetable, ½ Fat

2 teaspoons olive or canola oil

1 medium bulb fennel, cut into thin wedges

1 small onion, cut into thin wedges

2 cups frozen whole green beans

¼ cup water

2 teaspoons packed brown sugar

¼ teaspoon salt

¼ teaspoon freshly ground pepper

1 tablespoon balsamic vinegar

1 In 12-inch nonstick skillet, heat oil over medium heat. Add fennel and onion; cook 7 to 8 minutes, stirring frequently, until fennel is light golden brown.

2 Add beans and water; heat to boiling. Stir; reduce heat to low. Cover; simmer 6 to 8 minutes or until beans are crisp-tender.

3 Stir in remaining ingredients; cook and stir 15 to 30 seconds longer or until vegetables are coated.

Betty's Success Tip

Fennel is cultivated in the Mediterranean and the United States. Both the bulb and the stems can be eaten raw or cooked. The flavor is a little bit like anise but is sweeter and more delicate. The feathery greenery can be used as a garnish or snipped like dill weed and used as a last-minute flavor enhancer.

Peas with Mushrooms and Thyme

PREP TIME: 10 min • **START TO FINISH:** 10 min • 6 servings

1 Carbohydrate Choice

2 teaspoons olive, canola or soybean oil

1 medium onion, diced (½ cup)

1 cup sliced fresh mushrooms

1 bag (16 oz) frozen sweet peas

¼ teaspoon coarse (kosher or sea) salt

⅛ teaspoon white pepper

1 teaspoon chopped fresh or ¼ teaspoon dried thyme leaves

1 In 10-inch skillet, heat oil over medium heat. Add onion and mushrooms; cook 3 minutes, stirring occasionally. Stir in peas. Cook 3 to 5 minutes, stirring occasionally, until vegetables are tender.

2 Sprinkle with salt, pepper and thyme. Serve immediately.

1 SERVING: Calories 80 (Calories from Fat 15); Total Fat 1.5g (Saturated Fat 0g; Trans Fat 0g); Cholesterol 0mg; Sodium 150mg; Total Carbohydrate 11g (Dietary Fiber 2g; Sugars 4g); Protein 4g

% DAILY VALUE: Vitamin A 30%; Vitamin C 6%; Calcium 2%; Iron 6%

EXCHANGES: ½ Starch, 1 Vegetable, ½ Fat

Diabetes Team Tip Peas are loaded with vitamin B_1, also called thiamin. We need thiamin for normal energy metabolism and to help keep the nervous system healthy. —Diane Reader, Dietitian

Betty's Success Tip Put a gourmet touch to this simple side dish by using an assortment of wild mushrooms like cremini, shiitake and portabellas.

1
Carbohydrate
Choice

Herb-Roasted Root Vegetables

PREP TIME: 15 min • **START TO FINISH:** 1 hr 10 min • 6 servings (½ cup each)

1 SERVING: Calories 70 (Calories from Fat 0); Total Fat 0g (Saturated Fat 0g; Trans Fat 0g); Cholesterol 0mg; Sodium 260mg; Total Carbohydrate 15g (Dietary Fiber 4g; Sugars 7g); Protein 1g

% DAILY VALUE:
Vitamin A 70%; Vitamin C 20%; Calcium 6%; Iron 4%

EXCHANGES:
½ Starch, 1 Vegetable

2   medium turnips, peeled, cut into 1-inch pieces (3 cups)

2   medium parsnips, peeled, cut into ½-inch pieces (1½ cups)

1   medium red onion, cut into 1-inch wedges (1 cup)

1   cup ready-to-eat baby-cut carrots

    Cooking spray

2   teaspoons Italian seasoning

½   teaspoon coarse salt

1   Heat oven to 425°F. Spray 15×10×1-inch pan with cooking spray. Arrange vegetables in single layer in pan. Spray with cooking spray (2 or 3 seconds). Sprinkle with Italian seasoning and salt.

2   Bake uncovered 45 to 55 minutes, stirring once, until vegetables are tender.

Diabetes Team Tip
Stress can lead to high glucose. Try to find ways to keep your life balanced and, although stress is a part of life, find time to relax and do things you enjoy. —Dr. Bergenstal

Betty's Success Tip
Roasting brings out the natural sweetness of vegetables and is a low-fat cooking option. As some of the moisture is evaporated in the high heat, the sugar is concentrated, so the food tastes sweeter.

Roasted Asparagus–Berry Salad

PREP TIME: 10 min • **START TO FINISH:** 30 min • 4 servings

½ Carbohydrate Choice

1   lb fresh asparagus spears
    Cooking spray

2   tablespoons chopped pecans

1   cup sliced fresh strawberries

4   cups mixed salad greens

¼   cup fat-free balsamic vinaigrette dressing
    Cracked pepper, if desired

1   Heat oven to 400°F. Line 15×10×1-inch pan with foil; spray with cooking spray. Break off tough ends of asparagus as far down as stalks snap easily. Cut into 1-inch pieces.

2   Place asparagus in single layer in pan; spray with cooking spray. Place pecans in another shallow pan.

3   Bake pecans 5 to 6 minutes or until golden brown, stirring occasionally. Bake asparagus 10 to 12 minutes or until crisp-tender. Cool pecans and asparagus 8 to 10 minutes or until room temperature.

4   In medium bowl, mix asparagus, pecans, strawberries, greens and dressing. Sprinkle with pepper.

1 SERVING: Calories 90 (Calories from Fat 25); Total Fat 3g (Saturated Fat 0g; Trans Fat 0g); Cholesterol 0mg; Sodium 180mg; Total Carbohydrate 11g (Dietary Fiber 4g; Sugars 6g); Protein 4g

% DAILY VALUE: Vitamin A 80%; Vitamin C 35%; Calcium 6%; Iron 20%

EXCHANGES:
2 Vegetable, ½ Fat

Betty's Success Tip

This recipe is made with strawberries, but you could vary the fruit to suit your taste. Why not add a few raspberries or blueberries, or even slice a peach for a change?

3

Carbohydrate Choices

Moroccan Carrot Salad

PREP TIME: 15 min • **START TO FINISH:** 2 hr 15 min • 5 servings

1 SERVING: Calories 310 (Calories from Fat 100); Total Fat 11g (Saturated Fat 1g; Trans Fat 0g); Cholesterol 0mg; Sodium 230mg; Total Carbohydrate 44g (Dietary Fiber 10g; Sugars 12g); Protein 10g

% DAILY VALUE: Vitamin A 410%; Vitamin C 20%; Calcium 10%; Iron 20%

EXCHANGES: 2 Starch, ½ Other Carbohydrate, 1½ Vegetable, 2 Fat

DRESSING

- ¼ cup orange juice
- 2 tablespoons olive oil
- 1 teaspoon orange peel
- 1 teaspoon ground cumin
- 1 teaspoon paprika
- ¼ teaspoon salt
- ⅛ to ¼ teaspoon ground red pepper (cayenne)
- ⅛ teaspoon ground cinnamon

SALAD

- 1 bag (10 oz) julienne (matchstick-cut) carrots (5 cups)
- 1 can (15 oz) chickpeas (garbanzo beans), drained, rinsed
- ¼ cup golden raisins
- 3 tablespoons salted roasted whole almonds, coarsely chopped
- ¼ cup coarsely chopped fresh cilantro or parsley

1 In small bowl, combine all dressing ingredients with whisk until blended; set aside.

2 In large bowl, combine carrots, chickpeas and raisins; toss to combine. Add dressing; mix thoroughly. Cover and refrigerate at least 2 hours or overnight, stirring occasionally. Just before serving, sprinkle with almonds and cilantro.

Betty's Success Tip You can shred carrots using the coarse side of a box grater, the shredding attachment on your food processor or a mandoline. You'll need 7 to 8 medium carrots to get 5 cups.

1 Carbohydrate Choice

Five-Layer Salad

PREP TIME: 10 min • **START TO FINISH:** 25 min • 6 servings

1 SERVING: Calories 100 (Calories from Fat 30); Total Fat 3.5g (Saturated Fat 0.5g; Trans Fat 0g); Cholesterol 0mg; Sodium 330mg; Total Carbohydrate 13g (Dietary Fiber 3g; Sugars 7g); Protein 3g

% DAILY VALUE: Vitamin A 150%; Vitamin C 40%; Calcium 6%; Iron 4%

EXCHANGES: ½ Starch, 1 Vegetable, ½ Fat

1	cup frozen sweet peas
1	tablespoon water
⅓	cup plain fat-free yogurt
¼	cup reduced-fat mayonnaise (do not use salad dressing)
1	tablespoon cider vinegar
2	teaspoons sugar
½	teaspoon salt
3	cups coleslaw mix (shredded cabbage and carrots; from 16-oz bag)
1	cup shredded carrots (2 medium)
1	cup halved cherry tomatoes

1 In small microwavable bowl, place peas and water. Cover with microwavable plastic wrap, folding back one edge ¼ inch to vent steam. Microwave on High 4 to 6 minutes, stirring after 2 minutes, until tender; drain. Let stand until cool.

2 Meanwhile, in small bowl, mix yogurt, mayonnaise, vinegar, sugar and salt.

3 In 1½- or 2-quart glass bowl, layer coleslaw mix, carrots, tomatoes and peas. Spread mayonnaise mixture over top. Refrigerate 15 minutes. Toss gently before serving.

Diabetes Team Tip
Vegetable salads are a great way to make a dent in your recommended daily servings of fresh vegetables.
—Diane Reader, Dietitian

Betty's Success Tip
For a complete light meal in a bowl, place 1½ cups chopped cooked chicken between the carrots and tomatoes—it's a six-layer salad.

Strawberry-Blueberry-Orange Salad

PREP TIME: 15 min • **START TO FINISH:** 15 min • 8 servings (½ cup each)

¼ cup fat-free or reduced-fat mayonnaise

3 tablespoons sugar

1 tablespoon white vinegar

2 teaspoons poppy seed

2 cups fresh strawberry halves

2 cups fresh blueberries

1 orange, peeled, chopped

Sliced almonds, if desired

1 In small bowl, mix mayonnaise, sugar, vinegar and poppy seed with whisk until well blended.

2 In medium bowl, mix strawberries, blueberries and orange. Just before serving, pour dressing over fruit; toss. Sprinkle with almonds.

1 SERVING: Calories 70 (Calories from Fat 5); Total Fat 1g (Saturated Fat 0g; Trans Fat 0g); Cholesterol 0mg; Sodium 60mg; Total Carbohydrate 16g (Dietary Fiber 2g; Sugars 12g); Protein 0g

% DAILY VALUE: Vitamin A 0%; Vitamin C 30%; Calcium 2%; Iron 0%

EXCHANGES: ½ Fruit, ½ Other Carbohydrate

Betty's Success Tip

Try this recipe with other favorite summer fruits, such as peaches and raspberries or kiwi and blackberries.

1
Carbohydrate
Choice

Triple-Berry and Jicama Spinach Salad

PREP TIME: 30 min • **START TO FINISH:** 30 min • 6 servings

1 SERVING: Calories 120 (Calories from Fat 45); Total Fat 5g (Saturated Fat 0g; Trans Fat 0g); Cholesterol 0mg; Sodium 125mg; Total Carbohydrate 18g (Dietary Fiber 5g; Sugars 9g); Protein 2g

% DAILY VALUE:
Vitamin A 60%; Vitamin C 70%; Calcium 6%; Iron 8%

EXCHANGES: 1 Fruit, ½ Vegetable, 1 Fat

DRESSING

¼ cup fresh raspberries

3 tablespoons hot pepper jelly

2 tablespoons canola oil

2 tablespoons raspberry vinegar or red wine vinegar

2 medium jalapeño chiles, seeded, finely chopped (2 tablespoons)

2 teaspoons finely chopped shallot

¼ teaspoon salt

1 small clove garlic, crushed

SALAD

1 bag (6 oz) fresh baby spinach leaves

1 cup bite-size strips (1×¼×¼ inch) peeled jicama

1 cup fresh blackberries

1 cup fresh raspberries

1 cup sliced fresh strawberries

1 In small food processor or blender, combine all dressing ingredients; process until smooth.

2 In large bowl, toss spinach and ¼ cup of the dressing. On 6 serving plates, arrange salad. To serve, top each salad with jicama, blackberries, raspberries, strawberries and drizzle with scant 1 tablespoon of remaining dressing.

Diabetes Team Tip Spinach is a super source of folic acid, needed for cells to function normally. Recent studies show that as many as 40% of Americans don't meet their folic acid requirement. —Diane Reader, Dietitian

Betty's Success Tip Like things spicy-hot? Try a serrano chile in place of the jalapeño chile.

1
Carbohydrate
Choice

Cucumber-Mango Salad

PREP TIME: 20 min • **START TO FINISH:** 20 min • 4 servings (½ cup each)

1 SERVING: Calories 50 (Calories from Fat 0); Total Fat 0g (Saturated Fat 0g; Trans Fat 0g); Cholesterol 0mg; Sodium 40mg; Total Carbohydrate 12g (Dietary Fiber 1g; Sugars 9g); Protein 0g

% DAILY VALUE: Vitamin A 15%; Vitamin C 15%; Calcium 0%; Iron 2%

EXCHANGES: ½ Fruit, ½ Vegetable

1	small cucumber
1	medium mango
¼	teaspoon grated lime peel
1	tablespoon lime juice
1	teaspoon honey
¼	teaspoon ground cumin
	Pinch salt
4	leaves Bibb lettuce

1 Cut cucumber lengthwise in half; scoop out seeds. Chop cucumber (about 1 cup).

2 Score skin of mango lengthwise into fourths with knife; peel skin. Cut peeled mango lengthwise close to both sides of pit. Chop mango into ½-inch cubes.

3 In small bowl, mix lime peel, lime juice, honey, cumin and salt. Stir in cucumber and mango. Place lettuce leaves on serving plates. Spoon mango mixture onto lettuce leaves.

Betty's Success Tip

Mango is a great fresh fruit, but you could use peaches instead. Or look for jars of sliced mango in the produce department.

Mediterranean Vegetable Salad

PREP TIME: 10 min • **START TO FINISH:** 1 hr 10 min • 6 servings

1/2 Carbohydrate Choice

⅓ cup tarragon vinegar or white wine vinegar

2 tablespoons canola or soybean oil

2 tablespoons chopped fresh or 2 teaspoons dried oregano leaves

½ teaspoon sugar

½ teaspoon salt

½ teaspoon ground mustard

½ teaspoon pepper

2 cloves garlic, finely chopped

3 large tomatoes, sliced

2 large yellow bell peppers, sliced into thin rings

6 oz fresh spinach leaves (from 10-oz bag), stems removed (about 1 cup)

½ cup crumbled feta cheese (2 oz)

Kalamata olives, if desired

1 In small bowl, mix vinegar, oil, oregano, sugar, salt, mustard, pepper and garlic. In glass or plastic container, place tomatoes and bell peppers. Pour vinegar mixture over vegetables. Cover and refrigerate at least 1 hour to blend flavors.

2 Line serving platter with spinach. Drain vegetables; place on spinach. Sprinkle with cheese; garnish with olives.

1 SERVING: Calories 110 (Calories from Fat 70); Total Fat 8g (Saturated Fat 2.5g; Trans Fat 0g); Cholesterol 10mg; Sodium 340mg; Total Carbohydrate 8g (Dietary Fiber 1g; Sugars 6g); Protein 3g

% DAILY VALUE: Vitamin A 25%; Vitamin C 100%; Calcium 8%; Iron 4%

EXCHANGES: 1½ Vegetable, 1½ Fat

Diabetes Team Tip Research shows that spinach and other leafy green vegetables contain antioxidants. Spinach is an excellent source of the antioxidant lutein, vitamin C and folic acid—all beneficial nutrients for your health. —Diane Reader, Dietitian

½
Carbohydrate
Choice

Thai Broccoli Slaw

PREP TIME: 20 min • **START TO FINISH:** 1 hr 20 min • 8 servings (½ cup each)

1 SERVING: Calories 50 (Calories from Fat 15); Total Fat 1.5g (Saturated Fat 0g; Trans Fat 0g); Cholesterol 0mg; Sodium 75mg; Total Carbohydrate 7g (Dietary Fiber 1g; Sugars 3g); Protein 2g

% DAILY VALUE:
Vitamin A 50%; Vitamin C 60%; Calcium 2%; Iron 2%

EXCHANGES:
1½ Vegetable

DRESSING

2   tablespoons reduced-fat creamy peanut butter

1   tablespoon grated gingerroot

1   tablespoon rice vinegar

1   tablespoon orange marmalade

1½ teaspoons reduced-sodium soy sauce

¼   to ½ teaspoon chili garlic sauce

SLAW

3   cups broccoli slaw mix (from 10-oz bag)

½   cup bite-size thin strips red bell pepper

½   cup julienne (matchstick-cut) carrots

½   cup shredded red cabbage

2   tablespoons chopped fresh cilantro

1 In small bowl, combine all dressing ingredients. Beat with whisk, until blended.

2 In large bowl, toss all slaw ingredients. Pour dressing over slaw mixture; toss until coated. Cover and refrigerate at least 1 hour to blend flavors but no longer than 6 hours, tossing occasionally to blend dressing from bottom of bowl back into slaw mixture.

Betty's Success Tip

Ginger and chili garlic sauce contribute to the spicy heat in this dish. For a less spicy version, use a little less ginger and stick to the ¼ teaspoon chili garlic sauce. Look for chili garlic sauce among the other Asian condiments at your grocery store.

1 Carbohydrate Choice

BLT Potato Salad

PREP TIME: 20 min • **START TO FINISH:** 45 min • 6 servings

1 SERVING: Calories 100 (Calories from Fat 45); Total Fat 5g (Saturated Fat 1g; Trans Fat 0g); Cholesterol 10mg; Sodium 300mg; Total Carbohydrate 12g (Dietary Fiber 1g; Sugars 2g); Protein 3g

% DAILY VALUE: Vitamin A 25%; Vitamin C 8%; Calcium 0%; Iron 4%

EXCHANGES: ½ Starch, 1 Vegetable, 1 Fat

4	small new red potatoes (about 12 oz), cut into ½-inch cubes
¼	cup reduced-fat mayonnaise or salad dressing
1	teaspoon Dijon mustard
2	teaspoons chopped fresh or ½ teaspoon dried dill weed
¼	teaspoon salt
⅛	teaspoon pepper
½	cup grape tomatoes or halved cherry tomatoes
1½	cups bite-size pieces romaine lettuce
2	slices turkey bacon, cooked, crumbled

1 In 2-quart saucepan, place potatoes. Add enough water to cover. Heat to boiling; reduce heat to low. Cover; cook 10 to 15 minutes or until potatoes are tender. Drain; cool about 10 minutes.

2 Meanwhile, in medium bowl, mix mayonnaise, mustard, dill weed, salt and pepper. Stir in potatoes, tomatoes and lettuce until coated. Sprinkle with bacon.

Betty's Success Tip

You don't need to peel the potatoes for this recipe. The peel adds extra flavor, texture and nutrients. Be sure to wash the potatoes well before cooking.

FABULOUS FIBER

Fiber is the edible part of plants that isn't completely broken down by the digestive tract. Fiber is not the same as whole grain. And the truth is, most people don't eat enough fiber.

Sometimes it's easier to grab fruit juice instead of whole fruit, chips instead of vegetables, or white bread instead of whole wheat. And yet, fiber is so important for keeping the body regulated.

Fiber offers many health benefits. Since it's basically roughage, fiber provides a sense of fullness without the calories and satisfies your appetite without affecting your blood glucose levels. If you eat a food with 5 or more grams of fiber, you can subtract half the grams of fiber from the total grams of carbohydrate in the food. Choose foods high in fiber when you can—it will make sticking to your meal plan easier. Add fiber in these great ways:

- **Introduce it.**

   Slowly adding high-fiber cereal, such as Fiber One,® to your diet each day (until you reach up to ½ cup) will allow your body time to adjust. Remember to drink extra liquids because fiber acts like a sponge in the intestines—absorbing liquid to help keep things moving along.

- **Don't skin it.**

   The skins, seeds and hulls found in fruits, vegetables and grains are fiber. Eat pears, apples, peaches, potatoes and other fruits and vegetables with the skin. If they're too hard for you to bite into, use a knife to cut them into sections.

- **Top it.**

   When eating salads and soups, top with high-fiber cereals, popcorn or wheat germ. For pancakes, waffles or toast, use fruit sauces with seeds, such as raspberries, strawberries or kiwifruit, for topping.

- **Distribute it.**

   Eating fiber-rich foods throughout the day will help you achieve your goal. Start the day by eating a banana for breakfast, a pear with lunch, baby carrots for a snack, green beans at dinner. Aim for at least five servings of fruits or vegetables a day.

- **Stuff it.**

   Place tomato slices, shredded cabbage, sliced bell peppers and spinach leaves between slices of whole-grain bread. Whole wheat pita, whole-grain breadsticks and whole-grain crackers are also fiber rich.

- **Combine it.**

   Have high-fiber cereal with strawberries for breakfast, a whole wheat bread sandwich with veggies for lunch and vegetable soup or split pea soup with whole-grain crackers for dinner.

- **Bake it.**

   When baking, use whole wheat flour, add fiber cereals, such as Fiber One,® or bran to muffins, cookies and snack mixes.

- **Snack it.**

   Snack on fiber-rich foods such as high-fiber cereal, air-popped popcorn, raw vegetables, fruits, nuts and soy nuts, raisins or other dried fruit.

1
Carbohydrate
Choice

Celery and Apple Salad with Cider Vinaigrette

PREP TIME: 20 min • **START TO FINISH:** 20 min • 4 servings

1 SERVING: Calories 130 (Calories from Fat 60); Total Fat 6g (Saturated Fat 1g; Trans Fat 0g); Cholesterol 0mg; Sodium 410mg; Total Carbohydrate 17g (Dietary Fiber 3g; Sugars 13g); Protein 2g

% DAILY VALUE: Vitamin A 45%; Vitamin C 15%; Calcium 6%; Iron 4%

EXCHANGES: ½ Fruit, 2 Vegetable, 1 Fat

DRESSING

2 tablespoons apple cider or apple juice

1 tablespoon cider vinegar

2 teaspoons canola oil

2 teaspoons finely chopped shallots

½ teaspoon Dijon mustard

½ teaspoon honey

½ teaspoon salt

SALAD

2 cups chopped romaine lettuce

2 cups diagonally sliced celery

½ medium apple, unpeeled, sliced very thin (about 1 cup)

⅓ cup sweetened dried cranberries

2 tablespoons chopped walnuts

2 tablespoons crumbled blue cheese

1 In small bowl, beat all dressing ingredients with whisk until blended; set aside.

2 In medium bowl, place lettuce, celery, apple and cranberries; toss with dressing. To serve, arrange salad on 4 plates. Sprinkle with walnuts and blue cheese. Serve immediately.

Betty's Success Tip Blue cheese can be purchased already crumbled in the refrigerator section at the grocery store. Crumbled feta cheese would also be a great alternative.

1/2
Carbohydrate
Choice

Garden-Fresh Greek Salad

PREP TIME: 20 Min • **START TO FINISH:** 20 Min • 6 servings (1⅓ cups each)

1 SERVING: Calories 45 (Calories from Fat 15); Total Fat 1.5g (Saturated Fat 0.5g, Trans Fat 0g); Cholesterol 0mg; Sodium 340mg; Total Carbohydrate 6g (Dietary Fiber 2g, Sugars 3g); Protein 3g

% DAILY VALUE:
Vitamin A 30%; Vitamin C 40%; Calcium 6%; Iron 6%

EXCHANGES:
1 Vegetable, ½ Fat

DRESSING

- 3 tablespoons fresh lemon juice
- 1 tablespoon chopped fresh or 1 teaspoon dried oregano leaves
- ½ teaspoon salt
- ½ teaspoon sugar
- ½ teaspoon Dijon mustard
- ¼ teaspoon pepper
- 1 clove garlic, finely chopped

SALAD

- 1 bag (10 oz) ready-to-eat romaine lettuce
- ¾ cup chopped seeded peeled cucumber
- ½ cup sliced red onion
- ¼ cup sliced kalamata olives
- 2 medium tomatoes, seeded, chopped (1½ cups)
- ¼ cup reduced-fat feta cheese

1 In small bowl, beat all dressing ingredients with whisk.

2 In large bowl, toss all salad ingredients except cheese. Stir in dressing until salad is well coated. Sprinkle with cheese.

Betty's Success Tip

Feta cheese is often made from cow's milk, although traditionally it is made from sheep's or goat's milk. Either type will work in this recipe.

THE VALUE OF VEGETABLES

When you have diabetes, knowing the many health benefits of vegetables is more important than ever. Veggies are colorful and fun, add fiber and important vitamins and minerals and are naturally low in calories. To maximize your vegetable options:

- **Make vegetables fun.**

  Try dipping carrots, cucumber slices, celery and bell pepper strips into colorful low-fat dips.

- **Drink your veggies.**

  Try your hand at juicing, or if you'd rather, drink tomato, carrot, eight-vegetable or other vegetable juices.

- **Try new recipes with vegetables.**

  Adding a simple new low-fat sauce, topping with bread or cereal crumbs or teaming with other veggies creates interest and variety for everyone in the family.

- **Take advantage of convenience.**

  Buy baby carrots and pea pods to keep on hand for anytime snacking.

- **Keep fresh veggies at the ready.**

  Wash and cut broccoli, cucumbers, celery and bell peppers ahead of time. Place in individual storage bags to easily carry to work.

- **Add veggie variety to sandwiches.**

  Stuff lettuce leaves along with chicken chunks into pita breads; slice a cucumber or red bell pepper for your tuna sandwich; add tomato to your grilled cheese.

- **Top omelets, scrambled eggs and potato dishes.**

  Cooked onions, mushrooms, zucchini and bell peppers make great toppers or stir-ins.

- **Keep bagged salads on hand.**

  Or wash and dry lettuce, chop up other salad ingredients and keep in containers or food-storage bags in the refrigerator. Washed and well dried, salad greens will keep for several days.

- **Save leftover cooked vegetables.**

  Add them to soups, salads, egg dishes and casseroles.

- **Stock frozen and canned vegetables.**

  That way you'll always have vegetables on hand, even when you don't have time to shop.

A RAINBOW OF COLORS

When it comes to choosing vegetables, looks do count! Choosing produce that's rich in color often means that it's rich in vitamins and other nutrients. When you're grocery shopping, include:

- Dark green veggies such as broccoli, Brussels sprouts, spinach, romaine lettuce, green beans and asparagus.
- Orange veggies such as carrots, sweet potatoes, pumpkin and winter squash.
- Red veggies such as tomatoes, beets and radishes.

CHAPTER 7

Best
Gluten-Free
Recipes

1½ Carbohydrate Choices

Sandwich Bread

PREP TIME: 30 min • **START TO FINISH:** 3 hr 15 min • 1 loaf (16 slices)

1 SLICE: Calories 140 (Calories from Fat 40); Total Fat 4.5g (Saturated Fat 0.5g; Trans Fat 0g); Cholesterol 25mg; Sodium 280mg; Total Carbohydrate 22g (Dietary Fiber 1g; Sugars 3g); Protein 2g

% DAILY VALUE: Vitamin A 0%; Vitamin C 0%; Calcium 4%; Iron 2%

EXCHANGES: 1 Starch, ½ Other Carbohydrate, 1 Fat

- ¾ cup warm water (105°F to 115°F)
- 1 tablespoon fast-rising dry yeast
- ¾ cup plus 1 tablespoon tapioca flour
- ½ cup white rice flour
- ¼ cup sorghum flour
- ¼ cup garbanzo and fava flour
- ½ cup plus 2 tablespoons potato starch
- 1½ teaspoons salt
- 1½ teaspoons gluten-free baking powder
- 1 teaspoon xanthan gum
- 2 eggs
- ¼ cup sugar
- ¼ cup sunflower oil
- 1 teaspoon guar gum
- ½ teaspoon apple cider vinegar
- Cooking spray without flour

1 Spray bottom and sides of 8×4-inch loaf pan with cooking spray without flour. In small bowl, mix water and yeast; set aside.

2 In another small bowl, stir together all flours, the potato starch, salt, baking powder and xanthan gum; set aside.

3 In medium bowl, beat remaining ingredients except cooking spray with electric mixer on medium speed 1 to 2 minutes. Beat in yeast mixture. Add flour mixture; beat on medium speed until thoroughly mixed. Pour into pan. Spray top of dough with cooking spray; if necessary, smooth top of dough with spatula. Cover with plastic wrap; let rise in warm place (80°F to 85°F) 1 hour to 1 hour 30 minutes or until dough rises to top of pan.

4 Heat oven to 375°F. Carefully remove plastic wrap from pan; bake 30 minutes. Reduce oven temperature to 350°F. Cover loaf with parchment paper; bake 25 to 30 minutes longer or until instant-read thermometer inserted in center of loaf reads 207°F. Cool 5 minutes. Remove loaf from pan; place on cooling rack. Cool completely, about 40 minutes.

Jean Duane | Alternative Cook | http://www.alternativecook.com

Cooking gluten-free? Always read labels to make sure each recipe ingredient is gluten-free. Products and ingredient sources can change.

Betty's Success Tip
Don't omit the xanthan gum! It's necessary to hold the bread together. Look for it in the gluten-free section of your grocery store or a natural foods store.

Betty's Success Tip
Gluten-free bread looks "done" long before it is done, so don't be afraid to bake it for an hour.

Soft Pretzels

PREP TIME: 30 min • **START TO FINISH:** 2 hr 15 min • 12 pretzels

2
Carbohydrate
Choices

PRETZELS

4½	teaspoons regular active dry yeast
⅔	cup warm water (105°F to 115°F)
1	cup finely ground tapioca flour
⅔	cup sweet white sorghum flour
¼	cup garbanzo and fava flour
1	cup cornstarch
1½	teaspoons xanthan gum
½	teaspoon guar gum
1	teaspoon salt
3	eggs
1	tablespoon sugar
1	tablespoon honey
	Additional garbanzo and fava flour
	Cooking spray without flour

SODA BATH

⅔	cup baking soda
10	cups water

TOPPING

1	egg, beaten
1	tablespoon kosher (coarse) salt

1 Line cookie sheet with cooking parchment paper; spray paper with cooking spray without flour. In small bowl, dissolve yeast in warm water; set aside.

2 In another small bowl, mix flours, cornstarch, xanthan gum, guar gum and salt with whisk; set aside. In medium bowl, beat eggs, sugar and honey with electric mixer on medium speed about 1 minute or until well blended. Add yeast mixture and flour mixture; beat about 1 minute or until blended.

3 Divide dough into 12 equal-size balls. On work surface sprinkled with additional garbanzo and fava flour, roll each ball into 13×¾-inch rope. Carefully place ropes on cookie sheet; form into U shape and twist in middle. Spray tops of pretzels with cooking spray without flour. Cover with plastic wrap; let rise in warm place 1 hour to 1 hour 30 minutes or until doubled in size.

4 Heat oven to 375°F. In 4-quart saucepan or Dutch oven, stir baking soda into water until dissolved. Heat to full rolling boil. Carefully place 1 pretzel at a time in water; boil 25 seconds. Remove with slotted spoon and return to cookie sheet. Brush tops of pretzels with egg, being careful not to fill openings with egg; sprinkle with kosher salt. Bake 12 to 15 minutes or until golden brown. Immediately transfer pretzels to cooling rack.

Jean Duane | Alternative Cook | http://www.alternativecook.com

Betty's Success Tip

The xanthan gum combined with the guar gum makes a nicely textured baked item. If you don't have guar gum, add an extra ½ teaspoon of xanthan gum in this recipe.

1 PRETZEL: Calories 160 (Calories from Fat 20); Total Fat 2.5g (Saturated Fat 0.5g; Trans Fat 0g); Cholesterol 70mg; Sodium 2080mg; Total Carbohydrate 29g (Dietary Fiber 2g; Sugars 3g); Protein 4g

% DAILY VALUE: Vitamin A 0%; Vitamin C 0%; Calcium 2%; Iron 4%

EXCHANGES: 1½ Starch, ½ Other Carbohydrate, ½ Fat

4
Carbohydrate
Choices

Blueberry Pancakes

PREP TIME: 20 min • **START TO FINISH:** 20 min • 6 servings (2 pancakes and 3 tablespoons syrup each)

1 SERVING: Calories 280 (Calories from Fat 10); Total Fat 1g (Saturated Fat 0g; Trans Fat 0g); Cholesterol 35mg; Sodium 260mg; Total Carbohydrate 62g (Dietary Fiber 1g; Sugars 43g); Protein 4g

% DAILY VALUE: Vitamin A 4%; Vitamin C 2%; Calcium 10%; Iron 0%

EXCHANGES: 1 Starch, 3 Other Carbohydrate

1	cup Bisquick® Gluten Free mix
⅓	cup plain fat-free Greek yogurt
¾	cup fat-free (skim) milk
2	tablespoons packed brown sugar
1	egg, beaten
1	teaspoon grated orange peel
1	cup fresh blueberries
1	cup gluten-free blueberry or maple syrup

1 Spray griddle with cooking spray without flour; heat to 375°F. In medium bowl, stir Bisquick® mix, yogurt, milk, brown sugar, egg and orange peel until blended. Stir in blueberries.

2 Pour batter by ¼ cupfuls onto hot griddle. Cook until pancakes are bubbly on top and puffed and dry around edges. Turn and cook other sides until golden brown. Serve pancakes with syrup.

Betty's Success Tip

For a special touch, sprinkle pancakes with gluten-free powdered sugar and extra blueberries. Serve with warm syrup.

Waffles

4
Carbohydrate
Choices

2 eggs

½ cup gluten-free almond, rice, soy or regular milk

3 tablespoons sunflower oil or melted ghee

¼ cup sugar

2 teaspoons gluten-free vanilla

½ cup tapioca flour

½ cup white rice flour

½ cup sorghum flour

2 tablespoons garbanzo and fava flour

2 tablespoons potato starch

½ teaspoon gluten-free baking powder

½ teaspoon salt

¼ teaspoon baking soda

1 cup gluten-free maple syrup

1 Heat waffle maker as directed by manufacturer. In blender, place eggs, milk, oil, sugar and vanilla. Cover; blend until mixed. Add all flours, the potato starch, baking powder, salt and baking soda; blend until well mixed.

2 Pour batter by slightly less than 1 cupful onto center of hot waffle maker. Bake about 5 minutes or until browned on both sides. Remove from waffle maker. Serve immediately with syrup.

Jean Duane | Alternative Cook | http://www.alternativecook.com

1 SERVING: Calories 320 (Calories from Fat 60); Total Fat 7g (Saturated Fat 1g; Trans Fat 0g); Cholesterol 55mg; Sodium 240mg; Total Carbohydrate 59g (Dietary Fiber 1g; Sugars 31g); Protein 3g

% DAILY VALUE: Vitamin A 0%; Vitamin C 0%; Calcium 8%; Iron 6%

EXCHANGES: 1 Starch, 3 Other Carbohydrate, 1½ Fat

2
Carbohydrate
Choices

Lemon-Blueberry Muffins

PREP TIME: 15 min • **START TO FINISH:** 40 min • 12 muffins

1 MUFFIN: Calories 190 (Calories from Fat 70); Total Fat 8g (Saturated Fat 1g; Trans Fat 0g); Cholesterol 55mg; Sodium 250mg; Total Carbohydrate 27g (Dietary Fiber 1g; Sugars 11g); Protein 3g

% DAILY VALUE:
Vitamin A 2%; Vitamin C 0%; Calcium 6%; Iron 0%

EXCHANGES: 1 Starch, 1 Other Carbohydrate, 1½ Fat

2 cups Bisquick® Gluten Free mix

⅓ cup sugar

¾ cup fat-free (skim) milk

⅓ cup canola oil or melted butter

3 eggs, beaten

1 tablespoon grated lemon peel

1 cup fresh blueberries

2 tablespoons sugar

1 Heat oven to 400°F. Spray bottom only of 12 regular-size muffin cups with cooking spray without flour, or place paper baking cup in each muffin cup.

2 In large bowl, stir Bisquick® mix, ⅓ cup sugar, the milk, oil, eggs and lemon peel just until moistened. Fold in blueberries. Divide batter evenly among muffin cups. Sprinkle 2 tablespoons sugar evenly over batter in each muffin cup.

3 Bake 14 to 16 minutes or until set and lightly browned. Cool 5 minutes; transfer from pan to cooling rack. Serve warm.

Diabetes Team Tip
Developing and sticking to a schedule for monitoring blood sugar is one of the best tools you can use to learn how food and exercise affect your diabetes. —Dr. Bergenstal

Betty's Success Tip
Frozen blueberries may be substituted for fresh. Thaw completely and pat away excess moisture with a paper towel.

Apple-Gingerbread Muffins

PREP TIME: 20 min • **START TO FINISH:** 50 min • 16 muffins

2
Carbohydrate
Choices

1 cup white rice flour

¼ cup sweet white sorghum flour

¼ cup tapioca flour

1 teaspoon xanthan gum

1½ teaspoons gluten-free baking powder

¾ teaspoon salt

2 teaspoons ground ginger

1 teaspoon ground cinnamon

¼ cup canola oil

2 eggs

3 tablespoons unsulphured molasses

¾ cup packed light brown sugar

¼ cup water

1½ cups chopped peeled apple (about 1 large)

2 tablespoons gluten-free powdered sugar, if desired

1 Heat oven to 375°F. Place paper baking cup in each of 16 regular-size muffin cups.

2 In small bowl, mix flours, xanthan gum, baking powder, salt, ginger and cinnamon with whisk. In medium bowl, beat oil, eggs, molasses, brown sugar and water with electric mixer on medium speed until well blended. Gradually add flour mixture, beating on low speed just until combined. Stir in apple. Divide batter evenly among muffin cups.

3 Bake 20 to 25 minutes or until toothpick inserted in center comes out clean. Cool 5 minutes; remove from pan to cooling rack. Sprinkle powdered sugar over muffin tops. Serve warm.

1 MUFFIN: Calories 150 (Calories from Fat 40); Total Fat 4.5g (Saturated Fat 0.5g; Trans Fat 0g); Cholesterol 25mg; Sodium 170mg; Total Carbohydrate 26g (Dietary Fiber 0g; Sugars 13g); Protein 1g

% DAILY VALUE: Vitamin A 0%; Vitamin C 0%; Calcium 4%; Iron 4%

EXCHANGES: 1 Starch, 1 Other Carbohydrate, 1 Fat

Betty's Success Tip
No sorghum flour in your pantry? Increase the white rice flour to 1¼ cups.

2
Carbohydrate
Choices

Cornbread

PREP TIME: 10 min • **START TO FINISH:** 50 min • 12 servings

1 SERVING: Calories 180 (Calories from Fat 50); Total Fat 6g (Saturated Fat 0.5g; Trans Fat 0g); Cholesterol 35mg; Sodium 400mg; Total Carbohydrate 29g (Dietary Fiber 1g; Sugars 7g); Protein 2g

% DAILY VALUE: Vitamin A 2%; Vitamin C 0%; Calcium 8%; Iron 4%

EXCHANGES: 1 Starch, 1 Other Carbohydrate, 1 Fat

¾   cup cornmeal

½   cup tapioca flour

¼   cup white rice flour

¼   cup sorghum flour

¼   cup potato starch

2   teaspoons gluten-free baking powder

1   teaspoon baking soda

1   teaspoon salt

½   teaspoon xanthan gum

½   teaspoon guar gum

1¼   cups gluten-free almond, rice, soy or regular milk

1   teaspoon apple cider vinegar

⅓   cup sugar

2   eggs

¼   cup canola oil or melted ghee

1   Heat oven to 400°F. Spray bottom and sides of 8-inch square (2-quart) glass baking dish with cooking spray without flour.

2   In medium bowl, stir together cornmeal, all flours, the potato starch, baking powder, baking soda, salt and both gums; set aside.

3   In another medium bowl, beat milk, vinegar, sugar and eggs with electric mixer on medium speed until frothy. Gradually add oil, beating continuously until thoroughly mixed. Add cornmeal mixture; beat on low speed about 1 minute or until well blended. Pour into baking dish.

4   Bake 20 to 25 minutes or until top springs back when touched lightly in center and cornbread pulls away from sides of baking dish. Cool 15 minutes. Serve warm.

Jean Duane | Alternative Cook | http://www.alternativecook.com

Best-Ever Banana Bread

PREP TIME: 10 min • **START TO FINISH:** 2 hr 15 min • 1 loaf (24 slices)

½ cup tapioca flour

½ cup white rice flour

¼ cup garbanzo and fava flour

¼ cup sorghum flour

½ cup potato starch

1 teaspoon xanthan gum

½ teaspoon guar gum

1 teaspoon gluten-free baking powder

1 teaspoon baking soda

1 teaspoon ground cinnamon

1 teaspoon salt

¾ cup packed brown sugar

1 cup mashed very ripe bananas (2 medium)

½ cup canola oil or melted ghee

¼ cup gluten-free almond, rice, soy or regular milk

1 teaspoon gluten-free vanilla

2 eggs

1 Heat oven to 350°F. Generously spray bottom and sides of 9×5-inch loaf pan with cooking spray without flour. In small bowl, stir together all flours, the potato starch, both gums, baking powder, baking soda, cinnamon and salt; set aside.

2 In medium bowl, beat remaining ingredients with whisk until blended. Add flour mixture; stir until thoroughly mixed. Pour into pan.

3 Bake 30 minutes. Cover with foil; bake 25 to 30 minutes longer or until toothpick inserted in center comes out almost clean. Cool 5 minutes. Remove loaf from pan; place on cooling rack. Cool completely, about 1 hour. Wrap tightly and store in refrigerator.

Jean Duane | Alternative Cook | http://www.alternativecook.com

1 SLICE: Calories 130 (Calories from Fat 45); Total Fat 5g (Saturated Fat 0g; Trans Fat 0g); Cholesterol 20mg; Sodium 180mg; Total Carbohydrate 19g (Dietary Fiber 1g; Sugars 8g); Protein 1g

% DAILY VALUE: Vitamin A 0%; Vitamin C 0%; Calcium 2%; Iron 0%

EXCHANGES: ½ Starch, 1 Other Carbohydrate, 1 Fat

Diabetes Team Tip
When possible, select fortified versions of gluten-free flours, breads, cereals and crackers. —Diane Reader, Dietitian

Betty's Success Tip
To make Pumpkin Bread, substitute canned pumpkin (not pumpkin pie mix) for the mashed bananas and add ¼ teaspoon ground cloves and ¼ teaspoon ground nutmeg.

1
Carbohydrate Choice

Pumpkin–Chocolate Chip Cookies

PREP TIME: 30 min • **START TO FINISH:** 1 hr • 3 dozen cookies

1 COOKIE: Calories 80 (Calories from Fat 25); Total Fat 2.5g (Saturated Fat 1.5g; Trans Fat 0g); Cholesterol 10mg; Sodium 80mg; Total Carbohydrate 13g (Dietary Fiber 0g; Sugars 7g); Protein 0g

% DAILY VALUE: Vitamin A 15%; Vitamin C 0%; Calcium 0%; Iron 0%

EXCHANGES: 1 Other Carbohydrate, ½ Fat

¾ cup canned pumpkin (not pumpkin pie mix)

¼ cup butter, softened (not melted)

1 teaspoon gluten-free vanilla

1 egg

1 box Betty Crocker® Gluten Free chocolate chip cookie mix

½ cup raisins, if desired

¼ teaspoon ground cinnamon

Gluten-free powdered sugar, if desired

1 Heat oven to 350°F. Grease cookie sheets with shortening. In large bowl, stir pumpkin, butter, vanilla and egg until blended. Stir in cookie mix, raisins and cinnamon until soft dough forms.

2 On cookie sheets, drop dough by rounded tablespoonfuls 2 inches apart.

3 Bake 10 to 12 minutes or until almost no indentation remains when lightly touched in center and edges are golden brown. Immediately remove from cookie sheets to cooling racks. Cool completely, about 15 minutes. Sprinkle with powdered sugar.

Peppermint-Frosted Brownies

PREP TIME: 15 min • **START TO FINISH:** 45 min • 16 brownies

1½ Carbohydrate Choices

BROWNIES

- ⅓ cup unsweetened baking cocoa
- ¼ cup white rice flour
- ¼ cup potato starch flour
- ½ teaspoon xanthan gum
- ¼ teaspoon gluten-free baking powder
- ⅓ cup canola or sunflower oil or melted ghee (measured melted)
- ¾ cup granulated sugar
- 2 eggs
- 2 teaspoons gluten-free vanilla

FROSTING

- ¼ cup canola or sunflower oil or melted ghee (measured melted)
- ½ teaspoon gluten-free vanilla
- ¼ teaspoon pure peppermint extract or oil
- 1 cup gluten-free powdered sugar
- 2½ teaspoons gluten-free almond, soy or regular milk
- 2 tablespoons miniature semisweet chocolate chips

1 Heat oven to 350°F. Line 8-inch square pan with foil, leaving 1 inch of foil overhanging at 2 opposite sides of pan; spray foil with cooking spray without flour.

2 In small bowl, mix cocoa, flours, xanthan gum and baking powder. In medium bowl, beat oil, granulated sugar, eggs and vanilla with electric mixer on medium speed until well blended. Gradually add flour mixture, beating until well blended. Pour batter into pan.

3 Bake about 25 minutes or until toothpick inserted in center comes out clean. Cool completely in pan on cooling rack.

4 For frostings, in medium bowl, beat oil, vanilla and peppermint extract with electric mixer on medium speed. Gradually add powdered sugar and milk, beating until frosting is smooth and spreadable. If frosting is too thick, stir in additional milk, 1 teaspoon at a time. Stir in chocolate chips. Using foil, lift brownies out of pan; peel off foil. Frost brownies. Cut into 4 rows by 4 rows.

Jean Duane | Alternative Cook | http://www.alternativecook.com

1 BROWNIE: Calories 180 (Calories from Fat 80); Total Fat 9g (Saturated Fat 1g; Trans Fat 0g); Cholesterol 25mg; Sodium 15mg; Total Carbohydrate 23g (Dietary Fiber 0g; Sugars 17g); Protein 1g

% DAILY VALUE: Vitamin A 0%; Vitamin C 0%; Calcium 0%; Iron 2%

EXCHANGES: ½ Starch, 1 Other Carbohydrate, 1½ Fat

Betty's Success Tip

Peppermint oil is found in the spice aisle of most supermarkets and does not contain alcohol. Peppermint extract contains peppermint oil and alcohol. Either will work in this recipe.

½ Carbohydrate Choice

Glazed Meat Loaf

PREP TIME: 20 min • **START TO FINISH:** 1 hr 40 min • 6 servings (1 slice each)

1 SERVING: Calories 230 (Calories from Fat 90); Total Fat 10g (Saturated Fat 4g; Trans Fat 0.5g); Cholesterol 105mg; Sodium 530mg; Total Carbohydrate 10g (Dietary Fiber 0g; Sugars 6g); Protein 23g

% DAILY VALUE:
Vitamin A 4%; Vitamin C 2%; Calcium 4%; Iron 15%

EXCHANGES: ½ Other Carbohydrate, 3½ Lean Meat

MEAT LOAF

1½ lb extra-lean (at least 90%) ground beef

½ cup gluten-free cracker crumbs

2 tablespoons fat-free (skim) milk

2 tablespoons gluten-free ketchup

1 tablespoon gluten-free Dijon mustard

1 teaspoon dried sage leaves

½ teaspoon salt

¼ teaspoon pepper

1 small onion, finely chopped (⅓ cup)

1 egg

GLAZE

½ cup gluten-free ketchup

1 teaspoon gluten-free Dijon mustard

1 tablespoon packed brown sugar

1 Heat oven to 350°F. In large bowl, mix meat loaf ingredients. Spread mixture in ungreased 8×4- or 9×5-inch loaf pan.

2 In small bowl, mix glaze ingredients. Spread over meat loaf.

3 Bake uncovered 1 hour to 1 hour 15 minutes or until thermometer inserted in center of loaf reads 160°F. Drain and discard drippings from pan. Let stand 5 minutes before slicing.

Diabetes Team Tip
Be sure to take your medications as prescribed. If you have any questions, ask your doctor or pharmacist. Know when to take them and with what, how to store them and how to avoid side effects. Take a list of all your medications, the doses and how often you take them to each doctor visit.
—Dr. Bergenstal

Betty's Success Tip
To crush crackers, place a few crackers at a time in a plastic bag. Seal the bag, and crush crackers into fine crumbs with a rolling pin or the flat side of a meat mallet.

Hearty Chicken Pot Pie

PREP TIME: 15 min • **START TO FINISH:** 45 min • 6 servings

2
Carbohydrate
Choices

CHICKEN MIXTURE

1	tablespoon butter or margarine
1	medium onion, chopped (½ cup)
1	bag (12 oz) frozen mixed vegetables
1½	cups cut-up cooked chicken
1¾	cups reduced-sodium chicken broth
1	teaspoon seasoned salt
½	teaspoon dried thyme leaves
¾	cup fat-free (skim) milk
3	tablespoons cornstarch

TOPPING

¾	cup Bisquick® Gluten Free mix
½	cup fat-free (skim) milk
1	egg
2	tablespoons butter or margarine, melted
1	tablespoon chopped fresh parsley

1 Heat oven to 350°F. In 3-quart saucepan, melt butter over medium heat. Add onion; cook, stirring frequently, until tender. Stir in frozen vegetables, chicken, chicken broth, salt and thyme. Heat to boiling.

2 In small bowl, mix milk and cornstarch with whisk until smooth; stir into chicken mixture. Heat just to boiling. Pour into ungreased 2-quart casserole.

3 In small bowl, stir all topping ingredients except parsley with fork until blended. Drop topping mixture by small spoonfuls over chicken mixture. Sprinkle with parsley.

4 Bake uncovered 25 to 30 minutes or until toothpick inserted in center of topping comes out clean.

1 SERVING: Calories 260 (Calories from Fat 80); Total Fat 8g (Saturated Fat 4.5g; Trans Fat 0g); Cholesterol 80mg; Sodium 680mg; Total Carbohydrate 29g (Dietary Fiber 2g; Sugars 7g); Protein 16g

% DAILY VALUE: Vitamin A 25%; Vitamin C 4%; Calcium 10%; Iron 6%

EXCHANGES: 1 Starch, 1 Other Carbohydrate, 1½ Very Lean Meat, 1 Fat

1½ Carbohydrate Choices

Creamy Chicken and Broccoli Fettuccine

PREP TIME: 30 min • **START TO FINISH:** 30 min • 6 servings (1⅓ cups each)

1 SERVING: Calories 300 (Calories from Fat 100); Total Fat 11g (Saturated Fat 3.5g; Trans Fat 0g); Cholesterol 80mg; Sodium 350mg; Total Carbohydrate 25g (Dietary Fiber 2g; Sugars 3g); Protein 24g

% DAILY VALUE: Vitamin A 20%; Vitamin C 40%; Calcium 6%; Iron 10%

EXCHANGES: 1 Starch, 1½ Vegetable, 2½ Very Lean Meat, 2 Fat

6	oz uncooked gluten-free fettuccine
1	tablespoon canola oil
1	lb boneless skinless chicken breasts, cut into 1-inch pieces
1	medium onion, chopped (½ cup)
1	teaspoon gluten-free seasoned salt
2	cups broccoli florets
1	package (8 oz) sliced fresh mushrooms (about 3 cups)
1	medium red bell pepper, cut into 2- to 3-inch strips
4	oz (half of 8-oz package) ⅓-less-fat cream cheese (Neufchâtel), cut into cubes
1	teaspoon gluten-free garlic-pepper blend

1 Cook and drain fettuccine as directed on package.

2 Meanwhile, in 12-inch nonstick skillet, heat oil over medium heat. Add chicken and onion; sprinkle with seasoned salt. Cook about 4 minutes, stirring occasionally. Stir in broccoli, mushrooms and bell pepper. Cook 6 to 8 minutes, stirring occasionally, until chicken is no longer pink in center and vegetables are crisp-tender.

3 Add cream cheese and garlic-pepper blend to chicken mixture in skillet; stir to blend. Stir in cooked fettuccine; cook until thoroughly heated.

Betty's Success Tip

For added convenience, substitute frozen broccoli florets for the fresh. Gluten-free spaghetti may be used instead of fettuccine.

Chicken Noodle Soup

PREP TIME: 30 min • **START TO FINISH:** 30 min • 6 servings (1¼ cups each)

2
Carbohydrate
Choices

1   tablespoon canola oil

2   boneless skinless chicken breasts (about ¾ lb), cut into ½-inch pieces

¼   teaspoon gluten-free seasoned salt

½   teaspoon gluten-free garlic-pepper blend

1   medium onion, chopped (½ cup)

4   cups reduced-sodium chicken broth

1½ cups water

3   medium carrots, sliced (1½ cups)

1   medium stalk celery, sliced (½ cup)

1½ cups uncooked gluten-free quinoa rotelle pasta or other gluten-free spiral pasta

1   tablespoon chopped fresh or 1 teaspoon dried thyme leaves

1   In 4-quart saucepan, heat oil over medium-high heat. Cook chicken in oil 4 to 6 minutes, stirring occasionally, until no longer pink in center. Sprinkle chicken with seasoned salt and garlic-pepper blend. Add onion; cook 2 to 3 minutes, stirring occasionally, until tender.

2   Stir in broth, water, carrots and celery. Heat to boiling; reduce heat to medium. Cook 5 minutes.

3   Add pasta and thyme. Simmer uncovered 8 to 10 minutes, stirring occasionally, until pasta and vegetables are tender (do not overcook pasta).

1 SERVING: Calories 250 (Calories from Fat 45); Total Fat 5g (Saturated Fat 1g; Trans Fat 0g); Cholesterol 35mg; Sodium 490mg; Total Carbohydrate 30g (Dietary Fiber 2g; Sugars 3g); Protein 20g

% DAILY VALUE: Vitamin A 100%; Vitamin C 4%; Calcium 4%; Iron 10%

EXCHANGES: 2 Starch, ½ Vegetable, 2 Very Lean Meat, ½ Fat

Betty's Success Tip

Gluten-free pasta is more fragile than regular pasta and will break apart, so be careful to not overcook it or stir it too much.

2½ Carbohydrate Choices

Cheesy Vegetable Pizza with Basil

PREP TIME: 10 min • **START TO FINISH:** 1 hr 25 min • 2 pizzas (6 servings each)

1 SERVING: Calories 250 (Calories from Fat 60); Total Fat 7g (Saturated Fat 2g; Trans Fat 0g); Cholesterol 10mg; Sodium 340mg; Total Carbohydrate 39g (Dietary Fiber 4g; Sugars 6g); Protein 9g

% DAILY VALUE: Vitamin A 8%; Vitamin C 10%; Calcium 15%; Iron 8%

EXCHANGES: 2½ Starch, 1 Vegetable, 1 Fat

CRUST

1¾	cups lukewarm water (about 95°F)
2	teaspoons unflavored gelatin
1	tablespoon fast-rising dry yeast
2	tablespoons olive oil
2	tablespoons honey
1	teaspoon apple cider vinegar
1	cup sorghum flour
¾	cup brown rice flour
½	cup garbanzo and fava flour
½	cup white rice flour
½	cup potato starch
1	teaspoon salt
1	teaspoon guar gum
1	teaspoon xanthan gum
	Cooking spray without flour

TOPPINGS

1	can (15 oz) gluten-free pizza sauce
1	bell pepper, cut into thin slices
1	package (8 oz) sliced fresh mushrooms
¼	cup sliced fresh basil
1½	cups shredded reduced-fat mozzarella cheese (6 oz)

1 Spray 2 (12-inch) pizza pans with cooking spray without flour. In small bowl, stir warm water, gelatin, yeast, oil, honey and vinegar until yeast is dissolved; set aside.

2 In medium bowl, stir together remaining crust ingredients except cooking spray without flour. Add yeast mixture; beat with electric mixer on low speed 1 minute.

3 Divide dough in half. Spread half of dough in each pizza pan. Lightly spray dough with cooking spray; cover with plastic wrap. Let rise in warm place (80°F to 85°F) until doubled in height, about 45 minutes.

4 Heat oven to 425°F. Uncover dough; bake about 10 minutes or until surface is dry. Remove from oven. Spread half of pizza sauce over each crust. Top each with half of the remaining toppings, ending with cheese. Bake 15 to 20 minutes longer or until crust is browned and cheese is melted.

Jean Duane | Alternative Cook | http://www.alternativecook.com

Diabetes Team Tip Choose plain versions of fruits and vegetables, as anything in a sauce may contain thickeners or flavorings that contain gluten. —Diane Reader, Dietitian

Betty's Success Tip Garbanzo and fava flour or garfava flour is a mixture of garbanzo and fava beans. It can be substituted with soybean or white bean flour. Also, cornstarch may be substituted for the potato starch.

Champagne Shrimp Risotto

PREP TIME: 50 min • **START TO FINISH:** 50 min • 6 servings

3
Carbohydrate
Choices

1 lb medium shrimp in shells, thawed if frozen

1 tablespoon butter or margarine

1 medium onion, thinly sliced

½ cup brut Champagne, dry white wine or reduced-sodium chicken broth

1½ cups uncooked Arborio or other short-grain white rice

2 cups reduced-sodium chicken broth, warmed

1 cup clam juice or water, warmed

2 cups chopped arugula, watercress or spinach

⅓ cup grated Parmesan cheese

½ teaspoon pepper

Chopped fresh parsley, if desired

1 Peel shrimp. Make a shallow cut lengthwise down back of each shrimp; wash out vein.

2 In 12-inch skillet or 4-quart Dutch oven, melt butter over medium-high heat. Add onion; cook, stirring frequently, until tender. Reduce heat to medium. Add shrimp; cook uncovered about 8 minutes, turning once, until shrimp are pink. Remove shrimp from skillet; keep warm.

3 Add Champagne to onion in skillet; cook until liquid has evaporated. Stir in rice. Cook uncovered over medium heat about 5 minutes, stirring frequently, until edges of rice kernels are translucent. In 4-cup glass measuring cup, mix chicken broth and clam juice; pour ½ cup of the mixture over rice. Cook uncovered, stirring occasionally, until liquid is absorbed. Repeat with remaining broth mixture, ½ cup at a time, until rice is tender and creamy.

4 About 5 minutes before risotto is done, stir in shrimp, arugula, cheese and pepper. Sprinkle with parsley before serving.

1 SERVING: Calories 290 (Calories from Fat 40); Total Fat 4.5g (Saturated Fat 2.5g; Trans Fat 0g); Cholesterol 80mg; Sodium 470mg; Total Carbohydrate 43g (Dietary Fiber 1g; Sugars 1g); Protein 15g

% DAILY VALUE: Vitamin A 8%; Vitamin C 4%; Calcium 15%; Iron 20%

EXCHANGES: 2½ Starch, 1 Vegetable, 1 Very Lean Meat, ½ Fat

Betty's Success Tip

Even though you may be tempted, don't rush the process! When making risotto, adding the broth a little at a time ensures that the dish will be creamy while allowing the grains to remain separate.

Living Gluten-Free

ALL ABOUT GLUTEN AND CELIAC DISEASE

Gluten describes several proteins naturally found in certain grains such as wheat, barley, rye and some oats. Any foods that are made with these grains also contain gluten including foods such as bagels, breads, cakes, cereals, cookies, crackers, pasta, pizza and more.

About 3 million Americans suffer from a serious medical condition called celiac disease (or celiac sprue). With celiac disease, eating gluten or gluten-containing foods triggers an autoimmune reaction that leads to inflammation and damage to the lining of the small intestine. This damage makes it very difficult for the body to absorb nutrients from foods.

Over time, a damaged small intestine can lead to malnourishment and other possible complications such as loss of bone density, iron deficiency anemia, gastrointestinal and neurological symptoms and quality-of-life issues. Eating gluten-free is the best way to prevent any further damage to the small intestine. However, managing celiac disease is not just about eliminating gluten from the diet. People affected with celiac disease must take extra care to ensure that they get all the vitamins and nutrients they need—particularly calcium, iron, fiber, whole grains and B vitamins. In many cases, a gluten-free vitamin and mineral supplement may be recommended to provide extra assurance that nutrition needs are being met. Your healthcare provider can help determine what is right for you or your family.

READING LABELS TO AVOID GLUTEN

The best way to know if a product is gluten-free is to read the ingredients label. To determine if a product contains gluten, there are four foods to look for: wheat, barley, oats and rye. And since ingredients and products can change over time, you'll need to monitor ingredient labels regularly to know which foods are gluten-free. Even if a product does not contain these obvious sources of gluten, you may wish to contact the product manufacturer to confirm gluten-free status.

FOR MORE INFORMATION:

- Celiac Sprue Association www.csaceliacs.org

- Celiac Disease Foundation www.celiac.org

- University of Chicago Celiac Disease Center www.celiacdisease.net

- University of Maryland Center for Celiac Research www.celiaccenter.org

- Bell Institute of Health and Nutrition www.bellinstitute.com

- Visit www.glutenfreely.com

FINDING GLUTEN-FREE FOODS AT THE GROCERY STORE

With a bounty of food choices, how do you know what's gluten-free? To help you get started, here's a general grocery guide to help steer you toward foods that are smart choices for a gluten-free lifestyle.

Produce: Fruits and vegetables are a colorful place to start for gluten-free living. These foods in their fresh form are naturally gluten-free, plus they contain vitamins and minerals as well as fiber. Enjoy citrus fruits, bell peppers, strawberries and kiwifruit for a burst of vitamin C. Serve dark green and leafy green veggies such as asparagus and broccoli that contain

B vitamins. Choose colorful apples, beets, carrots, grapes, peaches, plums, tomatoes, watermelon and zucchini. Starchy vegetables that are naturally gluten-free, including potatoes, sweet potatoes and winter squash, can fill you up and take the place of pasta or other gluten-containing side dishes. And don't forget about frozen, canned and dried options—but read labels to be sure your selections are indeed gluten-free.

Meats, Poultry and Fish: Vitamin B_{12} from naturally gluten-free fish, meat and poultry plays a role in brain and nervous system health. Choose plain chicken breasts, ground turkey, beef tenderloin and pork loin as well as fresh salmon or flounder. Canned salmon and sardines (with bones) can provide protein as well as calcium. Check labels and ask questions at the grocery store, as some meat products can be enhanced with broths and flavorings that may contain gluten. Imitation crab (surimi), for example, is one such culprit. Marinated meats, unless specifically labeled "gluten-free," are another place to double-check for hidden gluten.

Dairy and Eggs: Calcium is important to everyone for bone development and strength—but even more so if you are living gluten-free. Go for fresh, natural choices such as low-fat milk, natural cheeses and plain yogurt. Read labels carefully on processed cheeses, yogurt and enhanced milks to be sure they don't contain thickeners or additives with gluten. Choose whole eggs in shells or gluten-free egg products.

Flours, Pastas and Grains: The choices for gluten-free flours and pastas are becoming greater as interest in eating gluten-free has risen. Look for fortified versions of grain foods whenever possible to help you get all the important nutrients they provide. Gluten-free grains like quinoa, amaranth, millet, sorghum and buckwheat can help fill your plate, and your appetite, without adding hidden gluten. Other whole-grain options such as brown rice, hominy, grits and cornmeal are good choices too. Steer clear of the bulk bins, where cross-contamination with other non-gluten-free bins can easily happen. For example, if someone uses the same scoop to get wheat-based pasta (which isn't gluten-free) and then it's used for rice flour (which is gluten-free)—oops! The rice flour has been contaminated!

Cereals, Breads and Crackers: Choose gluten-free flours, breads, cereals and crackers that do not contain wheat, oats, barley or rye. These foods are good sources of B vitamins, fiber, folic acid and iron. Today there are more and more gluten-free grain foods on store shelves with lots of options to choose from. Select fortified versions whenever possible and those with extra fiber to boost nutritional value. Read labels carefully, as "wheat-free" doesn't necessarily mean gluten-free as gluten is found in oats, barley and rye.

Prepared Foods, Soups and Legumes: Look for prepared foods and soups that are labeled gluten-free, as broths, thickeners and flavorings added to these foods can contain gluten. Legumes, such as beans, lentils and split peas, are a naturally gluten-free choice for carbohydrates, iron and fiber—especially if you cook them yourself. If you buy the canned varieties, choose the plain type without sauces, as the sauces may contain thickeners with gluten.

Spices, Condiments and Sauces: Gluten is prevalent in many of these products. Even if the foods don't contain gluten, they may have been processed in facilities that process foods that contain gluten. When in doubt, call the manufacturer, as some seasonings can have gluten-based starches to prevent clumping. Flavorings, gravies, salad dressings, sauce mixes and sauces such as barbecue, soy, teriyaki or sweet and sour can also be hidden sources of gluten.

Frozen Foods: Choose plain versions of fruits and vegetables—as anything in sauce may contain thickeners or flavorings with gluten. Frozen entrées, French fries and breaded items like chicken fingers or fish sticks may contain gluten unless specifically labeled gluten-free. Even ice creams, frozen yogurt and frozen novelties may contain hidden gluten! They can contain gluten-based starches to help prevent ice crystals from forming—so read those labels to be sure.

CHAPTER 8

Delightful Desserts

2½ Carbohydrate Choices

Baked Berry Cups with Crispy Cinnamon Wedges

PREP TIME: 25 min • **START TO FINISH:** 1 hr 5 min • 4 servings

1 SERVING: Calories 180 (Calories from Fat 20); Total Fat 2g (Saturated Fat 0g; Trans Fat 0g); Cholesterol 0mg; Sodium 60mg; Total Carbohydrate 37g (Dietary Fiber 7g; Sugars 25g); Protein 3g

% DAILY VALUE: Vitamin A 0%; Vitamin C 15%; Calcium 4%; Iron 4%

EXCHANGES: ½ Starch, 1½ Fruit, ½ Other Carbohydrate, ½ Fat

2	teaspoons sugar
¾	teaspoon ground cinnamon
	Butter-flavor cooking spray
1	balanced carb whole wheat tortilla (6 inch)
¼	cup sugar
2	tablespoons white whole wheat flour
1	teaspoon grated orange peel, if desired
1½	cups fresh blueberries
1½	cups fresh raspberries
	About 1 cup fat-free whipped cream topping (from aerosol can)

1 Heat oven to 375°F. In sandwich-size resealable food-storage plastic bag, combine 2 teaspoons sugar and ½ teaspoon of the cinnamon. Using cooking spray, spray both sides of tortilla, about 3 seconds per side; cut tortilla into 8 wedges. In bag with cinnamon-sugar, add wedges; seal bag. Shake to coat wedges evenly.

2 On ungreased cookie sheet, spread out wedges. Bake 7 to 9 minutes, turning once, until just beginning to crisp (wedges will continue to crisp while cooling). Cool about 15 minutes.

3 Meanwhile, spray 4 (6-oz) custard cups or ramekins with cooking spray; place cups on another cookie sheet. In small bowl, stir ¼ cup sugar, the flour, orange peel and remaining ¼ teaspoon cinnamon until blended. In medium bowl, gently toss berries with sugar mixture; divide evenly among custard cups.

4 Bake 15 minutes; stir gently. Bake 5 to 7 minutes longer or until liquid is bubbling around edges. Cool at least 15 minutes.

5 To serve, top each cup with about ¼ cup whipped cream topping; serve tortilla wedges with berry cups. Serve warm.

Diabetes Team Tip Keeping a daily log of the foods you eat and any higher-than-normal glucose levels can help you stay in control of your diabetes. —Dr. Bergenstal

Betty's Success Tip By dunking tortilla wedges into the fruit mixture, it will seem like you're eating pie! To cut wedges quickly and easily, use a pizza cutter.

0
Carbohydrate Choices

Dulce de Leche Fillo Cups

PREP TIME: 15 min • **START TO FINISH:** 15 min • 15 servings

1 SERVING: Calories 40 (Calories from Fat 20); Total Fat 2g (Saturated Fat 0.5g; Trans Fat 0g); Cholesterol 0mg; Sodium 35mg; Total Carbohydrate 4g (Dietary Fiber 0g; Sugars 2g); Protein 0g

% DAILY VALUE: Vitamin A 0%; Vitamin C 2%; Calcium 0%; Iron 0%

EXCHANGES: ½ Other Carbohydrate, ½ Fat

2   oz ⅓-less-fat cream cheese (Neufchâtel), softened
2   tablespoons dulce de leche (caramel) syrup
1   tablespoon reduced-fat sour cream
1   package frozen mini fillo shells (15 shells)
⅓   cup sliced fresh strawberries
2   tablespoons diced mango

1   In medium bowl, beat cream cheese with electric mixer on low speed until creamy. Beat in dulce de leche syrup and sour cream until blended.

2   Spoon cream cheese mixture into each fillo shell. Top each with strawberries and mango.

Betty's Success Tip
Dulce de leche is similar to sweetened condensed milk, but it has been caramelized and is much thicker. It can be found near the sweetened condensed milk section in the grocery store.

Mixed-Berry Snack Cake

PREP TIME: 15 min • **START TO FINISH:** 1 hr • 8 servings

2 Carbohydrate Choices

¼ cup low-fat granola

½ cup buttermilk

⅓ cup packed brown sugar

2 tablespoons canola oil

1 teaspoon vanilla

1 egg

1 cup whole wheat flour

½ teaspoon baking soda

½ teaspoon ground cinnamon

⅛ teaspoon salt

1 cup mixed fresh berries (such as blueberries, raspberries and blackberries)

1 Heat oven to 350°F. Spray 8- or 9-inch round pan with cooking spray. Place granola in resealable food-storage plastic bag; seal bag and slightly crush with rolling pin or meat mallet. Set aside.

2 In large bowl, stir buttermilk, brown sugar, oil, vanilla and egg until smooth. Stir in flour, baking soda, cinnamon and salt just until moistened. Gently fold in half of the berries. Spoon into pan. Sprinkle with remaining berries and the granola.

3 Bake 28 to 33 minutes or until golden brown and top springs back when touched in center. Cool in pan on cooling rack 10 minutes. Serve warm.

1 SERVING: Calories 160 (Calories from Fat 45); Total Fat 5g (Saturated Fat 0.5g; Trans Fat 0g); Cholesterol 30mg; Sodium 140mg; Total Carbohydrate 26g (Dietary Fiber 1g; Sugars 12g); Protein 3g

% DAILY VALUE: Vitamin A 0%; Vitamin C 2%; Calcium 4%; Iron 6%

EXCHANGES: 1 Starch, 1 Other Carbohydrate, 1 Fat

Betty's Success Tip

The low-fat granola and whole wheat flour in this tasty coffee cake give you two whole grains. The vanilla, cinnamon and nutmeg add flavor and help bring out the natural sweetness in baked goods so you don't need to add a lot of extra sugar.

1
Carbohydrate
Choice

Lemon Dessert Shots

PREP TIME: 30 min • **START TO FINISH:** 1 hr • 12 servings

1 SERVING: Calories 110 (Calories from Fat 25); Total Fat 3g (Saturated Fat 1.5g; Trans Fat 0g); Cholesterol 15mg; Sodium 70mg; Total Carbohydrate 18g (Dietary Fiber 0g; Sugars 14g); Protein 2g

% DAILY VALUE: Vitamin A 2%; Vitamin C 2%; Calcium 4%; Iron 0%

EXCHANGES: ½ Starch, ½ Other Carbohydrate, ½ Fat

10 gingersnap cookies

2 oz ⅓-less-fat cream cheese (Neufchâtel), softened

½ cup marshmallow crème (from 7-oz jar)

1 container (6 oz) fat-free Greek honey vanilla yogurt

½ cup lemon curd (from 10-oz jar)

36 fresh raspberries

½ cup frozen (thawed) lite whipped topping

1 In 1-quart resealable food-storage plastic bag, place cookies; seal bag. Crush with rolling pin or meat mallet; place in small bowl.

2 In medium bowl, beat cream cheese and marshmallow crème with electric mixer on low speed until smooth. Beat in yogurt until blended. Place mixture in 1-quart resealable food-storage plastic bag; seal bag. In 1-pint resealable food-storage plastic bag, place lemon curd; seal bag. Cut ⅛-inch opening diagonally across bottom corner of each bag.

3 In bottom of each of 12 (2-oz) shot glasses, place 1 raspberry. For each glass, pipe about 2 teaspoons yogurt mixture over raspberry. Pipe ¼-inch ring of lemon curd around edge of glass; sprinkle with about 1 teaspoon cookies. Repeat.

4 Garnish each dessert shot with dollop of about 2 teaspoons whipped topping and 1 raspberry. Place in 9-inch square pan. Refrigerate 30 minutes or until chilled but no longer than 3 hours.

Betty's Success Tip Shot glasses often have some kind of writing on them. For a prettier presentation, purchase plain shot glasses at your local party store or online.

½
Carbohydrate
Choice

Pomegranate–Tequila Sunrise Jelly Shots

PREP TIME: 30 min • **START TO FINISH:** 4 hr • 12 servings

1 SERVING: Calories 60 (Calories from Fat 0); Total Fat 0g (Saturated Fat 0g; Trans Fat 0g); Cholesterol 0mg; Sodium 0mg; Total Carbohydrate 9g (Dietary Fiber 0g; Sugars 9g); Protein 1g

% DAILY VALUE: Vitamin A 0%; Vitamin C 25%; Calcium 0%; Iron 0%

EXCHANGES: ½ Fruit

¾   cup pulp-free orange juice

2   envelopes unflavored gelatin

6   tablespoons silver or gold tequila

½   cup 100% pomegranate juice

¼   cup sugar

¼   cup water

Whole orange slices or orange slice wedges

1   Lightly spray 12 (2-oz) shot glasses with cooking spray; gently wipe any excess with paper towel. In 1-quart saucepan, pour orange juice; sprinkle 1 envelope gelatin evenly over juice to soften. Heat over low heat, stirring constantly, until gelatin is completely dissolved; remove from heat. Stir in tequila. Divide orange juice mixture evenly among shot glasses (about 2 tablespoons per glass). In 9-inch square pan, place shot glasses. Refrigerate 30 minutes or until almost set.

2   Meanwhile, in same saucepan, combine pomegranate juice, sugar and water. Sprinkle remaining 1 envelope gelatin evenly over juice to soften. Heat over low heat, stirring constantly, until gelatin is completely dissolved; remove from heat.

3   Remove shot glasses from refrigerator (orange layer should appear mostly set). Pour pomegranate mixture evenly over top of orange layer in glasses (about 4 teaspoons per glass). Refrigerate at least 3 hours until completely chilled and firm.

4   Just before serving, dip a table knife in hot water; slide knife along inside edge of shot glass to loosen. Shake jelly shot out of glass onto plate; repeat with remaining jelly shots. Serve each jelly shot on top of whole orange slice or serve jelly shots with orange slice wedges.

Betty's Success Tip

Be sure to pay attention to the 30-minute chilling time for the orange juice layer before adding the steaming pomegranate layer. The timing helps to give the two-layer appearance and also ensures your dessert shots will release from the glasses in one piece, rather than in two separate layers.

2½ Carbohydrate Choices

Ginger Cake with Caramel-Apple Topping

PREP TIME: 15 min • **START TO FINISH:** 1 hr • 15 servings

1 SERVING: Calories 230 (Calories from Fat 50); Total Fat 6g (Saturated Fat 0.5g; Trans Fat 0g); Cholesterol 15mg; Sodium 220mg; Total Carbohydrate 40g (Dietary Fiber 2g; Sugars 21g); Protein 3g

% DAILY VALUE: Vitamin A 4%; Vitamin C 0%; Calcium 8%; Iron 8%

EXCHANGES: 1 Starch, 1½ Other Carbohydrate, 1 Fat

2	cups harvest peach or vanilla fat-free yogurt
½	cup caramel fat-free topping
1¼	cups whole wheat flour
1	cup all-purpose flour
¼	cup sugar
1	teaspoon baking soda
1	teaspoon ground cinnamon
1	teaspoon ground ginger
½	teaspoon salt
½	cup molasses
⅓	cup canola oil
1	egg
1	medium tart apple, chopped
	Lemon juice

1 Heat oven to 350°F. Grease and flour 9-inch square pan. In medium bowl, mix ¾ cup of the yogurt and the caramel topping; cover and refrigerate until serving time.

2 In large bowl, beat remaining 1¼ cups yogurt and all remaining ingredients except apple and lemon juice with electric mixer on low speed 45 seconds, scraping bowl constantly. Beat on medium speed 1 minute, scraping bowl occasionally, until well blended. Stir in half of the chopped apple. Pour batter into pan. Sprinkle lemon juice over remaining apple; cover and refrigerate until serving time.

3 Bake 38 to 43 minutes or until toothpick inserted in center comes out clean. Cool slightly. Serve with topping mixture and remaining chopped apple.

Betty's Success Tip

Molasses, a thick syrup, is a by-product of making sugar. Blackstrap molasses is the most concentrated type, full of vitamins and minerals such as iron and calcium.

Creamy Key Lime Pie

PREP TIME: 30 min · **START TO FINISH:** 3 hr 30 min · 8 servings

1½ Carbohydrate Choices

CRUST

2 cups Fiber One® cereal

¼ cup butter or margarine, melted

1 tablespoon corn syrup

1 teaspoon vanilla

FILLING

2 tablespoons cold water

1 tablespoon lime juice

1½ teaspoons unflavored gelatin

4 oz (half of 8-oz package) ⅓-less-fat cream cheese (Neufchâtel), softened

3 containers (6 oz each) Key lime pie low-fat yogurt

½ cup frozen (thawed) reduced-fat whipped topping

2 teaspoons grated lime peel

1 Heat oven to 350°F. Place cereal in resealable food-storage plastic bag; seal bag and finely crush with rolling pin or meat mallet until cereal looks like graham cracker crumbs (or finely crush in food processor).

2 In medium bowl, mix crust ingredients until blended. Press crust mixture evenly and firmly in bottom and up side of ungreased 9-inch glass pie plate. Bake 10 to 12 minutes or until firm. Cool completely, about 1 hour.

3 In 1-quart saucepan, mix water and lime juice. Sprinkle gelatin on lime juice mixture; let stand 1 minute. Heat over low heat, stirring constantly, until gelatin is dissolved. Cool slightly, about 2 minutes.

4 In medium bowl, beat cream cheese with electric mixer on medium speed until smooth. Add yogurt and lime juice mixture; beat on low speed until well blended. Fold in whipped topping and lime peel. Spoon into crust. Refrigerate until set, about 2 hours.

1 SERVING: Calories 210 (Calories from Fat 90); Total Fat 10g (Saturated Fat 6g; Trans Fat 0g); Cholesterol 25mg; Sodium 180mg; Total Carbohydrate 24g (Dietary Fiber 7g; Sugars 8g); Protein 4g

% DAILY VALUE: Vitamin A 10%; Vitamin C 4%; Calcium 15%; Iron 15%

EXCHANGES: 1 Starch, ½ Other Carbohydrate, 2 Fat

Diabetes Team Tip
A refreshing Key lime pie gets the benefit of high fiber when the crust is made with Fiber One® cereal. It's delicious! —Diane Reader, Dietitian

2
Carbohydrate
Choices

Dark Chocolate Cupcakes

PREP TIME: 35 min • **START TO FINISH:** 1 hr 10 min • 12 cupcakes

1 CUPCAKE: Calories 170 (Calories from Fat 50); Total Fat 6g (Saturated Fat 1.5g; Trans Fat 0g); Cholesterol 0mg; Sodium 190mg; Total Carbohydrate 27g (Dietary Fiber 2g; Sugars 18g); Protein 3g

% DAILY VALUE:
Vitamin A 2%; Vitamin C 0%; Calcium 4%; Iron 6%

EXCHANGES: 1 Starch, 1 Other Carbohydrate, 1 Fat

CUPCAKES

1½	oz bittersweet baking chocolate (3 squares from 4-oz bar), finely chopped
6	tablespoons unsweetened dark baking cocoa
½	teaspoon instant espresso coffee powder
½	cup fat-free (skim) milk
¾	cup white whole wheat flour
¾	teaspoon baking soda
¼	teaspoon salt
¼	cup fat-free egg product
½	cup granulated sugar
¼	cup packed brown sugar
3	tablespoons canola oil
2	teaspoons vanilla

GLAZE

2	teaspoons fat-free (skim) milk
1	tablespoon unsweetened dark baking cocoa
1	oz fat-free cream cheese (from 8-oz package)
⅓	cup powdered sugar
⅛	teaspoon vanilla
	Pinch salt
¼	oz bittersweet baking chocolate (½ square from 4-oz bar), grated

1 Heat oven to 350°F. Place paper baking cup in each of 12 regular-size muffin cups.

2 In small bowl, add chocolate, cocoa and espresso powder. In small microwavable measuring cup, microwave milk uncovered on High 30 seconds or until steaming but not boiling. Pour over chocolate mixture; stir. Cover; let stand 5 minutes. Stir until smooth.

3 Meanwhile, in medium bowl, stir flour, baking soda and salt. In large bowl, beat egg product with electric mixer on medium speed 30 seconds. Gradually add sugars, about ¼ cup at a time, beating well after each addition. Beat 2 minutes longer. Beat in oil and vanilla. Beat about ⅓ of the flour mixture and about ½ of the chocolate mixture at a time alternately into sugar mixture on low speed until blended.

4 Divide batter evenly among muffin cups, filling each about ⅔ full. Bake 20 to 25 minutes or until tops spring back when touched lightly in center. Cool 5 minutes; transfer from muffin cups to cooling rack. Cool completely before glazing.

5 In small bowl or microwavable custard cup, heat milk uncovered on High about 10 seconds or until hot. Stir in cocoa until smooth.

6 In separate small bowl, stir cream cheese until smooth. Stir in cocoa mixture until blended. Stir in powdered sugar. Stir in vanilla and salt until mixture is smooth and shiny. Spoon about 1 teaspoon glaze over each cupcake; spread to edge with back of spoon. Sprinkle about ¼ teaspoon grated chocolate over each glazed cupcake.

2
Carbohydrate Choices

Mixed-Berry Cream Tart

PREP TIME: 20 min • **START TO FINISH:** 3 hr 30 min • 8 servings

1 SERVING: Calories 170 (Calories from Fat 30); Total Fat 3g (Saturated Fat 0.5g; Trans Fat 0g); Cholesterol 0mg; Sodium 340mg; Total Carbohydrate 27g (Dietary Fiber 3g; Sugars 17g); Protein 8g

% DAILY VALUE: Vitamin A 6%; Vitamin C 25%; Calcium 10%; Iron 4%

EXCHANGES: 1 Starch, 1 Other Carbohydrate, ½ Medium-Fat Meat

2   cups sliced fresh strawberries
½   cup boiling water
1   box (4-serving size) sugar-free strawberry gelatin
3   pouches (1.5 oz each) roasted almond crunchy granola bars (from 8.9-oz box)
1   package (8 oz) fat-free cream cheese
¼   cup sugar
¼   teaspoon almond extract
1   cup fresh blueberries
1   cup fresh raspberries
    Fat-free whipped topping, if desired

1 In small bowl, crush 1 cup of the strawberries with pastry blender or fork. Reserve remaining 1 cup strawberries.

2 In medium bowl, pour boiling water over gelatin; stir about 2 minutes or until gelatin is completely dissolved. Stir crushed strawberries into gelatin. Refrigerate 20 minutes.

3 Meanwhile, leaving granola bars in pouches, crush granola bars with rolling pin. Sprinkle crushed granola in bottom of 9-inch ungreased glass pie plate, pushing crumbs up side of plate to make crust.

4 In small bowl, beat cream cheese, sugar and almond extract with electric mixer on medium-high speed until smooth. Drop by spoonfuls over crushed granola; gently spread to cover bottom of crust.

5 Gently fold blueberries, raspberries and remaining 1 cup strawberries into gelatin mixture. Spoon over cream cheese mixture. Refrigerate about 3 hours or until firm. Serve topped with whipped topping.

Diabetes Team Tip   Research shows that antioxidants naturally found in blueberries may help prevent cell damage from oxygen. —Diane Reader, Dietitian

Betty's Success Tip   The same pigments that give strawberries and blueberries their intense colors are thought to help prevent disease. The great thing about having fruit in dessert is that it is likely to be eaten!

Creamy Pineapple-Pecan Dessert Squares

PREP TIME: 25 min • **START TO FINISH:** 4 hr 30 min • 18 servings

1
Carbohydrate Choice

¾ cup boiling water

1 package (4-serving size) lemon sugar-free gelatin

1 cup unsweetened pineapple juice

1½ cups graham cracker crumbs

½ cup sugar

¼ cup shredded coconut

¼ cup chopped pecans

3 tablespoons butter or margarine, melted

1 package (8 oz) fat-free cream cheese

1 container (8 oz) fat-free sour cream

1 can (8 oz) crushed pineapple, undrained

1 In large bowl, pour boiling water over gelatin; stir about 2 minutes or until gelatin is completely dissolved. Stir in pineapple juice. Refrigerate about 30 minutes or until mixture is syrupy and just beginning to thicken.

2 Meanwhile, in 13×9-inch (3-quart) glass baking dish, toss cracker crumbs, ¼ cup of the sugar, the coconut, pecans and melted butter until well mixed. Reserve ½ cup crumb mixture for topping. Press remaining mixture in bottom of dish.

3 In medium bowl, beat cream cheese, sour cream and remaining ¼ cup sugar with electric mixer on medium speed until smooth; set aside.

4 Beat gelatin mixture with electric mixer on low speed until foamy; beat on high speed until light and fluffy (mixture will look like beaten egg whites). Beat in cream cheese mixture just until mixed. Gently stir in pineapple (with liquid). Pour into crust-lined dish; smooth top. Sprinkle reserved ½ cup crumb mixture over top. Refrigerate about 4 hours or until set. For servings, cut into 6 rows by 3 rows.

1 SERVING: Calories 120 (Calories from Fat 40); Total Fat 4.5g (Saturated Fat 2g; Trans Fat 0g); Cholesterol 10mg; Sodium 180mg; Total Carbohydrate 18g (Dietary Fiber 0g; Sugars 11g); Protein 3g

% DAILY VALUE: Vitamin A 4%; Vitamin C 0%; Calcium 8%; Iron 2%

EXCHANGES: 1 Starch, 1 Fat

Betty's Success Tip

This is a light, refreshing treat reminiscent of the refrigerator desserts of the 1970s. The pecans lend a nutty, crunchy flavor and texture.

1½
Carbohydrate
Choices

Mini Chocolate Cheesecakes

PREP TIME: 20 min • **START TO FINISH:** 2 hr 25 min • 12 servings

1 SERVING: Calories 200 (Calories from Fat 80); Total Fat 9g (Saturated Fat 4.5g; Trans Fat 0g); Cholesterol 40mg; Sodium 160mg; Total Carbohydrate 25g (Dietary Fiber 0g; Sugars 19g); Protein 4g

% DAILY VALUE: Vitamin A 6%; Vitamin C 0%; Calcium 4%; Iron 4%

EXCHANGES: 1 Starch, ½ Other Carbohydrate, 1½ Fat

CHEESECAKES

12	foil baking cups
12	thin chocolate wafer cookies (from 9-oz package), crushed (⅔ cup)
12	oz ⅓-less-fat cream cheese (Neufchâtel), softened
⅔	cup sugar
2	teaspoons vanilla
¼	cup unsweetened baking cocoa
1	egg
1	egg white
1	oz bittersweet or semisweet baking chocolate, melted

TOPPING

⅓	cup fat-free hot fudge topping
	Fresh raspberries, if desired

1 Heat oven to 325°F. Place foil baking cup in each of 12 regular-size muffin cups. With back of spoon, firmly press slightly less than 1 tablespoon cookie crumbs in bottom of each foil cup.

2 In large bowl, beat cream cheese with electric mixer on medium speed until creamy. Beat in sugar and vanilla until fluffy. Beat in cocoa. Beat in whole egg and egg white until well blended. Stir in melted chocolate. Divide cheese mixture evenly among crumb-lined foil cups.

3 Bake 28 to 32 minutes or until set. Cool in pan on cooling rack 15 minutes. Remove cheesecakes from pan; cool 15 minutes longer. Refrigerate about 1 hour or until chilled.

4 To serve, carefully remove foil baking cups. Spread fudge topping on cheesecakes. Garnish with raspberries. Store cheesecakes covered in refrigerator until serving.

Diabetes Team Tip For your next doctor appointment, bring a three day food record to provide important information about your snack and meal selections. If you add your self-tested blood glucose numbers to the record, the information is even more useful. —Dr. Bergenstal

Betty's Success Tip When tested with fat-free cream cheese, the cheesecakes had poor texture and bland flavor. If you try fat-free cream cheese, we suggest using just 4 oz fat-free cream cheese with 8 oz ⅓-less-fat cream cheese for best results.

Sugar News

People with diabetes were once taught that the only way they could enjoy sweet foods was to use sugar substitutes. Times have changed! In 1994, the American Diabetes Association relaxed its ban on sugar because studies show that table sugar doesn't raise blood glucose any more quickly than other carbohydrates such as pasta, rice or potatoes.

Although you don't have to cut out all sugar, paying attention to the amount of sugar you eat and counting carbohydrates (see page 14) is still the key to maintaining blood glucose control. When eating sugar-containing foods:

- Substitute sweets for other carbohydrates in your food plan. Don't "add" them.
- Satisfy your sweet tooth with a small amount of your favorite treat.
- Eat smaller portions. A piece of fudge or candy can fit into your food plan—but that's only if you have a small serving of one or two pieces.
- Test your blood glucose after eating foods containing different sugars and sweets; let that determine how much or how often you consume these foods, or if you need to adjust your insulin dose.
- Share desserts with others when dining out. Restaurant desserts can be very rich—a bite or two is all you may need to feel like you've truly indulged!
- Choose an artificially sweetened (light) version of your favorite beverage. Most hot cocoas, colas, iced teas and other drinks come in sweetened versions that are sugar-free.
- Select a few favorites and make decisions about how often to eat them based on your personal goals, perhaps twice a week or only on special occasions.

SWEET SUBSTITUTES

You may want to use sugar substitutes once in a while. Here are a few things to remember:

- Calorie-free sweeteners such as aspartame, saccharin and sucralose won't increase your blood glucose level.
- Sugar alcohols, such as xylitol, mannitol and sorbitol, often found in sugar-free candies and gum, do provide carbohydrate and calories. Half the sugar alcohol amount should be considered carbohydrate.
- Stevia, a calorie-free sweetener made from the stevia plant, is also available as a sugar substitute. It does not raise blood glucose levels.
- When choosing what recipe to make, it's helpful to know that 1 tablespoon of sugar has 12 grams of carbohydrate.

1½
Carbohydrate
Choices

Dark Chocolate–Cherry Multigrain Cookies

PREP TIME: 40 min • **START TO FINISH:** 40 min • 18 cookies

1 COOKIE: Calories 160 (Calories from Fat 60); Total Fat 6g (Saturated Fat 1.5g; Trans Fat 0g); Cholesterol 10mg; Sodium 110mg; Total Carbohydrate 23g (Dietary Fiber 2g; Sugars 13g); Protein 2g

% DAILY VALUE:
Vitamin A 0%; Vitamin C 0%; Calcium 0%; Iron 6%

EXCHANGES: 1 Starch, ½ Other Carbohydrate, 1 Fat

½   cup packed brown sugar
3   tablespoons granulated sugar
⅓   cup canola oil
1   egg or ¼ cup fat-free egg product
2   teaspoons vanilla
1   cup white whole wheat flour
¾   cup uncooked 5-grain rolled hot cereal
½   teaspoon baking soda
¼   teaspoon salt
½   cup dried cherries
⅓   cup bittersweet chocolate chips

1   Heat oven to 375°F. In medium bowl, mix sugars, oil, egg and vanilla. Stir in flour, cereal, baking soda and salt until blended (dough will be slightly soft). Stir in cherries and chocolate chips.

2   Onto ungreased cookie sheets, drop dough by rounded tablespoonfuls 2 inches apart. Bake 7 to 8 minutes or until light golden brown around edges (centers will look slightly underdone). Cool 1 minute; transfer from cookie sheets to cooling racks. Cool completely.

Diabetes Team Tip
Taking care of your diabetes requires many changes, and this can be challenging. Take time to adjust—your health is very important. —Dr. Bergenstal

Betty's Success Tip
If you can't find bittersweet chocolate chips, semisweet will work just fine in the recipe. Also, to form perfectly shaped cookies, try using a #40 cookie scoop. Look for this handy tool at a specialty kitchen store.

1/2
Carbohydrate
Choice

Double-Ginger Cookies

PREP TIME: 45 min • **START TO FINISH:** 2 hr 45 min • 5 dozen cookies

1 COOKIE: Calories 45 (Calories from Fat 10); Total Fat 1g (Saturated Fat 0.5g; Trans Fat 0g); Cholesterol 5mg; Sodium 40mg; Total Carbohydrate 9g (Dietary Fiber 0g; Sugars 5g); Protein 0g

% DAILY VALUE: Vitamin A 0%; Vitamin C 0%; Calcium 0%; Iron 0%

EXCHANGES: ½ Other Carbohydrate

¾	cup sugar
¼	cup butter or margarine, softened
1	egg or ¼ cup fat-free egg product
¼	cup molasses
1¾	cups all-purpose flour
1	teaspoon baking soda
½	teaspoon ground cinnamon
½	teaspoon ground ginger
¼	teaspoon ground cloves
¼	teaspoon salt
¼	cup sugar
¼	cup orange marmalade
2	tablespoons finely chopped crystallized ginger

1 In medium bowl, beat ¾ cup sugar, the butter, egg and molasses with electric mixer on medium speed, or mix with spoon. Stir in flour, baking soda, cinnamon, ground ginger, cloves and salt. Cover and refrigerate at least 2 hours, until firm.

2 Heat oven to 350°F. Lightly spray cookie sheets with cooking spray. Place ¼ cup sugar in small bowl. Shape dough into ¾-inch balls; roll in sugar. Place balls about 2 inches apart on cookie sheet. Make indentation in center of each ball, using finger. Fill each indentation with slightly less than ¼ teaspoon of the marmalade. Sprinkle with crystallized ginger.

3 Bake 8 to 10 minutes or until set. Immediately transfer from cookie sheets to cooling racks. Cool completely, about 30 minutes.

Betty's Success Tip

Be sure to use both kinds of ginger to get the double hit of ginger (and other spices) in these cute little cookies.

Chewy Barley-Nut Cookies

PREP TIME: 45 min • **START TO FINISH:** 45 min • 2 dozen cookies

1½
Carbohydrate
Choices

⅓   cup canola oil

½   cup granulated sugar

¼   cup packed brown sugar

¼   cup reduced-fat mayonnaise or salad dressing

1   teaspoon vanilla

1   egg

2   cups rolled barley flakes or 2 cups plus 2 tablespoons old-fashioned oats

¾   cup whole wheat flour

½   teaspoon baking soda

½   teaspoon salt

¼   teaspoon ground cinnamon

⅓   cup "heart-healthy" mixed nuts (peanuts, almonds, pistachios, pecans, hazelnuts)

1 Heat oven to 350°F. Spray cookie sheet with cooking spray.

2 In medium bowl, mix oil, sugars, mayonnaise, vanilla and egg with spoon. Stir in barley, flour, baking soda, salt and cinnamon. Stir in nuts.

3 Drop dough by rounded tablespoonfuls 2 inches apart onto cookie sheet.

4 Bake 10 to 14 minutes or until edges are golden brown. Cool 2 minutes; transfer from cookie sheet to cooling rack.

1 COOKIE: Calories 150 (Calories from Fat 50); Total Fat 5g (Saturated Fat 0.5g; Trans Fat 0g); Cholesterol 10mg; Sodium 110mg; Total Carbohydrate 23g (Dietary Fiber 3g; Sugars 7g); Protein 2g

% DAILY VALUE: Vitamin A 0%; Vitamin C 0%; Calcium 0%; Iron 4%

EXCHANGES: 1 Starch, ½ Other Carbohydrate, 1 Fat

Betty's Success Tip

If you haven't seen rolled barley flakes, look for it at your favorite co-op or health-food store. It works well in place of old-fashioned oats (also called rolled oats) in many recipes.

2
Carbohydrate Choices

Chewy Chocolate-Oat Bars

PREP TIME: 20 min • **START TO FINISH:** 2 hr 15 min • 16 bars

1 BAR: Calories 180 (Calories from Fat 60); Total Fat 7g (Saturated Fat 2g, Trans Fat 0g); Cholesterol 0mg; Sodium 115mg; Total Carbohydrate 27g (Dietary Fiber 1g, Sugars 18g); Protein 3g

% DAILY VALUE: Vitamin A 0%; Vitamin C 0%; Calcium 4%; Iron 6%

EXCHANGES: 1 Starch, 1 Other Carbohydrate, 1 Fat

¾ cup semisweet chocolate chips
⅓ cup fat-free sweetened condensed milk (from 14-oz can)
1 cup whole wheat flour
½ cup quick-cooking oats
½ teaspoon baking powder
½ teaspoon baking soda
¼ teaspoon salt
¼ cup fat-free egg product or 1 egg
¾ cup packed brown sugar
¼ cup canola oil
1 teaspoon vanilla
2 tablespoons quick-cooking oats
2 teaspoons butter or margarine, softened

1 Heat oven to 350°F. Spray 8-inch or 9-inch square pan with cooking spray.

2 In 1-quart saucepan, heat chocolate chips and milk over low heat, stirring frequently, until chocolate is melted and mixture is smooth. Remove from heat.

3 In large bowl, mix flour, ½ cup oats, the baking powder, baking soda and salt; set aside. In medium bowl, stir egg product, brown sugar, oil and vanilla with fork until smooth. Stir into flour mixture until blended. Reserve ½ cup dough in small bowl for topping.

4 Pat remaining dough in pan (if dough is sticky, spray fingers with cooking spray or dust with flour). Spread chocolate mixture over dough. Add 2 tablespoons oats and the butter to reserved ½ cup dough; mix with pastry blender or fork until well mixed. Place small pieces of mixture evenly over chocolate mixture.

5 Bake 20 to 25 minutes or until top is golden and firm. Cool completely, about 1 hour 30 minutes. For bars, cut into 4 rows by 4 rows.

Betty's Success Tip
When heating the chocolate chips and condensed milk for the filling, be sure to use low heat to keep the mixture from scorching.

Healthy Holidays

During the holidays, it may be tempting to go off your meal plan. At a special party or family dinner, you might have an extra helping or more dessert than usual. That's fine! Just get back on your plan the next day.

If you or a member of your family has diabetes, you don't have to completely cross off desserts or holiday goodies. The key is to find something delicious that fits into your (or their) food plan. Whether you're cooking a traditional holiday dinner, bringing a dish to a festive potluck or enjoying yourself at a holiday get-together:

- Keep up your daily walk or other exercise to help keep blood glucose down.

- Stay well rested, and take care of yourself. You'll be more in control and less tempted to overindulge if you practice healthy habits.

- Stick to your food plan by planning ahead. Give up a dinner roll or a helping of potatoes if you really want a wedge of pumpkin pie for dessert.

- Use lower-fat recipes. Bake pumpkin (or other) pie without the crust in individual custard cups; lower-fat quick breads, cookies, bars and desserts can be just as tasty as their high-fat counterparts.

- Eat fewer high-fat, high-calorie treats. Don't exclude treats altogether, but eat less of them less often.

- Keep portions small. If you really love cheesecake, have a small wedge to satisfy your sweet tooth and prevent overindulging on other desserts later.

- Choose a fun activity—like a tree-trimming party or an ice-skating party—to take the place of holiday events like cookie exchanges that are centered around food.

- Drink seltzer water or carbonated flavored waters (without sugar or sweetener)—but jazz them up! If everyone else is sipping eggnog or another holiday drink, try mixing seltzer with low-calorie cranberry juice for a festive alternative.

- Bring a dish that works in your food plan when you're toting something to a potluck dinner. If you like it, chances are everyone else will enjoy it, too.

Glossary of Diabetes Terms

Listed here are definitions of the nutrition and medical terms used in this cookbook.

Antioxidants: Substances that prevent cell damage from oxygen in plant and animal cells.

Blood Glucose: The main sugar the body uses for energy. Most of the glucose in the blood comes from carbohydrate foods in the diet. Without insulin, the cells cannot use glucose.

Calcium: Found in dairy foods, this mineral is important for maintaining strong bones and teeth and to help the heart, muscles and nerves function properly.

Carbohydrate: Providing quick energy, carbohydrates are the body's main fuel source. Carbohydrate food groups include milk/yogurt, starch, fruit and desserts.

Carbohydrate Counting: A system of "counting" carbohydrate foods (servings, grams or "choices"). Too much carbohydrate can cause high glucose levels; too little can cause low glucose levels if someone is on diabetes medications.

Cholesterol: A soft waxy substance that is important for cell structures, hormones and nerve coverings. It is found in animal foods and can also be made by the body. LDL (low-density lipoprotein), or "bad" cholesterol, increases the risk of heart disease. HDL (high-density lipoprotein), or "good" cholesterol, protects against heart disease.

ChooseMyplate.com: A food guide to healthy eating and healthy portions based on the current Dietary Guidelines. It encourages ½ plate of fruit and vegetables, ¼ plate of protein and ¼ plate of grains, and more whole grains, low-fat dairy and lower-sodium foods.

Chromium: An essential trace mineral that works with insulin to help the body use glucose and fat. It is found in meats, eggs, whole grains, cheese, brewers yeast and wheat germ.

Coronary Heart Disease (CHD): A buildup of fatty, cholesterol-filled deposits in the arteries of the heart that block the normal flow of blood and can ultimately cause a heart attack.

Diabetes: A disease that occurs when the body cannot make enough (or any) insulin in order to use glucose for energy. Glucose can't get in the cells, and glucose levels get too high.

Diabetes Care Team: Doctor, nurse, registered dietitian, health psychologist, pharmacist and others that may be involved in the care and management of diabetes.

Dietitian: A registered dietitian (RD) is a food and nutrition expert who has achieved academic and professional training and is recognized by the medical community as the primary provider of nutrition education and counseling.

Fat: A necessary nutrient, fat is needed to build new cells, shuttles vitamins through the body and makes certain hormones that regulate blood pressure. Fat in the diet provides twice as many calories as carbohydrate or protein.

Fiber: Dietary fiber is a healthy part of the diet that helps with digestion, lowers LDL cholesterol and may help provide a full feeling after eating. It is not broken down before passing through the body.

Food Exchanges: Developed by the American Dietetic Association and the American Diabetes Association, foods are categorized by the amount of carbohydrate, protein and fat they contain. The six exchanges include starch, milk, meat, meat substitutes, fat and vegetable.

Free Foods: Food or drink that has less than 20 calories or less than 5 grams of carbohydrates per serving.

Gestational Diabetes: A type of diabetes that can occur in the second half of a woman's pregnancy.

Glucose: A simple sugar formed from carbohydrate foods during the digestion process or produced in the liver. It goes from the bloodstream to the body's cells, where it is the body's main source of energy.

Glycemic Index: A controversial rating system that predicts how high and how quickly the blood glucose level will rise after eating equal amounts of different carbohydrate foods. This is compared to eating glucose alone.

Hemoglobin A1C: A blood test that measures the average blood glucose over the past two to three months. This test tells you how well your treatment plan is working. If elevated for a long time, it is closely related to a person's risk for developing diabetes complications.

Herbs: Plants or parts of plants that impart flavor and may have medicine-like qualities.

High Blood Pressure (Hypertension): The force of blood against the blood vessels is too high, leading to damaged vessels or increased plaque formation. In diabetes, the target blood pressure is less than 130/80 millimeters of mercury because of the increased risk for heart disease.

Hyperglycemia: A glucose level higher than the target glucose level set by your health-care team. If high frequently, it can lead to other health problems and means the treatment plan needs changing.

Hypoglycemia: A glucose level lower than the target glucose level set by your health-care team, often less than 70 mg/dL. Additional carbohydrate must be added to bring the glucose level back up. It is a sign that food, exercise and medication are not properly balanced in diabetes and is characterized by sweatiness, shakiness and confusion.

Incretins: A natural substance produced by the digestive tract that signals the body to make more insulin after eating and causes the stomach to empty more slowly. With type 2 diabetes, both insulin levels and incretin levels drop over time.

Insulin: A hormone made by islet cells in the pancreas that helps the body use food and glucose for energy.

Insulin-Sensitizing Agents: Medications that help the body use insulin more efficiently. These medications reduce insulin resistance and help improve blood glucose control in type 2 diabetes.

Insulin-Stimulating Agents: Medications that stimulate the cells of the pancreas to release more insulin to help lower blood glucose levels in type 2 diabetes.

Iron: A mineral that carries oxygen to cells, iron is vital for life and is found in meats, spinach and fortified cereal.

Meditation: Quiet forms of contemplation and mindfulness used to establish a sense of peace, inner calm and relaxation.

Minerals: Essential substances that are needed in very small amounts for many processes in the body. Examples include sodium, potassium chloride, magnesium, calcium and phosphorus.

Monounsaturated Fat: Healthy (good) fat is found in canola oil, olive oil, nuts, avocados and fatty fish.

Nutrients: Substances necessary for life that build, repair and maintain body cells. Protein, carbohydrates, fats, water, vitamins and minerals are nutrients.

Phytochemicals: Many naturally occurring substances found in plant foods that may have positive benefits on health and might serve as disease-fighting agents.

Polyunsaturated Fat: Healthy (good) fat found in corn oil, soybean oil and sunflower oil.

Protein: One of three major nutrients in food. Essential for body structure and function. Important part of muscle, enzymes, hormones and antibodies.

Saturated Fat: Unhealthy fats. Usually solid at room temperature, these fats tend to elevate blood cholesterol levels and come from animal sources: beef, pork, poultry, eggs and dairy foods. Palm and coconut oils are also saturated fats, even though they are liquids.

Sugar Alcohols: Reduced-calorie sweeteners often used to make sugar-free or no-added-sugar desserts, candies or gums. These products may have a laxative effect. They do not contain alcohol.

Triglycerides: Major form of fat in the body. Too much triglyceride in the blood increases the risk for heart disease. Being overweight or consuming too much fat, alcohol or sugar can increase blood triglycerides.

Type 1 Diabetes: A chronic disease in which the body stops producing insulin. It can happen at any age but usually occurs in children and young adults. Insulin injections are required.

Type 2 Diabetes: A chronic disease in which the pancreas makes insulin, but the body doesn't use it properly. The body "resists" the action of insulin. It is the most common form of diabetes. Typically seen in adults, but it is becoming more common in children. Individuals will need a food and exercise plan and may also need pills or insulin injections.

Unsaturated Fat: Liquid at room temperature, these fats do not tend to elevate blood cholesterol levels. They are from plant sources and include olive oil, sunflower oil, corn oil, nuts and avocados.

Vitamins: A group of vital nutrients, found in small amounts in a variety of foods, that are key to developing cells, controlling body functions and helping release energy from fuel sources.

Whole Grains: The entire edible part of any grain: bran, endosperm and germ. Rich in fiber, vitamins, minerals and phytochemicals. Experts recommend eating at least three servings of whole grains every day for optimal health. Look for the term "whole grain" on the food label.

Yoga: An ancient practice based on deep breathing, stretching and strengthening exercises to balance the mind, body and spirit.

Diabetes Tips at a Glance

Day-Starter Breakfasts

- **Whole-Grain Strawberry Pancakes:** Look for sugar-free syrup at the grocery store. The carbohydrate content is lower than regular syrup. If it's 20 calories or less per serving, it's a free food for you. —Diane Reader, Dietitian

- **Corn, Egg and Potato Bake:** As your steps (or other physical activity) add up, so do the health benefits. Research shows that walking helps control blood pressure and cholesterol, while reducing the risk of diabetes, stroke and certain types of cancer. —Diane Reader, Dietitian

- **Breakfast Panini:** Breakfast eaters usually eat better overall than those who skip—it's so important to eat early in the day. Even when you're in a hurry, take time to grab a slice of toast, a container of yogurt and a small piece of fruit on your way out the door. —Diane Reader, Dietitian

- **Raspberry Lemonade Smoothies:** Because blood glucose levels can vary at different times of the day, test your blood sugar throughout the day, not just in the morning. Good times to check it are before lunch or two hours after dinner. —Dr. Bergenstal

- **Carrot-Lemon Bread:** At 4 grams per slice, this bread is a great source of fiber. Fiber can help with blood glucose management. Fruits, vegetables and whole grains, along with beans and other legumes, contain good amounts of fiber. —Diane Reader, Dietitian

Smart Snacks and Breads

- **Three-Seed Flatbread:** Nuts and seeds are great little nuggets of nutrients, but adding them in moderation is wise because they can be high in fat. Fortunately a little goes a long way in terms of flavor. —Diane Reader, Dietitian

- **Mini Rosemary Scones:** If you haven't already, consider an activity that has an impact on your body to help strengthen your bones, such as walking, jogging or dancing; try anything where you're on your feet, working against gravity. —Diane Reader, Dietitian

- **Sweet Potato Oven Fries with Spicy Sour Cream:** If you love seasoned sweet potato fries but don't want the fat, then you will like this easy recipe for making them in the oven. They're delicious and full of beta-carotene. —Diane Reader, Dietitian

- **Greek Salad Kabobs:** Do you drink enough water? Quench your thirst with water or carbohydrate-free beverages like herbal teas. Juices and milk contain carbohydrates, so limit portions to 4 to 8 ounces. —Dr. Bergenstal

- **Crunchy Chicken Chunks with Thai Peanut Sauce:** Snacks are not required just because you have diabetes since they often add extra calories and fat. Check with your doctor or diabetes educator to determine if you need between-meal snacks. —Dr. Bergenstal

Pleasing Poultry, Fish and Meat

- **Citrus-Glazed Salmon:** Salmon is a super source of vitamin B_{12}, which is needed for all body cells to function properly. Salmon also contains omega-3 fats, the good-for-you fats that are so beneficial for your heart and overall health. —Dr. Bergenstal

- **Halibut with Lime and Cilantro:** Eating fish at least once or twice a week is recommended by health experts because most fish is low in fat and calories and contains heart-healthy nutrients. —Dr. Bergenstal

- **Slow Cooker Chipotle Beef Stew:** Beef is a super source of the mineral zinc, which is important for growth, wound healing and your ability to taste foods. —Diane Reader, Dietitian

- **Broiled Dijon Burgers:** Broiling, braising and roasting are healthy, low-fat techniques to use when cooking meats. Grilling is another great method, as it allows the fat to drip away from the meat. —Diane Reader, Dietitian

- **Swiss Steak Casserole:** Although protein will not raise your blood glucose levels, it's still wise to eat only one serving of 3 to 4 ounces per meal to control your total calorie and fat intake. —Diane Reader, Dietitian

- **Beef Roast with Onions and Potatoes:** Beef is a great source of vitamin B_{12} and the mineral iron. Both of these are important for proper body function. —Diane Reader, Dietitian

- **Flank Steak with Smoky Honey Mustard Sauce:** You don't have to avoid all red meat if you're trying to lose weight. By selecting lean cuts, trimming all visible fat and eating small portions, you can enjoy meat as part of a healthy diet. —Diane Reader, Dietitian

- **Asian Steak Salad:** Just the colors of fruits and vegetables tell us that they are good for us. So choose the most colorful ones. Fruits and veggies contain vitamins and minerals which are good for our bodies in many ways. —Diane Reader, Dietitian

Stand-Out Meatless Meals

- **Stir-Fried Tofu with Almonds:** Tofu is a great alternative to meat. Made from soybeans, it provides protein, iron and calcium, but it's a bit high in carbohydrates, so plan accordingly. —Diane Reader, Dietitian
- **Southwestern Bean Skillet:** Eating cheese is a tasty, satisfying way to get your calcium, a nutrient needed to maintain bone density. Good lower-fat choices are part-skim mozzarella and reduced-fat Cheddar cheese. —Diane Reader, Dietitian
- **Lentil-Corn Burgers:** To reduce fat, calories and cholesterol, eat meatless meals often; aim for one or two times per week. Continue to count carbohydrates, as meatless meals often provide more carbohydrates than meat-based meals. —Diane Reader, Dietitian
- **Chipotle and Black Bean Burritos:** A small increase in physical activity can have a big effect on your diabetes and in your general health. It can help lower glucose levels and create a feeling of well being. —Dr. Bergenstal
- **Veggie-Tofu Pizza:** When picking out your pizza crust, think thin. The thicker crust type is much higher in carbohydrates per serving. —Diane Reader, Dietitian

Great Grains, Legumes and Pasta

- **Coconut-Ginger Rice:** Choosing low-fat foods if you are trying to lose weight is a good rule to follow. Don't forget to balance your healthy eating habits with 30 to 60 minutes of aerobic exercise at least five times per week. —Dr. Bergenstal
- **Farmers' Market Barley Risotto:** Risotto is traditionally made by stirring small amounts of broth into rice throughout the cook time to get the chewy texture. This recipe uses barley instead of rice. Barley is high in soluble fiber and may have the same cholesterol-lowering properties as oats. —Diane Reader, Dietitian
- **Thai Beef Noodle Bowls:** A person with diabetes can drink alcohol in moderation. Alcohol temporarily lowers blood glucose, however, so it's best to have just one glass of wine and have it with your meal. —Dr. Bergenstal

- **African Squash and Chickpea Stew:** Boost your fiber with beans. Filled with many other important nutrients, beans are an excellent source of fiber that's so important for good blood glucose management and to keep your digestive system moving. —Diane Reader, Dietitian
- **Edamame-Tabbouleh Salad:** Soy foods like the edamame in this recipe or tofu contain high-fiber carbohydrates, low-fat protein and heart-healthy fat. —Diane Reader, Dietitian

Vital Vegetables and Salads

- **Chipotle Twice-Baked Sweet Potatoes:** Sweet potatoes, squash, carrots and other bright orange vegetables contain beta-carotene, which your body converts to vitamin A. It's vital for proper eyesight. —Dr. Bergenstal
- **Broccoli and Squash Medley:** Broccoli, part of the same vegetable family that includes Brussels sprouts, cabbage and cauliflower, is nutrient rich. These tasty gems are thought to help protect against diseases, particularly certain cancers. —Dr. Bergenstal
- **Asparagus-Pepper Stir-Fry:** Vegetables are loaded with the nutrients you need each day to be healthy. It's recommended to have three to five servings of veggies each day. —Diane Reader, Dietitian
- **Peas with Mushrooms and Thyme:** Peas are loaded with vitamin B_1, also called thiamin. We need thiamin for normal energy metabolism and to help keep the nervous system healthy. —Diane Reader, Dietitian
- **Herb-Roasted Root Vegetables:** Stress can lead to high glucose. Try to find ways to keep your life balanced and, although stress is a part of life, find time to relax and do things you enjoy. —Dr. Bergenstal
- **Five-Layer Salad:** Vegetable salads are a great way to make a dent in your recommended daily servings of fresh vegetables. —Diane Reader, Dietitian
- **Triple-Berry and Jicama Spinach Salad:** Spinach is a super source of folic acid, needed for cells to function normally. Recent studies show that as many as 40% of Americans don't meet their folic acid requirement. —Diane Reader, Dietitian
- **Mediterranean Vegetable Salad:** Research shows that spinach and other leafy green vegetables contain antioxidants. Spinach is an excellent source of the antioxidant lutein, vitamin C and folic acid — all beneficial nutrients for heart health. —Diane Reader, Dietitian

Best Gluten-Free Recipes

- **Lemon-Blueberry Muffins:** Developing and sticking to a schedule for monitoring blood sugar is one of the best tools you can use to learn how food and exercise affect your diabetes. —Dr. Bergenstal

- **Best-Ever Banana Bread:** When possible, select fortified versions of gluten-free flours, breads, cereals and crackers. —Diane Reader, Dietitian

- **Glazed Meat Loaf:** Be sure to take your medications as prescribed. If you have any questions, ask your doctor or pharmacist. Know when to take them, with what, how to store them and how to avoid side effects. Take a list of all your medications, the doses and how often you take them to each doctor visit. —Dr. Bergenstal

- **Cheesy Vegetable Pizza with Basil:** Choose plain versions of fruits and vegetables, as anything in a sauce may contain thickeners or flavorings that contain gluten. —Diane Reader, Dietitian

Delightful Desserts

- **Baked Berry Cups with Crispy Cinnamon Wedges:** Keeping a daily log of the foods you eat and any higher-than-normal glucose levels can help you stay in control of your diabetes. —Dr. Bergenstal

- **Creamy Key Lime Pie:** A refreshing key lime pie gets the benefit of high fiber when the crust is made with Fiber One® cereal. It's delicious. —Diane Reader, Dietitian

- **Mixed-Berry Cream Tart:** Research shows that antioxidants naturally found in blueberries may help prevent cell damage from oxygen. —Diane Reader, Dietitian

- **Mini Chocolate Cheesecakes:** For your next doctor appointment, bring a three day food record to provide important information about your snack and meal selections. If you add your self-tested blood glucose numbers to the record, the information is even more useful. —Dr. Bergenstal

- **Dark Chocolate–Cherry Multigrain Cookies:** Taking care of your diabetes requires many changes, and this can be challenging. Take time to adjust—your health is very important. —Dr. Bergenstal

A Leader in Diabetes Education and Care

International Diabetes Center
Park Nicollet

International Diabetes Center at Park Nicollet provides world-class diabetes management, education and research programs to meet the needs of people with diabetes and their families. Located in Minneapolis, Minnesota, the center is internationally recognized for its range of clinical, motivational and educational programs, products and services. Founded in 1967, International Diabetes Center's mission is to ensure that every individual with diabetes or at risk for diabetes receives the best possible care.

Helping People Live Well with Diabetes

The center's guiding principle is that patient-centered team care is the key to excellent diabetes management. Its outpatient-care programs, educational products and professional training programs reflect this philosophy. From classes that teach basic self-care skills to consulting services that improve clinical care systems, the center provides education and support for adults, children and their families, and their health care providers.

Expertise Based on Research and Innovation

International Diabetes Center has conducted nearly 300 clinical trials to date, including the landmark *Diabetes Control and Complications Trial* and groundbreaking work demonstrating the important roles that dietitians and diabetes nurse specialists have in diabetes care. Results of this work and extensive clinical experience are the foundations of its evidence-based approaches to education and care. The center is dedicated to sharing its methods and knowledge with other health-care organizations to help them achieve the best possible outcomes for patients with diabetes.

Worldwide Training

The center trains health professionals in the most current diabetes-care practices, works to improve diabetes screening and detection practices and educates the public about the disease—all on a worldwide basis. International Diabetes Center professionals travel across the country and around the world to consult with, train and coach health-care providers and administrators as they improve their own practices and patient outcomes. Today, health-care centers in China, India, Russia, Mexico, Brazil, Japan and the United States are among the many organizations that have embraced International Diabetes Center's education and care solutions.

Visit Us Online

To learn more about International Diabetes Center, or for comprehensive information about diabetes prevention, care, education and research, visit www .internationaldiabetescenter.com or call 888-825-6315.

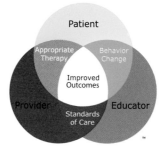

Patient Services
- Classes and educational materials
- Counseling
- Clinical research
- Health and care store

Professional Services
- Medical education and training
- Patient education curricula
- Clinical guidelines and tools
- Care systems consulting

Index

A

African Squash and Chickpea Stew, 162, *163*
Almond(s)
  blueberry-, brown bread, 68, *69*
  stir-fried tofu with, 131
Apple
  celery and, salad, 204, *205*
  -cinnamon quesadilla, 71
  -gingerbread muffins, 215
Asiago Mac and Cheese, 172, *173*
Asian Mushroom-Chicken Soup, 96, 97
Asian Sloppy Joes, 146
Asian Steak Salad, 117
Asian-Stuffed Portabellas, 128, *129*
Asian Turkey Burgers, 98
Asparagus
  -pepper stir-fry, 187
  roasted, and berry salad, 191
  and salmon, quinoa pilaf with, 100

B

Bacon and Tomato Frittata, 52
Banana bread, best-ever, 217
Barley
  -nut cookies, chewy, 249
  risotto, farmers' market, 159
Bars, chocolate-oat, chewy, 250
Bean(s). *See also* Black bean
  green, and fennel, balsamic, 188
  soup, Italian, with greens, 136
  Southwestern, skillet, 140
Beef dishes
  Asian Steak Salad, 117
  Beef Roast with Onions and Potatoes, 114
  Broiled Dijon Burgers, 112
  Flank Steak with Smoky Honey Mustard Sauce, 115
  Sirloin Steaks with Cilantro Chimichurri, 116

Slow Cooker Chipotle Beef Stew, 110, *111*
  Swiss Steak Casserole, 113
  Thai Beef Noodle Bowls, 160, *161*
Berry(ies). *See also individual berries*
  asparagus–, salad, 191
  cups, baked, 230, *231*
  double-, muffins, 59
  –French toast stratas, 38, *39*
  mixed-, cream tart, 242
  mixed-, snack cake, 233
  triple-, and jicama spinach salad, 196, *197*
  triple-, oatmeal muesli, 55
Black bean
  chipotle and, burritos, 148
  salsa, calypso shrimp with, 108
BLT Potato Salad, 202
Blueberry
  -almond brown bread, 68, *69*
  lemon-, muffins, 214
  pancakes, 212
Bread(s). *See also* Sandwiches; Scones
  banana, best-ever, 217
  blueberry-almond brown, 68, *69*
  carrot-lemon, 60
  cornbread, 216
  flatbread, three-seed, 66
  sandwich, gluten-free, 210
Breakfast Panini, 50, *51*
Broccoli
  chicken and, fettuccine, 222
  slaw, Thai, 200, *201*
  and squash medley, 186
  sweet potato–, soup, 134, *135*
Brown rice
  herbed, pork chops with, 118, *119*
  –stuffed butternut squash, 156, *157*
Brownies, peppermint-frosted, 219
Buffalo Chicken Pizza, 88, *89*

Burgers
  chicken, Greek, 92, *93*
  Dijon, broiled, 112
  Italian Veggie Sliders, 149
  lentil-corn, 144, *145*
  turkey, Asian, 98
Burrito(s)
  chipotle and black bean, 148
  pork, bowls, slow-cooked, 120
Butternut squash
  broccoli and, medley, 186
  brown rice–stuffed, 156, *157*
  and chickpea stew, African, 162, *163*

C

Cajun onion dip, spicy, 80
Cake(s)
  ginger, with caramel-apple topping, 238
  Mini Chocolate Cheesecakes, 244
  mixed-berry snack, 233
Calypso Shrimp with Black Bean Salsa, 108
Carbohydrate Choices, about, 12–16
  carbohydrate counting, 11–12
  great snacks, 61
Carrot
  and herb spread, roasted, 75
  -lemon bread, 60
  salad, Moroccan, 192, *193*
Casserole(s)
  jerk chicken, 94
  Mediterranean minestrone, 174
  Swiss steak, 113
  wild rice and turkey, 95
Celery and Apple Salad with Cider Vinaigrette, 204, *205*
Champagne Shrimp Risotto, 225
Cheese, Asiago, mac and, 172, *173*
Cheesecakes, chocolate, mini, 244
Cherry(ies)
  chocolate chip–, scones, 70
  dark chocolate–, multigrain cookies, 246, *247*
  dried, chicken–wild rice salad with, 166
Chicken dishes
  Asian Mushroom-Chicken Soup, 96, *97*
  Baked Chicken Dijon, 91
  Buffalo Chicken Pizza, 88, *89*
  Chicken and Vegetables with Quinoa, 167
  Chicken Noodle Soup, 223
  Chicken–Wild Rice Salad with Dried Cherries, 166
  Creamy Chicken and Broccoli Fettuccine, 222
  Crunchy Chicken Chunks with Thai Peanut Sauce, 81
  Greek Chicken Burgers with Tzatziki Sauce, 92, *93*
  Hearty Chicken Pot Pie, 221
  Jerk Chicken Casserole, 94
  Mandarin Chicken Salad, 90
Chickpea(s)
  and couscous salad, spicy, 170
  in Slow Cooker Mediterranean Minestrone Casserole, 174
  in spinach hummus, 76, *77*
  and squash stew, African, 162, *163*
Chimichurri, cilantro, 116
Chipotle
  beef stew, slow cooker, 110, *111*
  and black bean burritos, 148
  sweet potatoes, twice-baked, 184, *185*
Chocolate. *See also* Chocolate chip
  cheesecakes, mini, 244
  dark, cupcakes, 240, *241*
  dark,–cherry multigrain cookies, 246, *247*
  -oat bars, chewy, 250
  pancakes with strawberries, 40
Chocolate chip
  –cherry scones, 70
  pumpkin–, cookies, 218
Chorizo Mexican Breakfast Pizzas, 44, *45*
Cinnamon, apple-, quesadilla, 71
Cinnamon wedges, crispy, baked berry cups with, 230, *231*
Cobia with Lemon-Caper Sauce, 106, *107*
Coconut-Ginger Rice, 158
Cookies
  barley-nut, 249
  dark chocolate–cherry multigrain, 246, *247*
  double-ginger, 248
  pumpkin–chocolate chip, 218
Corn, Egg and Potato Bake, 43
Corn, lentil-, burgers, 144, *145*
Cornbread, 216
Couscous
  and chickpea salad, spicy, 170
  and sweet potatoes with pork, 121
Cucumber-Mango Salad, 198
Cupcakes, dark chocolate, 240, *241*
Curried Lentils with Rice, 142

D

Dark chocolate. *See* Chocolate
Date-bran muffins, upside-down, 58
Dessert shots, lemon, 234, *235*
Diabetes
    lifestyle, 18, 27, 49, 137, 153, 175, 181, 203, 207, 226–227, 245, 251
    living with, 8–35, 245
    tips at a glance, 254–256
Dijon
    burgers, broiled, 112
    chicken, baked, 91
Dip
    ginger and mint, with fruit, 79
    mustard, 78
    onion, spicy Cajun, 80
Dulce de Leche Fillo Cups, 232

E

Edamame
    in Spicy Couscous and Chick Pea Salad, 170
    and tabbouleh Salad, 171
Egg dishes. *See also* Frittata
    Breakfast Panini, 50, *51*
    Corn, Egg and Potato Bake, 43
    Veggie-Stuffed Omelets, 46, *47*
Eggplant, in The Great Greek Sandwiches, 143
Exchange lists, about, 16

F

Fajitas, spicy shrimp, 109
Falafel Sandwiches with Yogurt Sauce, 147
Farmers' Market Barley Risotto, 159
Fennel, balsamic green beans and, 188
Fettuccine, creamy chicken and broccoli, 222
Fillo cups, dulce de leche, 232
Fish. *See* Seafood
Flank Steak with Smoky Honey Mustard Sauce, 115
Flatbread, three-seed, 66
French toast, berry–, stratas, 38, *39*
Fries, sweet potato oven, with spicy sour cream, 72, *73*
Frittata
    bacon and tomato, 52
    potato, egg and sausage, 48
Fruit. *See also* Berry(ies); *individual types*
    Tropical Fruit 'n Ginger Oatmeal, 56, *57*

G

Garden-Fresh Greek Salad, 206
Ginger, double-, cookies, 248
Ginger and Mint Dip with Fruit, 79
Gingerbread, apple-, muffins, 215
Ginger Cake with Caramel-Apple Topping, 238
Gluten-free recipes, 208–227
Greek Chicken Burgers with Tzatziki Sauce, 92, *93*
Greek Salad Kabobs, 74
Greek sandwiches, the great, 143

H

Halibut with Lime and Cilantro, 104
Holidays, tips for diabetics, 251
Hummus, spinach, smoky, 76, *77*

I

Italian Bean Soup with Greens, 136
Italian Veggie Sliders, 149

J

Jelly shots, pomegranate–tequila sunrise, 236, *237*
Jerk Chicken Casserole, 94
Jicama
    salsa, grilled fish with, 101
    spinach salad, triple berry and, 196, *197*

K

Kabobs
    Greek salad, 74
    vegetable, with mustard dip, 78
Kasha, veggies and, 165
Key lime pie, creamy, 239
Kiwi, strawberry, parfaits, crunchy-topped, 54

L

Lasagna wheels, whole wheat, 176, *177*
Lemon, carrot-, bread, 60
Lemonade smoothies, raspberry, 53
Lemon-Blueberry Muffins, 214
Lemon Dessert Shots, 234, *235*
Lentil-Corn Burgers, 144, *145*
Lentils, curried, with rice, 142
Lollipops, Vietnamese meatball, 82, *83*

M

Mac and cheese, Asiago, 172, *173*
Mandarin Chicken Salad, 90
Mango, cucumber-, salad, 198
Meatball lollipops, Vietnamese, 82, *83*
Meat loaf, glazed, 220
Mediterranean minestrone casserole, slow cooker, 174
Mediterranean Vegetable Salad, 199
Menus, 22–23. *See also* Snack tips,
Minestrone casserole, Mediterranean, 174
Mini Chocolate Cheesecakes, 244
Mini Rosemary Scones, 67
Mole, pork, quesadillas, 122, *123*
Moroccan Carrot Salad, 192, *193*
Muffins
  apple-gingerbread, 215
  double-berry, 59
  lemon-blueberry, 214
  upside-down date-bran, 58
Multigrain cookies, dark chocolate–cherry, 246, *247*
Mushroom
  -chicken soup, Asian, 96, *97*
  peas with thyme and, 189
  portabellas, Asian-stuffed, 128, *129*
  -spinach stroganoff, 132
Mustard dip, 78. *See also* Dijon
MyPlate, about, 14

N

Noodle(s)
  bowls, Thai beef, 160, *161*
  chunky garden, 178, *179*

O

Oatmeal
  fruit 'n ginger
  muesli, triple-berry, 55
Omelet, veggie-stuffed, 46, *47*
Onion
  caramelized, potato and polenta pizza, 130
  caramelized, –shrimp spread, 84
  dip, spicy Cajun, 80
  –poppy seed scones, 64, *65*
  potatoes and, roast with, 114

P

Pancakes
  blueberry, 212
  chocolate, with strawberries, 40
  whole-grain strawberry, 41
Panini, breakfast, 50, *51*
Parfaits, strawberry-kiwi, 54
Pasta. *See also* Noodle(s); Pizza(s)
  Asiago Mac and Cheese, 172, *173*
  Slow Cooker Mediterranean Minestrone Casserole, 174
  Stuffed Pasta Shells, 180
Peanut sauce, Thai, crunchy chicken chunks with, 81
Peas with Mushrooms and Thyme, 189
Pecan, pineapple-, dessert squares, creamy, 243
Pepper(s)
  asparagus-, stir-fry, 187
  red, soup, with mozzarella, 138, *139*
  stuffed, smoky brown rice–, 141
Peppermint-Frosted Brownies, 219
Pie, key lime, creamy, 239
Pineapple-pecan dessert squares, 243
Pizza(s)
  Buffalo chicken, 88, *89*
  caramelized onion–potato and polenta, 130
  cheesy vegetable, with basil, 224
  chorizo Mexican breakfast, 44, *45*
  veggie, homemade, 152
  veggie-tofu, 150, *151*
Polenta, caramelized onion–potato and, pizza, 130
Pomegranate–Tequila Sunrise Jelly Shots, 236, *237*
Poppy seed, onion–, scones, 64, *65*
Pork dishes
  Chorizo Mexican Breakfast Pizzas, 44, *45*
  Couscous and Sweet Potatoes with Pork, 121
  Pork Chops with Raspberry-Chipotle Sauce and Herbed Rice, 118, *119*
  Pork Medallions with Cherry Sauce, 124
  Pork Mole Quesadillas, 122, *123*
  Slow-Cooked Pork Burrito Bowls, 120
Portabellas, Asian-stuffed, 128, *129*
Potato(es). *See also* Sweet potato
  salad, BLT, 202
  caramelized onion–, and polenta pizza, 130
  corn, and egg bake, 43
  Egg and Sausage Frittata, 48
  smashed, stew, 133
  onions and, beef roast with, 114

Pot pie, hearty chicken, 221
Pretzels, soft, 211
Pumpkin–Chocolate Chip Cookies, 218

Q

Quesadilla(s)
  creamy apple-cinnamon, 71
  pork mole, 122, *123*
Quinoa
  chicken and vegetables with, 167
  pilaf with salmon and asparagus, 100
  salad, Southwestern, 168, *169*

R

Ragout, turkey–butternut squash, 99
Raspberry Lemonade Smoothies, 53
Rice. *See also* Brown rice; Wild rice
  Coconut-Ginger Rice, 158
  Curried Lentils with Rice, 142
Risotto
  barley, farmers' market, 159
  shrimp, champagne, 225
Rosemary scones, mini, 67

S

Sage and Garlic Vegetable Bake, 164
Salad(s)
  Asian steak, 117
  BLT potato, 202
  celery and apple, with cider vinaigrette, 204, *205*
  chicken–wild rice, with dried cherries, 166
  couscous and chickpea, 170
  cucumber-mango, 198
  edamame-tabbouleh, 171
  five-layer, 194
  garden-fresh Greek, 206
  Greek, kabobs, 74
  mandarin chicken, 90
  Mediterranean vegetable, 199
  Moroccan carrot, 192, *193*
  roasted asparagus–berry, 191
  Southwestern quinoa, 168, *169*
  strawberry-blueberry-orange, 195
  veggies and kasha with balsamic vinaigrette, 165

Salmon dishes
  Citrus-Glazed Salmon, 102, *103*
  Quinoa Pilaf with Salmon and Asparagus, 100
Salsa
  black bean, 108
  jicama, 101
Sandwich Bread, 210
Sandwiches. *See also* Burgers
  Asian Sloppy Joes, 146
  Breakfast Panini, 50, *51*
  falafel, 147
  Greek, 143
Sauces
  cherry, 124
  cilantro chimichurri, 116
  dipping, 82, *83*
  honey mustard, 115
  lemon-caper, 106, *107*
  peanut, 81
  raspberry-chipotle, 118, *119*
  tzatziki, 92, *93*
  yogurt, 147
Scones
  chocolate chip–cherry, 70
  mini rosemary, 67
  onion–poppy seed, 64
Seafood. *See also individual types*
  Cobia with Lemon-Caper Sauce, 106, *107*
  Grilled Fish with Jicama Salsa, 101
  Halibut with Lime and Cilantro, 104
  Roasted Tilapia and Vegetables, 105
Seed, three-, flatbread, 66
Shrimp
  with black bean salsa 108
  caramelized onion–, spread, 84
  fajitas, spicy, 109
  risotto, champagne, 225
Sick days, what to do, 125
Sirloin Steaks with Cilantro Chimichurri, 116
Slaw, Thai broccoli, 200, *201*
Sliders, Italian veggie, 149
Sloppy Joes, Asian, 146
Smashed Potato Stew, 133
Smoothies, raspberry lemonade, 53
Snacking tips, 61, 85

Soft Pretzels, 211
Soup(s)
  Asian mushroom-chicken, 96, *97*
  Italian bean, with greens, 136
  red pepper, roasted, with mozzarella, 138, *139*
  sweet potato–broccoli, 134, *135*
Southwestern Bean Skillet, 140
Southwestern Quinoa Salad, 168, *169*
Spinach hummus, smoky, 76, *77*
Spinach, mushroom-, stroganoff, 132
Spread
  caramelized onion–shrimp, 84
  roasted carrot and herb, 75
Squash. *See* Butternut squash
Steak. *See* Beef dishes
Stew(s)
  chipotle beef, 110, *111*
  smashed potato, 133
  squash and chickpea, 162, *163*
Stratas, berry–French toast, 38, *39*
Strawberry(ies)
  -blueberry-orange salad, 195
  chocolate pancakes with, 40
  -kiwi parfaits, 54
  pancakes, whole-grain, 41
Stroganoff, mushroom-spinach, 132
Sweet potato dishes
  Chipotle Twice-Baked Sweet Potatoes, 184, *185*
  Couscous with Sweet Potatoes with pork, 121
  Sweet Potato–Broccoli Soup, 134, *135*
  Sweet Potato Oven Fries with Spicy Sour Cream, 72, *73*
  Swiss Steak Casserole, 113

T

Tabbouleh, edamame-, salad, 171
Tart, mixed-berry cream, 242
Tequila sunrise, pomegranate–, jelly shots, 236, *237*
Thai Beef Noodle Bowls, 160, *161*
Thai Broccoli Slaw, 200, *201*
Tilapia and vegetables, roasted, 105
Tofu
  with almonds, stir-fried, 131
  veggie-, pizza, 150, *151*
Tomato
  and bacon frittata, 52
  in BLT Potato Salad, 202

Topping, caramel-apple, 238
Turkey dishes
  Asian Turkey Burgers, 98
  Brown Rice–Stuffed Butternut Squash, 156, *157*
  Stuffed Pasta Shells, 180
  Turkey–Butternut Squash Ragout, 99
  Vietnamese Meatball Lollipops with Dipping Sauce, 82, *83*
  Wild Rice and Turkey Casserole, 95

U

Upside-Down Date-Bran Muffins, 58

V

Vegetable(s), value of, 206–207
Vegetable dishes. *See also* Salads; *specific vegetables*
  Cheesy Vegetable Pizza with Basil, 224
  Herb-Roasted Root Vegetables, 190
  Homemade Veggie Pizza, 152
  Italian Veggie Sliders, 149
  Mediterranean Vegetable Salad, 199
  Vegetable Kabobs with Mustard Dip, 78
  Veggies and Kasha with Balsamic Vinaigrette, 165
  Veggie-Stuffed Omelet, 46, *47*
  Veggie-Tofu Pizza, 150, *151*
Vietnamese Meatball Lollipops with Dipping Sauce, 82, *83*
Vinaigrette
  balsamic, 165
  cider, 204, *205*

W

Waffles, 213
  whole wheat, with honey–peanut butter drizzle, 42
Wild rice
  and turkey casserole, 95
  chicken–, salad, 166

Y

Yogurt. *See also* Dips; Sauces
  in Crunchy-Topped Strawberry-Kiwi Parfaits, 54
  in Raspberry Lemonade Smoothies, 53
  in Triple-Berry Oatmeal Muesli, 55
  in Tropical Fruit 'n Ginger Oatmeal, 56, *57*

Metric Conversion Guide

Note: The recipes in this cookbook have not been developed or tested using metric measures. When converting recipes to metric, some variations in quality may be noted.

Volume

U.S. Units	Canadian Metric	Australian Metric
¼ teaspoon	1 mL	1 ml
½ teaspoon	2 mL	2 ml
1 teaspoon	5 mL	5 ml
1 tablespoon	15 mL	20 ml
¼ cup	50 mL	60 ml
⅓ cup	75 mL	80 ml
½ cup	125 mL	125 ml
⅔ cup	150 mL	170 ml
¾ cup	175 mL	190 ml
1 cup	250 mL	250 ml
1 quart	1 liter	1 liter
1½ quarts	1.5 liters	1.5 liters
2 quarts	2 liters	2 liters
2½ quarts	2.5 liters	2.5 liters
3 quarts	3 liters	3 liters
4 quarts	4 liters	4 liters

Weight

U.S. Units	Canadian Metric	Australian Metric
1 ounce	30 grams	30 grams
2 ounces	55 grams	60 grams
3 ounces	85 grams	90 grams
4 ounces (¼ pound)	115 grams	125 grams
8 ounces (½ pound)	225 grams	225 grams
16 ounces (1 pound)	455 grams	500 grams
1 pound	455 grams	0.5 kilogram

Measurements

Inches	Centimeters
1	2.5
2	5.0
3	7.5
4	10.0
5	12.5
6	15.0
7	17.5
8	20.5
9	23.0
10	25.5
11	28.0
12	30.5
13	33.0

Temperatures

Fahrenheit	Celsius
32°	0°
212°	100°
250°	120°
275°	140°
300°	150°
325°	160°
350°	180°
375°	190°
400°	200°
425°	220°
450°	230°
475°	240°
500°	260°